Baxter & Stevenson, Women's History

Selected Reading Lists and Course Outlines from American Colleges and Universities

Women's History

edited by Annette K. Baxter
Barnard College, Columbia University

Louise L. Stevenson
Franklin and Marshall College

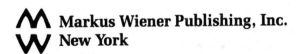 Markus Wiener Publishing, Inc.
New York

Library of Congress Cataloging-in-Publication Data

Women's history.

(Selected course outlines and reading lists from
American colleges and universities ; vol. 10)
    Bibliography: p.
    1. Women--United States--History--Outlines, syllabi,
etc. I. Stevenson, Louise L. II. Baxter, Annette Kar.
III. Title.
HQ1410.W683 1987   305.4'07'1173   87-8286
ISBN 0-910129-78-9

Printed in America

Foreword

In assembling the syllabi for this edition, I let the example of the previous editor, the late Annette K. Baxter, guide me. She always encouraged innovations in the teaching of women's history and welcomed new scholars to the field. There are more than thirty contributors to this volume, and over sixty historians received invitations to contribute. Sabbaticals, leaves of absence, and changes in teaching assignments played a large role in determining whose names appear in the "Table of Contents." Nevertheless, if Annette could read it, I think she would be pleased. With but four exceptions, all the reading lists and syllabi in this edition either represent new work or revised versions of syllabi from the first edition. Readers should be aware that this edition does not replace its predecessor as much as complement it. Many of the earlier syllabi retain their integrity and interest.

The syllabi reprinted here evidence several new emphases in the teaching of women's history. Whereas an initial contribution of women's history was the discovery of women's private lives and the explication of their meaning, increasingly the focus is shifting toward women's engagement with public life, whether through work, professional or social commitment, or politics. In the 1984 edition of this volume the term *gender* did not appear in any of the syllabi titles, but in the current edition gender appears as an organizing principle in one out of nine. And in many syllabi, consideration of gender opens the door to new initiatives in comparative and interdisciplinary studies.

3

The richness and diversity of the syllabi presented in this volume speak to the value of women's history. Rather than feeling, as one reviewer did, that a separate volume for women's history represents its ghettoization, I believe that the current edition again confirms women's history as one of the most vital and vibrant developments in the center city of historical studies.

Table of Contents

C. Courses, 1820-1987

D. Experiences of Religious, Racial and Ethnic Groups

E. Social History

F. Women and Work

G. Gender and Sexuality

H. Feminism: History, Theory, and Methodology

I. Topics Courses

Documents have been reproduced from the originals as submitted.

PACE UNIVERSITY

History 280D1.
The Changing Role of Women
in American Society

Dr. Harris
Office: 41 Park Row, 1105
Extension: 1463
Hours: Mon. 2:50-3:50; 5:00-6:00
Tue. 2:50-3:50; 5:00-6:00
Thu. 2:50-3:50

REQUIRED BOOKS
Mary Ryan, Womanhood in America, 3rd edition
Nancy Cott, Root of Bitterness
Alice Rossi, Feminist Papers
Nancy Cott and Elizabeth H. Pleck, Heritage of Her Own
Barbara Harris and Jo Ann McNamara, Women and the Structure of Society
Charlotte Perkins Gilman, Herland
Alice Walker, The Color Purple

Readings that need to be done in the library are indicated by **

COURSE REQUIREMENTS
1. Class participation on a regular basis; I take attendance and consider
    it when I make up final grades.
2. Short quizzes on assigned reading; some announced and some unannounced.
3. Mid-term examination, October 24th
4. One 3-6 page paper on Charlotte Perkins Gilman, Herland DUE NOVEMBER 11
5. One 3-6 page paper on Alice Walker, The Color Purple DUE DECEMBER 10.
6. Regularly scheduled final examination

WARNINGS
1. No late papers accepted.
2. No make-up exams on mid-term or final. I count missed exams as an F
    unless I have an excuse I can verify. In the case of the final I do allow
    students to take the regularly scheduled make-up if the excuse seems to
    warrent it.
3. Papers must be typed and double-spaced.
4. Plagiarism: to take or pass off as one's own the ideas, writings, etc.
    of another; to copy the exact words or to use key phrases from another
    author; to steal key ideas, even if you put them in your own words. If you
    do any of these things, without using a footnote to indicate your source,
    you are guilty of plagiarism. The exact words of another author must be
    put in quotation marks. **If you are guilty of plagiarism in this course, you**
    will receive a failing grade for the semester.
5. **Any student who cheats on a mid-term or final examination will receive a**
    failing grade for the semester.

SEPTEMBER

Thurs, 5th   Introduction

Mon, 9th   Women in Early Colonial Society: Family
              & Work

              Ryan, Womanhood in America, ch. 1 to p. 53.

              Lois Carr and Lorena Walsh, "The Planter's Wife," #1 in
              Cott & Pleck, A Heritage of Her Own.

              Suggested additional reading:
              Gwen Gampel, "The Planter's Wife Revisited: Women,
              Equity Law, and the Chancery Court in Seventeenth
              Century Maryland," in Harris & McNamara, Women and the
              Structure of Society

              Edmund Morgan, The Puritan Family

              John Demos, A Little Commonwealth

              Laurel Thatcher Ulrich, Good Wives

              Lyle Koehler, A Search for Power: The 'Weaker Sex' in
              Seventeenth Century New England

              D. Kelly Weisburg, "Under Great Temptations Heer":
              Women and Divorce in Puritan Massachusetts," Feminist
              Studies, vol. 2, no. 2/3, 1975

              Linda Speth, "More Than Her 'Thirds': Wives and Widows
              in Colonial Virginia", Women and History, vol. V, 1982.

              Gwen Gample and Joan Gunderson, "Married Women's Legal
              Status in Eighteenth Century New York and Virginia,"
              William and Mary Quarterly, vol. 39, Jan. 1982

              Marylynn Salmon, "Equality or Submersion? Feme Covert
              Status in Early Pennsylvania," in Mary Beth Norton and
              Carol Berkin, Women of America, A History

              Catherine M. Scholten, Childbearing in American Society
              1650-1850

Women in Early Colonial Society: The Public
Sphere and Female Rebellion

Ryan, Womanhood in America, ch. 1, 53-67.

Cott, Root of Bitterness, pp. 34-73

Poems by Anne Bradstreet, to be distributed

Suggested additional reading:
Lyle Koehler, "The Case of the American Jezebels:
Anne Hutchinson and Female Agitation During the
Antinomian Turmoil, 1636-1640," in Linda Kerber and
Jane Mathews, Women's America (on reserve); Esther Katz
and Anita Rapone, Women's Experience in America (on
reserve); and William and Mary Quarterly, 3rd series,
vol. 30 (1974) in periodical collection

Mary Maples Dunn, "Saints and Sinners: Congregational
and Quaker Women in the Early Colonial Period,"
American Quarterly, 30 (Winter 1978), 582-601.

Paul Boyer and Stephen Nissenbaum, Salem Possessed

Ben Barker-Benfield, "Anne Hutchinson and the Puritan
Attitude Toward Women," Feminist Studies, vol. 1, fall
1972, 65-96

Carol V. R. George, "Anne Hutchinson and the Revolution
Which Never Happened," in Remember the Ladies, edited
by same.

John Demos, Entertaining Satan: Witchcraft and the
Culture of Early New England

Gerald Moran, "Sister in Christ: Women and the Church
in Seventeenth Century New England," in Janet Wilson
James, ed., Women in American Religion

Margaret Masson, "The Typology of the Female as a Model
for the Regenerate: Puritan Preaching, 1690-1730,"
Signs, vol, 3, no. 2 (1975-76).

Changing Roles of Women in Late 18th Century
Society: The Family and Work

Ryan, Womanhood in America, ch. 2.

Mary Beth Norton, "Eighteenth-Century Women in Peace
and War: The Case of the Loyalists," #5 in Cott and
Pleck, A Heritage of Her Own.

Suggested additional reading:
Catherine Scholten, "'On the Importance of the
Obstetrik Art:' Changing Customs of Childbirth in
America," in Kerber & Mathew, Women's America (on
reserve) or William and Mary Quarterly, 3rd series,
vol. 34 (1977) in periodical collection.

J. William Frost, Quaker Family in Colonial America

Nancy Cott, "Eighteenth Century Family Life & Social
Life Revealed in Massachusetts Divorce Records,"
Journal of Social History, Fall 1976.

Nancy Cott, "Divorce and the Changing Status of Women
in Eighteenth Century Massachusetts," William and Mary
Quarterly, 3rd series, vol. 32, October 1976.

Daniel B. Smith, Inside the Great House: Planter
Family Life in Eighteenth Century Chesapeake Society

Marylynn Salmon, "Women and Property in South Carolina:
The Evidence from Marriage Settlement, 1730-1830,"
William and Mary Quarterly, 3rd series, vol. 39, 1982.

Mary Beth Norton, "A Cherished Spirit of Independence:
The Life of An Eighteenth-Century Businesswoman," in
Norton and Berkin, Women of America, A History

Nancy Schrom Dye, "History of Childbirth in America,"
Signs, vol. 10 (1980), 97-108.

Richard and Dorothy Wertz, Lying-In: A History of
Childbirth in America

Catherine M. Scholten, Childbearing in American
Society 1650-1850

Impact of the American Revolution: Education
and Politics

**Linda Kerber, "Daughters of Columbia: Educating Women
for the Republic, 1787-1805," in Kerber and Mathews (on
reserve) or Stanley Elkins and Eric McKitrick, The
Hofstadter Aegis (on reserve)

Alice Rossi, The Feminist Papers, pp. 3-24
(on Abigail Adams and Judith Sargent Murray)

Suggested additional reading:
Linda Kerber, "The Republican Mother: Women and the
Enlightenment--An American Perspective," American
Quarterly, 28 (Summer 1976), 187-205.

Linda Kerber, Women of the Republic: Intellect and
Ideology in Revolutionary America

Mary Beth Norton, Liberty's Daughters: The
Revolutionary Experience of American Women, 1750-1800

Joan Hoff Wilson, "The Illusion of Change: Women in
the American Revolution" in Alfred F. Young, ed., The
American Revolution: Explorations in the History of
American Radicalism

Ann D. Gordon, "The Young Ladies Academy of
Philadelphia," in Carol R. Berkin and Mary Beth Norton,
Women of America, A History

Women and the Transition to Industrial Society

Ryan, Womanhood in America, pp. 113-25

Gerda Lerner, "Lady and the Mill Girl," #7 in Cott
and Pleck, A Heritage of Her Own

**Thomas Dublin, "Women, Work and the Family: Female
Operatives in the Lowell Mills, 1830-1860," Feminist
Studies, vol. 3, no. 1/2, Fall 1975 in periodical
collection; also copy at reserve desk

Suggested additional reading:
**Ruth H. Bloch, "Untangling the Roots of Modern Sex
Roles: A Survey of Four Centuries of Change," Signs,
vol. 4, no. 2 (Winter 1978), 237-52

**Mary P. Ryan, "Femininity and Capitalism in Antebellum
America," in Zillah Eisenstein, Capitalism Patriarchy
and the Case for Socialist Feminism (on reserve)

Thomas Dublin, Women at Work

Bernita Eisler, The Lowell Offering

Harriet Robinson et. al., Women of Lowell

Faye Dudden, Serving Women, Household Service in
Nineteenth Century America

Susan Strasser, Never Done: A History of American
Housework

Mary H. Blewett, "Work, Gender, and the Artisan
Tradition in New England Shoemaking, 1780-1860,"
Journal of Social History, vol. 17, no. 2 (Winter 1983)
Joan M. Jensen and Sue Davidson, A Needle, A Bobbin, A
Strike

Donald Sutherland, Americans and their Servants:
Domestic Service in the United States from 1800 to 1920
Thomas Dublin, ed., Farm to Factory, Women's Letters
1830-1860

David M. Katzman, Seven Days a Week, Women and Domestic
Service in Industrializing America

Bernard, Richard and Vinovskis, Maris A., "The Female
School Teacher in Antebellum Massachusetts," Journal of
Social History, vol. 10, no. 3 (March 1977).

Allis Wolfe, ed., "Letters of a Lowell Mill Girl and
Friends," Labor History, 17 (Winter 1976)

Female Nature: Views of Female Sexuality

Nancy Cott, "Passionlessness: An Interpretation of
Victorian Sexual Ideology, 1790-1850," #6 in Cott and
Pleck, A Heritage of Her Own

**Carl Degler, "What Ought To Be and What Was: Women's
Sexuality in the Nineteenth Century," American
Historical Review, vol. 79, Dec. 1974 in periodical
collection or in Michael Gordon, American Family in
Social-Historical Persepctive, 2nd edition (on reserve)

Cott, Root of Bitterness, pp. 285-91; 299-303

Suggested additional reading:
B. J. Barker Benfield, The Horrors of the Half-Known
Life

John S. Haller and Robin Haller, Physician and
Sexuality in Victorian America

Charles Rosenberg, Sexuality, "Class and Role in
Nineteenth Century America," American Quarterly, vol.
25 (May 1973)

Female Nature: Medical Views of Women and Health
Reform

**Carroll Smith-Rosenberg, "The Hysterical Woman: Sex
Roles and Role Conflict in 19th Century America," in
Esther Katz and Anita Rapone, Women's Experience in
America

Cott, Root of Bitterness, pp. 63-84; 292-98

Suggested additional reading:
Charlotte Perkins Gilman, The Yellow Wallpaper

**Carroll Smith-Rosenberg, "Puberty to Menopause,"
Feminist Studies, vol. 1, no. 3/4 in periodical
collection or in Mary Hartman and Lois Banner, Clio's
Consciousness Raised (on reserve)

**Ann Douglas Wood, "The Fashionable Diseases: Women's
Complaints and Their Treatment in Nineteenth Century
America," Journal of Interdisciplinary History, vol. 4
(Summer 1973), 25-52 in p[eriodical collection or in
Mary Hartman and Lois Banner, Clio's Consciousness
Raised (on reserve)

R. C. Smith and R. G. Smith, "The Female Animal:
Medical and Biological Views of Women in the Nineteenth
Century," Journal of American History, vol. 60 (Sept.
1973)

Jean Strouse, Alice James

17

Cult of Domesticity: Wife and Mother

Ryan, Womanhood in America, pp. 134-50

**Barbara Welter, "The Cult of True Womanhood," in Katz
and Rapone, Womanhood in America or Gordon, American
Family in Social-Historical Perspective or Barbara
Welter, Dimity Convictions (all on reserve)

Cott, Root of Bitterness, pp. 113-25, 141-47, 157-70

excerpt from Harriot Hunt, Glances and
Glimpses, #1 (to be distributed)

Suggested additional reading:
Catherine Beecher, A Treatise on Domestic Economy, ed.
Kathryn Kish Sklar

Elizabeth Stuart Phelps, Story of Avis

Nancy Cott, The Bonds of Womanhood

Mary Kelley, "At War With Herself: Harriet Beecher
Stowe as Woman in Conflict Within the Home," in Mary
Kelley, ed., Woman's Being, Woman's Place

Mary Grant, "Domestic Experience and Feminist Theory:
The Case of Julia Ward Howe," in Mary Kelley, Woman's
Being, Woman's Place

Carl Degler, At Odds: Women and the Family in America
from the Revolution to the Present. An Important
survey and work of synthesis. On this period see
especially chs. 1-5.

Mary Kelley, Private Woman, Public Stage, Literary
Domesticity in Nineteenth-Century America

Voluntary Motherhood

**Linda Gordon, "Voluntary Motherhood: The Beginnings of
Birth Control Ideas in the United States," in Mary
Hartman and Lois Banner, Clio's Consciousness Raised
(on reserve)

Daniel Scott Smith, "Family Limitation, Sexual Control
and Domestic Feminism," #9 in Cott and Pleck, A
Heritage of Her Own

Suggested additional reading:
Wilson Yates, "Birth Control Literature and the Medical
Profession in Nineteenth Century America," Journal of
the History of Medicine, vol. 31 (Jan. 76)

Cult of Domesticity: Daughters and Spinsters

Welter, "Coming of Age in America," in Welter, Dimity
Conviction (on reserve)

**Nancy Cott, "Young Women in the Second Great
Awakening," Feminist Studies, vol. 3, no. 1/2, Fall
1975, 14-29 in periodical collection

Cott, Root of Bitterness, pp. 130-40.

Louisa May Alcott, "How I Went Out to Service" (to be
distributed)

Suggested additional reading:
Degler, At Odds, ch. 7.

Lee Chambers-Schiller, "The Single Woman: Family and
Vocation among Nineteenth Century Reformers," in Mary
Kelley, Woman's Being, Woman's Place

Lee Chambers-Schiller, Liberty, A Better Husband:
Single Women of America the Generations of 1780-1840

Susan Koppelman, Old Maids: Short Stories by
Nineteen Century United States Women Writers

Mary Wilkins Freeman, A New England Nun (short story)

Female Friendship

Carroll Smith-Rosenberg, "The Female World of Love and
Ritual: Relations Between Women in Nineteenth Century
America," # 14 in Cott and Pleck, A Heritage of Her Own

Rossi, "A Feminist Friendship," in Feminist Papers, pp.
378-96.

**Susan Glaspell, "A Jury of Her Peers," in American
Voices, American Women (on reserve)

Suggested additional reading:
Christopher Lasch and William R. Taylor, "Two 'Kindred
Spirits': Sorority and Family in New England 1839-40,"
New England Quarterly, 36 (March 1963

The Beginnings of Female Reform Movements

Ryan, Womanhood in America, 125-34, 150-54

Carroll Smith-Rosenberg, "Beauty, the Beast, and the Militant Woman: A Case Study in Sex Roles and Social Stress in Jacksonian America," #8 in Cott and Pleck, A Heritage of Her Own

Jean Friedman, "Piety and Kin: The Limits of Antebellum Southern Women's Reform," in Harris and McNamara, Women and the Structure of Society

Frances Harper, "The Double Standard" (to be distributed)

Suggested additional reading:
Barbara Berg, The Remembered Gate

Keith Melder, Beginnings of Sisterhood

Mary P. Ryan, "The Power of Women's Networks: A Case Study of Female Moral Reform in Antebellum America," Feminist Studies, vol. 5 (1979).

**Keith Melder, "Ladies Bountiful: Organized Women's Benevolence in Early Nineteenth Century America," in Katz and Rapone, Women's Experience in America (on reserve

Nancy A. Hewitt, Women's Activism and Social Change, Rochester, New York, 1822-1872

Helen Marshall, Dorothea Dix, Forgotton Samaritan

Beginnings of Female Education

**Kathryn Kish Sklar, "The Founding of Mount Holyoke College," in Carol Berkin and Mary Beth Norton, Women of America, A History

**Ronald Hogeland, "Coeducation of the Sexes at Oberlin College," Journal of Social History, vol. 6 (Winter 1972/73) in periodical collection; copy also at reserve desk.

Suggested additional reading:
Anne Firor Scott, "The Ever Widening Circle: The Diffusion of Feminist Values from the Troy Female Seminary 1822-1872," History of Education Quarterly, 19 (1979).

Keith Melder, "The Mask of Oppression: The Female
Seminary Movement in the United States," New York
History, vol. 55, no. 3 (July 1974).

David F. Allmendinger, "Mount Holyoke Students
Encounter the Need for Life Planning," History of
Education Quarterly, 19 (1979)

Nancy Green, "Female Education and School Competition:
1820-1850," in Mary Kelley, Woman's Being, Woman's
Place

Kathryn Kish Sklar, "Catharine Beecher: Transforming
the Teaching Profession," in Linda Kerber and Jane De
Hart Mathews, Women's America, Refocusing the Past

Alma Lutz, Emma Willard, Daughter of Democracy

Elizabeth Aldren Green, Mary Lyon and Mount Holyoke:
Opening the Gates

Helene Horowitz, Alma Mater

Mary Gilchrist, Life of Mary Lyon

Barbara M. Cross, The Educated Woman in America

Kathryn Kish Sklar, Catharine Beecher, A Study in
American Domesticity

Joan Burstyn, "Catharine Beecher and the Education of
American Women," in Esther Katz and Anita Rapone,
Women's Experience in America

Women in Slavery

Ryan, Womanhood in America, pp. 158-63

Cott, Root of Bitterness, pp. 186-93; 200-16

**Jacqueline Jones, "My Mother Was Much of a Woman:
Black Women, Work, and the Family Under Slavery,"
Feminist Studies, vol. 8, no. 2 (Summer 1982), in
periodical collection

Frances Harper, "The Slave Mother" (to be distributed)

Suggested additional reading:
Jacqueline Jones, Labor of Love, Labor of Sorrow:
Black Women, Work, and the Family from Slavery to the
Present

21

Mattie Griffiths, Autobiography of a Female Slave

Dorothy Sterling, We Are Your Sisters: Black Women in the Nineteenth Century

Jean Fagin Yellin, "Written by Herself: Harriet Jacobs Slave Narrative," American Literature, vol. 55, no. 3 (November 1981).

Loren Schweineger, "A Slave Family in the Ante-Bellum South," in Jean Friedman and William Shade, eds., Our American Sisters

Bert J. Lowenberg and Ruth Bogin, Black Women in Nineteenth Century American Life

Michael P. Johnson, "Smothered Slave Infants: Were Slave Mothers at Fault?" in Linda Kerber and Jane De Hart Mathews, Women's America, Refocusing the Past

Free Black Women

Jean Humez, "'My Spirit Eye'" Some Functions of Spiritual and Visionary Experience in the Lives of Five Black Women Preachers, 1810-1880," in Harris and McNamara, Women and the Structure of Society

**Suzanne Lebsock, "Free Black Women and the Question of Matriarchy: Petersburg, Virginia, 1784-1820, Feminist Studies, vol. 8, no. 2 (Summer 1982) in periodical collection

Abolitionism and the Beginnings of Women's Rights

Ryan, Womanhood in America, pp. 163-65

Harris, Beyond Her Sphere, ch. 3

Rossi, Feminist Papers, pp. 282-322

Cott, Root of Bitterness, pp. 194-99

Suggested additional reading:
**Gerda Lerner, "The Political Activities of Anti-Slavery Women," in The Majority Finds Its Past (on reserve)

Olive Gilbert, Narrative of Sojourner Truth

Helen Griffith, Dauntless in Mississippi: The Life of Sarah Dickey 1838-1904

Gerda Lerner, The Grimke Sisters from South Carolina

Katherine Lumpkin, The Emancipation of Angelina Grimke

Lydia Maria Child, Selected Letters, 1817-80, edited by
Milton Meltzer and Patricia Holland

Sarah Bradford, Harriet Tubman, The Moses of Her People

Milton Meltzer, Tongue of Flame: The Life of Lydia
Maria Child

Blanche Glassman Hersh, "The 'True Woman' and the 'New
Woman" in Nineteenth-Century America: Feminists-
Abolitionists and a New Concept of True Womanhood," in
Mary Kelley, Woman's Being, Woman's Place

Birth of the Woman's Movement

Rossi, Feminist Papers, pp. 241-81.

Suggested additional reading:
Ellen Dubois, Feminism and Suffrage, 1848-1869

Keith Melder, Beginnings of Sisterhood

Norma Basch, In the Eyes of the Law: Women, Marriage
and Property in Nineteenth-Century New York

Elizabeth Cady Stanton, Eighty Years and More

Miriam Gurko, The Ladies of Seneca Falls: The Birth of
the Woman's Rights Movement

Peggy Rabkin, Fathers to Daughters: The Legal
Foundations of Female Emancipation

Elizabeth Griffiths, In Her Own Right: The Life of
Elizabeth Cady Stanton

Celia Morris Eckhardt, Fanny Wright, Rebel in America

Elizabeth Cady Stanton, Susan B. Anthony, and Matilda
J. Gage, History of Women Suffrage

Leslie Wheeler, Loving Warriors, Selected Letters of
Lucy Stone and Henry B. Blackwell, 1853-93

Ellen Dubois, ed., Elizabeth Cady Stanton and Susan B.
Anthony, Correspondence, Writings, Speeches

Eleanor Flexner, Century of Struggle

Eleanor Rice Hays, Those Extraordinary Blackwells

Eleanor Rice Hays, Morning Star: A Biography of Lucy Stone

Elizabeth Cazden, Antoinette Brown Blackwell

Claudia L. Bushman, 'A Good Poor Man's Wife:' Being a Chronicle of Harriet Hanson Robinson and Her Family in Nineteenth Century New England

D. C. Bloomer, Life and Writings of Amelia Bloomer

Woman's Movement Before the Civil War: Ideology, Action and Accomplishments

**Eleanor Flexner, Century of Struggle, chs. 5 & 6

Rossi, Feminist Papers, 407-30

Harriot Hunt, Glances and Glimpses, IV & V (distributed earlier)

Suggested additional reading:
Michael Grossberg, "Who Gets the Child? Custody, Guardianship and the Rise of Judicial Patriarchy in Nineteenth Century America," Feminist Studies, vol. 9, no. 2 (Summer 1983).

Elisabeth Griffith, "Elizabeth Cady Stanton on Marriage and Divorce: Feminist Theory and Domestic Experience," in Mary Kelley, Woman's Being, Woman's Place

MID-TERM EXAMINATION

Women During the Civil War: Continuity and Change

John Faragher and Christine Stansell, "Women and Their Families on the Overland Trail, 1842-1867," #10 in Cott and Pleck, A Heritage of Her Own

**Carole Turbin, "And We Are Nothing But Women: Irish Working Women in Troy," in Carol Berkin and Mary Beth Norton, Women of America, A History

24

Suggested additional reading:
Julie R. Jeffrey, Frontier Women

John Faragher, Women and Men on the Overland Trail

Alice Kessler-Harris, Out to Work

Lillian Schlissel, ed. Women's Diaries of the Westward Journey

Dee Brown, Gentle Tamers: Women of the Old West

Mary Agnes Brown-Groover, "From Concord Mass. to the Wilderness: The Brown Family Letters, 1792-1852," New England Historical and Genealogical Record, vol. 131, Jan. & April 1977

Glenda Riley, "Images of the Frontierswoman: Iowa as a Case Study," Western Historical Quarterly, April 1977

Glenda Riley, ed., "Family Life on the Frontier: The Diary of Kitturah Penton Belknap," Annales of Iowa, Summer 1977

Glenda Riley, ed., Frontierswomen: The Iowa Experience

Christine Stansall, "Women on the Great Plains, 1865-1890," Women's Studies, vol. 4, no. 1 (1976)

Woman's Movement During the Civil War and the Struggle Over the 14th & 15th Amendments

Rossi, Feminist Papers, pp. 430-70.

Suggested additional reading:
Flexner, Century of Struggle, chs. 7, 10 (on reserve)

Mary Elizabeth Massey, Bonnet Brigades

Ann Douglas Wood, "The Was Within a War: Women Nurses in the Union Army," in Esther Katz and Anita Rapone, Women's Experience in America

Women After the Civil War: Breakthrough in Higher Education

Matthew Vassar's Statement to the Trustees of Vassar Female College, 1861 (to be distributed)

**Roberta Wein, "Women's Colleges and Domesticity, 1875-1918," History of Education Quarterly, vol. 14, Spring 1975 (copies on reserve)

**Lynn D. Gordon, "Coeducation on Two Campuses: Berkeley and Chicago, 1890–1912," in Mary Kelley, Woman's Being, Woman's Place (on reserve)

**Patricia Graham, "Expansion and Exclusion: A History of Women in American Higher Education," Signs, vol. 3, no. 4 (1978), 759–73, in periodical collection

Suggested additional reading:
Edith Finch, M. Carey Thomas of Bryn Mawr

Marjorie H. Dobkin, The Making of a Feminist: Early Journal and Letters of M. Carey Thomas

Mabel Newcomer, A Century of Higher Education for American Women

Roberta Frankfort, Collegiate Women

Charlotte W. Conable, Women at Cornell, The Myth of Equal Education

George Herbert Palmer, The Life of Alice Palmer

Elizabeth Alden Green, Mary Lyon and Mount Holyoke: Opening the Gates

Helene Horowitz, Alma Mater

Nancy Sahli, "Smashing: Women's Relationships Before the Fall," Chrysalis, #8, Summer 1979.

Sally G. Kohlstadt, "Maria Mitchell: The Advancement of Women in Science," The New England Quarterly, March 1978

Jill Conway, "Perspective on the History of Women's Education in the United States," History of Education Quarterly, vol. 14 (Spring 1974)

Annie Nathan Meyer, Barnard Beginnings

Florence Converse, Wellesley College: A Chronicle of the Years 1875–1938

Marion Talbot, The History of the American Association of University Women

Joan Burstyn, "Educational Experience for Women at Carnegie-Mellon University: A Brief History," Western Pennsylvania History, April 1973

26

Women After the Civil War: Struggling to Enter the
Professions

Harris, Beyond Her Sphere, pp. 104-21

Rossi, Feminist Papers, pp. 323-55.

Regina Morantz, "Feminism, Professionalism, and Germs:
A Study of the Thought of Mary Putnam Jacobi and
Elizabeth Blackwell," in Harris and McNamara, Women and
the Structure of Society.

Suggested additional reading:
Dee Garrison, "The Tender Technicians," in Mary Hartman
and Lois Banner, Clio's Consciousness Raised

Elizabeth Blackwell, Pioneer Work in Opening the
Medical Profession to Women

Anna Howard Shaw, Story of a Pioneer, chs. 1-6

Harriot Hunt, Glances and Glimpses

Jane B. Donegan, Wopmen and Men Midwives: Medicine,
Morality, and Misogyny in Early America

Judy Litoff, American Midwives, 1860 to the Present

Mary Roth Walsh, Doctors Wanted: No Woman Need Apply

Agnes Vietor, A Woman's Quest: The Life of Marie
Zakrzewska, MD

Virginia Drachman, "Female Solidarity and Professional
Success: The Dilemma of Women Doctors in the 19th
Century," Journal of Social History, vol. 15, no. 4
(Summer 1982)

Carl Degler, At Odds, chs. 15-16

N. Roth, "Personalities of Two Pioneer Medical Women:
Elizabeth Blackwell and Elizabeth Garrett Anderson,"
Bulletin of the New York Academy of Medicine, vol. 7
(Jan. 1971)

Judith Walzer Leavitt, Women and Health in America

John B. Blake, "Women and Medicine in Antebellum
America," Bulletin of the History of Medicine, vol. 39,
no. 2 (Mar-Ap, 1965).

Dee Garrison, Apostles of Culture: The Public Library and American Society 1870-1920

Regina Morantz, "The Connecting Link: The Case for the Woman Doctor in Nineteenth Century America," in Judith Waltzer Leavitt and Ronald L. Numbers, eds., Sickness and Health in America

Regina Morantz and Sue Zachoch, "Professionalism, Feminism and Gender Roles: A Comparative Study of Nineteenth Century Therapeutics," The Journal of American History, vol. 67 (1980), 569-88

Margaret Rossiter, Women Scientists in America, Struggles and Strategies to 1940

Ruth Putnam, ed., Life and Letters of Mary Putnam Jacobi, Pathfinder in Medicine

Working-Class and Immigrant Women in the Late 19th and Early 20th Century

Ryan, Womanhood in America, pp. 167-198

Alice Kessler-Harris, "Where Are the Organized Workers?", #15 in Cott and Pleck, A Heritage of Her Own

Suggested additional reading:
Elizabeth H. Pleck, "A Mother's Wages: Income Earning Among Married Italian and Black Women, 1896-1911," #16 in Cott and Pleck, A Heritage of Her Own

Judith E. Smith, "Our Own Kind: Family and Community Networks in Providence," #17 in Cott and Pleck, A Heritage of Her Own

Dana Frank, "Housewives, Socialists, and the Politics of Food: The 1917 New York Cost-of-Living Protests," Feminist Studies, vol. 11, no. 2 (Summer 1985)

Maxine Sellers, "The Education of the Immigrant Woman, 1900-35," in Linda Kerber and Jane De Hart Mathews, Women's America, Refocusing the Past

Kathleen Jones, "Sentiment and Science: The Late Nineteenth Century Pediatrician as Mother's Advisor," Journal of Social History, vol. 17, no. 1 (Fall 1973)

Nancy Schrom Dye, "Creating a Feminist Alliance: Sisterhood and Class Conflict in the New York Women's Trade Union Leauge, 1903-1914," in Jean Friedman and William Shade, Our American Sisters

Nancy Schrom Dye, As Equals and As Sisters: Feminism,
the Labor Movement and the Women's Trade Union League
of New York

Nancy Schrom Dye, "Sisterhood and Class Conflict in the
New York Women's Trade Union League," Feminist Studies,
vol. 2, 2/3, 1975.

Carl Degler, At Odds, ch. 13

Martha May, "The Historic Problem of the Family Wage:
The Ford Motor Company and the $5 Day," Feminist
Studies, vol. 8, no. 2 (Summer 1982)

Alice Kessler-Harris, Out to Work

Julie A Matthaei, An Economic History of Women in
America

David M. Katzman, Seven Days A Week

Dorothy Richardson, "The Long Day, The Story of a New
York Working Girl," in William O'Neill, ed. Women at
Work

Eylce J. Rotella, From Home to Office: United States
Women at Work, 1870-1930

Margery Davies, "Woman's Place Is At the Typewriter:
The Feminization of the Clerical Labor Force," in
Zillah R. Eisenstein, Capitalism Patriarchy and the
Case for Socialist Feminism

Susan Benson Porter, "The Clerking Sisterhood:
Rationalization and the Work Culture of Saleswomen in
American Department Stores, 1890-1960," Radical
America, March-April, 1978

Margery Davies, A Woman's Place is at the Typewriter

Mary H. Blewett, "The Union of Sex and Craft in the
Haverhill Shoe Strike of 1895," Labor History, vol. 20
(Summer 1979)

Nancy Schrom Dye, "Feminism or Unionism? The New York
Women's Trade Union League and the Labor Movment?",
Feminist Studies, vol. 3, 1/2, Fall 1975

Robin Miller Jacoby, "The Women's Trade Union League
and American Feminism," Feminist Studies, vol. 3, no.
1/2, Fall 1975

Andreia Hourwich and Gladys L. Palmer, I Am a Woman
Worker: A Scrapbook of Autobiographies

Mary Jones, Autobiography of Mother Jones

Rose Schneiderman and Lucy Goldthwaite, All for One

Ann Schofield, "Rebel Girls and Union Maids: The Woman
Question in the Journals of the AFL & IWW 1905-1920,"
Feminist Studies, vol. 9, no. 2 (Summer 1983).5

Mary Antin, The Promised Land: The Autobiography of a
Russian Immigrant

Hasia P. Diner, Erin's Daughters in America: Irish
Immigrant Women in the Nineteenth Century

Virginia Yans McLaughlin, Family and Community:
Italian Immigrants in Buffalo, 1880-1930

Susan J. Kleinberg, "Technology and Work: The Lives of
Working-Class Women in Pittsburgh, 1870-1900," Labor
History, 17 (Winter 1976).

Lucie Cheng Kirata, "Chinese Immigrant Women in
Nineteenth Century California," in Carol Berkin and
Mary Beth Norton, Women of America, A History

Alice Kessler Harris, "Organizing the Unorganizable,"
Three Jewish Women and Their Union" in Milton Cantor
and Bruce Laurie, eds., Class, Sex and the Woman Worker

Emma Goldman, Living My Life

Richard Drinnon, Rebel in Paradise

Emma Goldman, Red Emma Speaks: An Emma Goldman Reader,
ed. Alix Kates Schulman

Candace Falk, Love, Anarchy, and Emma Goldman

Alice Wexler, Emma Goldman: An Intimate Life

Social Reform, 1870-1920

Ryan, Womanhood in America, pp. 198-210

John Rousmaniere, "Cultural Hybrid in the Slums: The
College Woman and the Settlement House," in Esther Katz
and Anita Rapone, Women's Experience in America

Cott, Root of Bitterness, pp. 356-62

Rossi, Feminist Papers, pp. 599-612

Gayle Gullett, "City Mothers, City Daughters, and the Dance Hall Girls: The Limits of Female Political Power in San Francisco, 1913," in Harris and McNamara, Women and the Structure of Society

Suggested additional reading:
Charles E. Strickland, "Juliette Low, the Girl Scouts, and the Role of American Women," in Mary Kelley, Woman's Being, Woman's Place

Patricia Hill, The World Their Household: The American Women's Foreign Mission Movement and Cultural Transformation, 1870-1920

Alice Hamilton, Exploring the Dangerous Trades

Barbara Sicherman, Alice Hamilton: A Life in Letters

Lela Costin, Two Sisters for Social Justice: A Biography of Grace and Edith Abbott

Karen Blair, The Club Woman As Feminist: True Womanhood Redefined, 1868-1914

Gerda Lerner, "Community Work of Black Club Women," in The Majority Finds Its Past

Ruth Bordin, "'A Baptism of Power and Liberty': The Women's Crusade of 1873-1874, in Mary Kelley, Woman's Being, Woman's Place

Blanche Wiesen Cook, "Female Support Networks and Political Activism: Lillian Wald, Crystal Eastman, and Emma Goldman," #18 in Cott and Pleck, A Heritage of Her Own

Ruth Bordin, Woman and Temperance: The Quest for Power and Liberty, 1873-1900

Joan Jacobs Brumberg, "The Ethnological Mirror: American Evangelical Women and Their Heathan Sisters, 1870-1910," in Barbara Harris and Jo Ann McNamara, ed., Women and the Structure of Society

Kathryn Kish Skalr, "Hull House in the 1890s: A Community of Women Reformers," Signs, vol. 10, no. 4 (Summer 1985)

31

Marilyn T. Williams, "New York City's Public Baths: A Case Study in Urban Progressive Reform," Journal of Urban History, vol. 7, no. 1 (Nov. 1980)

Julie Roy Jeffrey, "Women in the Southern Farmers' Alliance: A Reconstruction of the Role and Status of Women in the Late Nineteenth Century South," Feminist Studies, vol. III, no. 1/2, Fall 1975

Florence Kelley, Life Story

Ida Wells Barnett, Crusade for Justice

Rackham Holt, Mary McLeod Bethune: A Biography

Mary Church Terrell, A Colored Woman in a White World

Christopher Lasch, ed., The Social Thought of Jane Addams

Robert Stinson, "Ida Tarbell and the Ambiguities of Feminism," Pennsylvania Magazine of Historical Biography, April 1977

Allen F. David, Spearheads for Reform: The Social Settlements and the Progressive Movement, 1890-1914

Jill Conway, "Women Reformers and American Culture," in Jean Friedman and William Shade, Our American Sisters, 2nd edition

Jane Addams, Twenty Years at Hull House

Jane Addams, My Friend, Julia Lathrop

Josephine Baker, Fighting for Life

Dorothy Rose Blumberg, Florence Kelley: The Making of a Social Pioneer

Mary E. Dreier, Margaret Dreier Robins: Her Life, Letters, and Work

Josephine Goldmark, Impatient Crusader

Barbara Epstein, The Politics of Domesticity: Women, Evangelicalism and Temperance in Nineteenth Century America

William Leach, True Love and Perfect Union

Mary Wood, History of the General Federation of Women's Clubs

Mary Earhart, Frances Willard: From Prayers to Politics

Frances Willard, Glimpses of Fifty Years

Ellen Condliffe Lageman, A Generation of Women: Education in the Lives of Progressive Reformers

Christopher Lasch, The New Radicalism in America, chs. 1 & 2.

William D. Jenkins, "Housewifery and Motherhood: The Question of Role Change in the Progressive Era," in Mary Kelley, Woman's Being, Woman's Place

Maud Nathan, Story of an Epoch-Making Movement

David Pivar, Purity Crusade

Agnes Nestor, Woman's Labor Leader

Mary K. Simkhovitch, Neighborhood: My Story of Greenwich House

Lillan Wald, House on Henry Street

New Feminist Theory: Charlotte Perkins Gilman

Rossi, Feminist Papers, pp. 566-98

PAPERS ON HERLAND DUE

Suggested additional reading:
Charlotte Perkins Gilman, Women & Economics

Charlotte Perkins Gilman, The Yellow Wallpaper

Carl Degler, "Charlotte Perkins Gilman on the Theory and Practice of Feminism," American Quarterly, Spring 1956.

Mary Hill, Charlotte Perkins Gilman, The Making of a Radical Feminist, 1860-1896

Carol Berkin, "Private Woman, Public Woman: The Contradictions of Charlotte Perkins Gilman," in Carol Berkin and Mary Beth Norton, Women of America, A History

33

The Suffrage Movement, 1870–1920

Ryan, Womanhood in America, pp. 210–16

Ellen DuBois, "The Limitations of Sisterhood: Elizabeth Cady Stanton and Vision in the American Suffrage Movement, 1875-1902," in Barbara Harris and JoAnn McNamara, Women and the Structure of Society

Elinor Lerner, "Jewish Involvement in the New York City Wom Suffrage Movement," in McNamara and Harris, Women and the Structure of Society

Suggested additional reading:
Eleanor Flexner, Century of Struggle, pts. II & III.

Ellen DuBois, "The Radicalism of the Woman Suffrage Movement," Feminist Studies, vol. 3, no. 1/2, Fall 1975 in periodical collection

Aileen S. Kraditor, The Ideas of the Woman Suffrage Movement, 1890–1929

Carl Degler, At Odds, ch. 14.

Margaret S. Marsh, "The Anarchist-Feminist Response to the 'Woman Question," in Late Nineteenth Century America," American Quarterly, 30, Fall 1978.

Margaret S. Marsh, Anarchist Women, 1870–1920

William O'Neill, "Feminism as a Radical Ideology," in Dissent, Explorations in the History of American Radicalism, ed. Alfred Young

Ruth Barnes Moynihan, Rebel for Rights, Abigail Scott Duniway

Deborah Pickman Clifford, Mine Eyes Have Seen the Glory: A Biography of Julia Ward Howe

Estelle B. Freedman, "Separatism as Strategy: Female Institution-Building and American Feminism, 1870–1930," Feminist Studies, vol. 5, 1979.

Evan Paulson Ross, Women's Suffrage and Prohibition

Alan P. Grimes, The Puritan Ethic and Woman Suffrage

The Fight for Birth Control, Sexual Freedom, and the "New Woman"

Ryan, Womanhood in America, pp. 227-44

Margaret Sanger, "My Fight for Birth Control," in Rossi, Feminist Papers, pp.517-36

Linda Gordon, "Birth Control and Social Revolution," #19 in Cott and Pleck, A Heritage of Her Own

Suggested additional reading:
Margaret Sanger, Autobiography

Margaret Sanger, My Fight for Birth Control

Linda Gordon, Woman's Body, Woman's Right

James Reed, From Private Vice to Public Virtue

Carl Degler, At Odds, chs. 8-12

David Kennedy, Birth Control in America

James McGovern, "The American Woman's Pre-World War I Freedom in Manners and Morals," Journal of American History, vol. 55, Sept. 1968 in periodical collection or in Esther Katz and Anita Rapone, Women's Experience in America

Nancy Folbre, "Of Patriarchy Born: The Political Economy of Fertility Decisions," Feminist Studies, vol. 9, no. 2 (Summer 1983)

John Paull Harper, "Be Fruitful and Multiply: Origins of Legal Restrictions on Planned Parenthood in Nineteenth-Century America," in Carol Berkin and Mary Beth Norton, Women of America, A History

Lois P. Rudnick, Mabel Dodge Luhan, New Woman, New Worlds

Mable Dodge Luhan, Intimate Memories, 1933-37

William O'Neill, Divorce in the Progressive Era

Elaine Tyler May, Great Expectations: Marriage and Divorce in Post Victorian America

F. Scott Fitzgerald, Tender is the Night

Zelda Fitzgerald, Save Me the Waltz

Paula S. Fass, The Damned and the Beautiful
John C. Burnham, "Progressive Era Revolution in
American Attitudes Toward Sex," Journal of American
History, vol. LIX (March 1973)

Sondra R. Herman, "Loving Courtship or the Marriage
Market? The Ideal and Its Critics 1871-1911," American
Quarterly, vol. XXV, no. 2, May 1973

Linda Gordon, "The Struggle for Reproductive Freedom:
Three Stages of Feminism," in Zillah Eisenstein,
Capitalist Patriarchy and the Case for Socialist
Feminism

18th   Women's Work and Feminism in the 1920s and 1930s

Ryan, Womanhood in America, pp. 217-27, 244-52

Frank Stricker, "Cookbooks and Lawbooks," #20 in Cott
and Pleck, A Heritage of Her Own

Joyce Antler, "Was She a Good Mother? Some Thoughts on
a New Issue for Feminist Biography," in Harris and
McNamara, Women and the Structure of Society

Suggested additional reading:
William Chafe, The American Woman, 1920-70

Maurine Greenwald, Women, War and Work: The Impact of
World War I on Women Workers in the United States

Estelle B. Freedman, "The New Woman: Changing Views of
Women in the 1920's," Journal of American History, vol.
61 (Sept. 1974)

Jacquelyn Dowd Hall, "'A Truly Subversive Affair':
Women Against Lynching in the Twentieth century South,"
in Carol Berkin and Mary Beth Norton, Women of America,
A History

Jacqueline Dowd Hall, Revolt Against Chivalry: Jesse
Daniel Ames and the Women's Campaign Against Lynching

Elaine Showalter, ed., These Modern Women

Patricia M. Hummer, The Decade of Elusive Promise:
Professional Women in the United States, 1920-1930

Winifred Wandersee, Women's Work and Family Values,
1920-1940

Lois Scharf and Joan Jenson, eds., Decades of
Discontent: The Woman's Movement, 1920-1940

Barbara Melosh, "'The Physician's Hand:' Nurses and
Nursing in the Twentieth Century

Dorothy Johnson, "Organized Women as Lobbyists in the
1920s," Capitol Studies, Spring 1972

Cheryl Townsend Gilkes, "'Together and in Harness'"
Women's Traditions in the Sanctified Church," Signs,
vol 10, no. 4 (Summer 1985), 678-699

American Women and the Great Depression

Ryan, Womanhood in America, pp. 253-59

Ruth Milkman, "Women's Work and the Economic Crisis:
Some Lessons from the Great Depression," #22 in Cott
and Pleck, A Heritage of Her Own

**Beverley W. Jones, "Race, Sex and Class: Black Female
Tobacco Workers in Durham, North Carolina, 1920-1940,
and the Development of Female Consciousness," Feminist
Studies, vol. 10, 3, Fall 1984 in periodical collection

Suggested additional reading:
William Chafe, The American Woman, 1920-70

Karen Anderson, Wartime Women: Sex Roles, Family
Relations, and the Status of Women During World War II

Winifred D. Wandersee Bolin, "Economics of Middle-
Income Family Life: Working Women During the Great
Depression," Journal of American History, vol. LXV
(1978)

Susan Ware, Holding Their Own: American Women in the
1930's

Lois Scharf, To Work and To Wed: Female Employment,
Feminism, and the Great Depression

Patterns of Employment 1940-1960

Ryan, Womanhood in America, pp. 278-90

Sheila Tobias and Lisa Anderson, "What Really Happened
to Rosie the Riveter? Demobilization and the Female
Labor Force, 1944-47 (to be distributed)

37

**Susan Reverby, "From Aide to Organizer: The Oral History of Lillan Roberts," in Carol Berkin and Mary Beth Norton, Women of America, A History

Suggested additional reading:
Elinor Langer, "Inside the New York Telephone Company," in William O'Neill, ed., Women at Work

Ruth Milkman, "Redefining Women's Work: The Sexual Division of Labor in the Auto Industry During World War II," Feminist Studies, vol. 8, no. 2 (Summer 1978)

William Chafe, The American Woman, 1920-70

Susan Hartmann, The Home Front and Beyond: American Women in the 1940s

Nancy Gabin, "They Have Placed a Penalty on Womanhood: The Protest Actions of Female Auto Workers in the Detroit-Area UAW Locals, 1945-1947," Feminist Studies, vol. 8, no. 2 (Summer 1982)

Susan Hartmann, "Women's Organizations During World War II: The Interaction of Class, Race and Feminism in Mary Kelley, Woman's Being, Woman's Place

The 1950s, the Feminine Mystique, and Simone de Beauvoir

Ryan, Womanhood in America, pp.259-78

"A Not-So-Rebellious Other: Simone de Beauvoir," in Rossi, Feminist Papers, pp. 672-705

Suggested additional reading:
Betty Friedan, The Feminine Mystique

Simone de Beauvoir, The Second Sex

Sandra Dijkstra, "Simone de Beauvoir and Betty Friedan: The Politics of Omission," Feminist Studies, vol. 6, no. 2, Summer 1980

Simone de Beauvoir, Memoirs of a Dutiful Daughter; Prime of Life, Force of Circumstances; All Said and Done (autobiographical volumes)

Leila J. Rupp, "The Women's Community in the National Woman's Party, 1945-1960," Signs, vol. 10, no. 4 (Summer 1985), 715-740

Rebirth of Feminism

Ryan, Womanhood in America, pp. 305-17

Phyllis M. Palmer, "White Woman/Black Woman: The
Dualism of Female Identity and Experience in the United
States," Feminist Studies, vol. 9, no. 1, Spring 1982,
in periodical collection

Suggested additional reaading:
Amy Swerdlow, "Ladies Day at the Capitol: Women's
Strike for Peace versus HUAC," Feminist Studies, vol.
8, no. 3 (Fall 1982) in periodical collection

Robin Morgan, ed., Sisterhood is Power

Juliet Mitchell, "Women the Longest Revolultion," New
Left Review, Nov.-Dec. 1966

Dolores Janiewski, Sisterhood Denied: Race, Gender,
and Class in a New South Community

Bell Hooks, Feminist Theory: From Margin to Center

Hester Eisenstein, Contemporary Feminist Thought

Nannerl O. Keohane, Feminist Theory: A Critique of
Ideology

Sara Evans, Personal Politics: The Roots of Women's
Liberation in the Civil Rights Movement

Zillah Eisenstein, The Radical Future of Liberal
Feminism

Gloria Joseph and Jill Lewis, Common Differences:
Conflicts in Black and White Feminist Perspectives

Nancy Hartsock, Money, Sex and Power: An Essay on
Domination and Community

Alison Jaggar, Feminist Politics and Human Nature

Albie Sachs, Sexism and the Law: A Study of Male
Beliefs and Legal Bias in Britain and the United States

Bonnie Thornton Dill, "Race, Class, and Gender:
Prospects for an All-inclusive Sisterhood," Feminist
Studies, 9, no. 1 (Spring 1983), pp. 131-50

Rosemarie Tong, Women, Sex, and the Law

Robin Morgan, Going Too Far: The Personal Chronicle
of a Feminist

Betty Friedan: It Changed My Life: Writings on the
Women's Movement

Robin Morgan, The Anatomy of Freedom: Feminism,
Physics, and Global Politics

Rosemary Ruether, Sexism and God-Talk: Toward a
Feminist Theology

William Chafe, Women and Equality: Changing Patterns
in American Culture

Mary Daly, The Church and the Second Sex

Mary Daly, Beyond God the Father

Mary Daly, Gyn/Ecology: The Metaethics of Radical
Feminism

Jo Freeman, The Politics of Women's Liberation: A Case
Study of an Emerging Social Movement and Its Relation
to the Social Policy Process

Carol Gilligan, In a Different Voice

Juliet Mitchell, Woman's Estate

Women and the Economy in Post-Industrial Capitalism

Ryan, Womanhood in America, pp. 317-21

**The following two essays in Capitalist Patriarchy and
the Case for Socialist Feministm, ed. by Zillah R.
Eisenstein, on reserve in the library:

Batya Weinbaum and Amy Bridges, The Other Side of the
Paycheck: Monopoly Capital and the Structure of
Consumption; also appeared in Monthly Review, July-
August 1976; not at Pace, but you might try public
libraries

Heidi Hartman, Capitalism, Patriarchy, and Job
Segregation by Sex; also in Signs, vol. 1, no. 3, part
2 (Spring 1976) in periodical collection

40

Suggested additional reading:
Jean Gardiner, Women's Domestic Labor; also in New Left
Review, 89 (January-February 1975); not at Pace, but
you might try public libraries

Ralph E. Smith, The Subtle Revolution

Carl Degler, At Odds, chs. 17-18.

Bettina Berch, The Endless Day: The Political Economy
of Women and Work

Leslie Tentler Woodcock, Wage Earning Women:
Industrial Work and Family Life in the United States

Louise Kapp Howe, Pink Collar Workers: Inside the
World of Women's Work

Jean Reith Schroedle, Alone in a Crowd: Women in the
Trades Tell Their Stories

Regina Markell Morantz, Cynthia S. Pomerleau, and Carol
H. Fenichel, In Her Own Words: Oral Histories of Women
Physicians

Diana M. Pearce, "Toil and Trouble: Women Workers and
Unemployment Compensation," Signs, 10, 3 (Spring 1985).

Sara Ruddick and Pamela Daniels, Working It Out

Cynthia Fuchs Epstein, Women in Law

Carl Degler, At Odds, chs. 17-18

Evelyn Fox Keller, A Feeling for the Organism: The
Life and Work of Barbara McClintock

Carol Lopate, Women in Medicine

Michael J. Carter and Susan Boslega Carter, "Women's
Recent Progress in the Professions or, Women Get a
Ticket to Ride After the Gravy Train Has Left the
Station," Feminist Studies, vol. 7, no. 3, Fall 1981 in
periodical collection

Mary Roth Walsh, "The Rediscovery of the Need for a
Feminist Medical Education," Harvard Educational
Review, vol. 49, 1979

Women and the Contemporary Family

Ryan, Womanhood in America, pp. 321-45

Nancy Chodorow, "Family Structure and Feminine Personality," in Michelle Z. Rosaldo and Louise Lamphere, eds., Woman, Culture and Society (on reserve)

Suggested additional reading:
Harold Benenson, "Women's Occupational and Family Achievements in the United States Class System," The British Journal of Sociology, vol. XXXV, no. 1, March 1984, copies at reserve desk

Janice Radeway, "Women Read the Romance," Feminist Studies, vol. 9, no. 1, Spring 1983 in periodical collection

Carol Smart, The Ties That Bind: Law, Marriage and the Reproduction of Patriarchal Relations

Lynn Carol Halem, Divorce Reform: Changing Legal and Social Perspectives

Lillian Rubin, Worlds of Pain: Life in the Working-Class Family

Letty Cottin Pogrebin, Family Politics: Love and Power on an Intimate Frontier

Adrienne Rich, Of Woman Born: Motherhood as Experience and Institution

Joyce Trebilcot, ed., Mothering: Essays in Feminist Theory

Dorothy Dinnerstein, The Mermaid and the Minotaur: Sexual Arrangements and Human Malaise

Nancy Chodorow, The Reproduction of Mothering: Psychoanalysis and the Sociology of Gender

Lenore J. Weitzman, The Divorce Revolution: The Unexpected Social and Economic Consequences for Women and Children in America

Nancy Chodorow, "Mothering, Male Dominance, and Capitalism," in Zillah Eisenstein, Capitalist Patriarchy and the Case for Socialist Feminism

Barrie Thorne, ed., Rethinking the Family: Some
Feminist Questions

Heather Rose and Isabel Sawbell, The Growth of Families
Headed by Women

Women's Bodies: The Control of Reproduction and Female
Sexuality

**Adrienne Rich, "Compulsory Heterosexuality and Lesbian
Experience," Signs, vol. 5, 1980

**Roe v. Wade in Linda Kerber and Jane DeHart Mathews,
Women's America (on reserve)

"Court Reaffirms Right to Abortion and Variety of Local
Curbs," New York Times, June 16, 1983 (to be
distributed)

Susan Harding, "Family Reform Movements: Recent
Feminism and Its Opposition," Feminist Studies, no. 7,
no. 1, Spring 1981 in periodical collection

Suggested additional reading:
Zillah Eisenstein, "Antifeminism in the Politics and
Election of 1980," Feminist Studies, vol. 7, no. 2,
Summer 1981

Rosalind Petchesky, "Abortion, Antifeminism, and the
Rise of the New Right," Feminist Studies, vol. 7, no.
2, Summer 1981.

Lee Rainwater and Karoe K. Weinstein, And The Poor Get
Children

Catherine Mackinnon, "The Male Ideology of Privacy: A
Feminist Perspective on the Right to Abortion," Radical
America, vol. 17, no. 4, July/August 1983 (copies on
reserve)

Edwin Schur, The Family and the Sexual Revolution

Susan Brownmiller, Against Our Will

Thomas Shapiro, Population Control Politics: Women,
Sterilization, and Reproductive Choice

R. Christian Johnson, "Feminism, Philanthropy and
Science in the Development of the Oral Contraceptive
Pill," Pharmacy History, vol. 19, no. 2, 1977

Catherine A. Mackinnon, Sexual Harassment of Working
Women

Carole Vance, ed., Pleasure and Danger: Exploring
Female Sexality

Ann Snitow, Christine Stansell, and Sharon Thomson,
Powers of Desire: The Politics of Sexuality

Mary O'Brien, Politics of Reproduction

Helen Roberts, Women, Health and Reproduction

Rosalind Petchesky, Abortion and Women's Choice: The
State, Sexuality and Reproductive Freedom

Beverly Harrison, Our Right to Choose: Towards a New
Ethic of Abortion

Kristin Luker, Abortion and the Politics of Motherhood

Susan T. Nicholson, Abortion and the Roman Catholic
Church

Black Women

PAPER ON COLOR PURPLE DUE

Carol Stack, "Sex Roles and Survival Strategies in the
Urban Black Community," in Michelle Z. Rosaldo and
Louise Lamphere, Women, Culture and Society

Two articles on Black Family that appeared in New York
Times in 1983 (to be distributed)

**Elizabeth M. Almquist and Juanita L. Wehrle-Einhorn,
"The Doubly Disadvantaged: Minority Women in the Labor
Force," in Ann H. Stromberg and Shirley Harkess, in
Women Working (on reserve)

Suggested additional reading:
Gerda Lerner, Black Women in White America

Joyce A. Ladner, Tomorrow's Tomorrow

Josephine Carson, Silent Voices, The Southern Negro
Woman Today

Toni Cade [Bambera], The Black Woman, An Anthology

Voices of Black Feminism, Issue of Radical America,
vol. 18, nos. 2-3.

Bell Hooks, Ain't I A Woman: Black Women and Feminism

Angela Davis, Women, Race and Class

Sharon Harley and Rosalyn Terborg-Penn, The Afro-American Woman

Carol Stack, All Our Kin: Strategies for Survival in a Black Community

Mari Evans, ed., Black Women Writers (1950-1980): A Critical Evaluation

Barbara Smith, Home Girls: A Black Feminist Anthology

Robert Staples, The Black Woman in America: Sex, Marriage, and the Family

Frances Beale, "Slave of a Slave No More: Black Women in Struggle," Black Scholar, vol. 6, no. 6, March 1975

Dexter Fisher, The Third Woman: Minority Women Writers of the United States

Gloria T. Hull, P. B. Scott, and Barbara Smith, But Some of Us Are Brave: Black Women's Studies

Alice Walker, In Search of Our Mothers' Gardens

Syracuse University   DEPARTMENT OF HISTORY

Women in American History
Spring, 1985

Course: History 302/600

This course is an introduction to women in the American
past. It is primarly for upper divison and graduate
students who seek an overview of the roles women have
secured, the images against which they have been matched,
and the social initiatives they have provided. There will
be an emphasis on methods of pursuing women's history and
attention given to the philosophical underpinnings of
particular authors.

Faculty: Sally Gregory Kohlstedt, Associate Professor
201 Maxwell Hall (ext 2349; 2210)
Office Hours: TTh 11-12 am and by appointment

Instruction:

There will be regular lectures, class presentations and
discussion. There will be two examinations, a mid-term on
February 28 and a final. Students will also write a review
of an autobiography and conduct an oral interview. Oral
presentations may include slides and recordings). These are
optional alternatives to a written paper and should be
accompanied by a brief outline and bibliography. Ideas for
projects may come from lectures, readings, or the "issues
and reports" sections listed below. Graduate students will
do one class project and a longer historiographical paper.

Texts: Linda Kerber and Jane DeHart Mathews, Women's America:
Refocusing the Past (Oxford, 1981)

Lauren Thatcher Ulrich, Goodwives: Image and Reality in the
Lives of Women in Northern New England, 1650-1750 (Oxford,
1980)

Thomas Dublin, ed., Farm to Factory, Women's Letters,
1830-1860 (Columbia, 1981)

Ellen Carol DuBois, Feminism and Suffrage: The Emergence of
an Independent Women's Movement in America, 1848-1869
(Cornell, 1978)

Virginia Woolf, A Room of One's Own (Harcourt, Brace, and
World [1928], 1981)

Anne Moody, Coming of Age in Mississippi: An Autobiography
(Dell, 1968)

Evaluation: Students will be evaluated on the basis of written assignments and class participation. They, in turn, will be given an opportunity to evaluate course content, instruction, and achievement of the objectives of the course.

Preparation: Careful, thoughtful reading is one important component of this class. Not all authors will agree with each other and you should try to clarify issues by considering every author's use of sources and point of view. It is best to complete a week's assignment in advance, and I highly recommend that you take written notes on readings. The questions listed below particular assignments (given for the first half of the course, after which you should be able to determine important issues on your own) are to guide you in your reading and prepare you for discussion.

Centuries Ago: Questions of Change and Continuity

(January 15, 17, 22, and 24)

Lectures: Introduction
Old World Legacies and New World Natives
Helpmeets
Innovators

Readings: Kerber and Mathews, _Women's America_, pages 1-64 and Document 1

Ulrich, _Goodwives_

Issues: Fundamental philosophical and methodological issues exist as we investigate the history of women. Should women's history be looked at as a seamless web, continuing personal and public experiences across centuries that are often described as periods of revolutionary change? Does the history of women reinforce or challenge theories about historical process, and how does it fit into "models" of history or other social sciences? How do we discover anonymous women and what do we write about those women who "made it in a man's world?" In our consideration of the colonial period we will develop alternative points of view by which we might assess later historical periods.

Rites and New Initiatives

(January 29 and 31)

47

Lectures: Liberty, Equality and Justice: The American Revolution
Bonds of Womanhood

Readings: Kerber and Mathews, pp. 65-94

Reports: Camp followers
Abigail Adams

Issues: Historians debate the extent to which the American
Revolution was a social revolution, but few deny that
political and legal opportunities and obligations were
different after the event. Consider what the
Revolution meant for women, of all classes and
conditions. What does Kerber mean by "Republican
Motherhood?"

Rites and New Initiatives

(February 5, 7, 12, and 14)

Lectures: Women's Sphere
Women Working for Wages
Minority Women's Lives
Women in Utopian Communities

Readings: Dublin, _Farm to Factory_
Kerber and Mathews, pp. 95-17

Reports: Sarah Bagley
Mother Ann Lee

Issues: Nineteenth century women frequently discussed their
sphere as through it existed in natural laws as well as
the particular social and intellectual environment in
which they found themselves. Consider the relative
limitations and also the relative freedoms which this
concept of spheres provided. For whom was the
so-called "cult of true womanhood" irrelevant? What
were the means of avoiding it?

Sentiments and Activism

(February 19, 21, and 26)

Lectures: Property and Politics
Organizing Women

Readings: DuBois, _Feminism and Suffrage_
Kerber and Mathews, complete Part IIa, documents 2 and

3

Reports: Sarah and Angelina Grimke
                Ernestine Rose
                Sojourner Truth

Issues: How does DuBois explain the emergence of a women's
                movement in the middle of the nineteenth century? On
                what assumptions did various activists built their
                programs? What tactics seemed to them appropriate and
                possible?

Education and Aspirations

(March 5, 7 and 19, 21)

Lectures: Collegiate Experience
                Emerging Professionalism
                Personal Clubs and Public Reform
                Catholic Churchwomen - guest lecture by Margaret
                Thompson

Readings: Kerber and Mathews, Part IIB, documents 5, 6, 7, and 8
                Margaret Rossiter, chapters 1-3

Projects: Women at Mount Holyoke, Oberlin, Vassar, or Syracuse
                Women physicians, lawyers, teachers, or
                    journalists
                Emily Dickinson
                Alice James

Theoretical Concerns in an Age of Science

(March 26 and 28, April 2 and 4)

Lectures: Feminism at the turn of the century
                Social Theory and Activism
                Suffragists, Anarchists, and Assorted Rebels
                Biology and Psychology "on women"

Readings: Kerber and Mathews, review Part IIB, document 9
                Virginia Woolf, A Room of One's Own
                Selections (on reserve) from Mary Wollstonecraft,
                Margaret Fuller, Elizabeth Cady Stanton, Charlotte
                Perkins Gilman

Projects: Gilman, The Yellow Wallpaper (a reading)
                Emma Goldman
                Margaret Sanger

The Industrial World

(April 9, 11, 16 and 18)

Lectures: Technology and Women's Work
             Changes in Domestic Technology
             Working Lives of Women
             War and Social Change

Readings: Kerber and Mathews, Part III to page 353, document 10
             Rossiter, chapters 9-11

Projects: Advertising and women (slides)
             New Deal for women?
             Hallie Flanagan

Establishing Agendas

(April 23, 25, and 30)

Lectures: Myth and Realities of Home Life
             Feminism and Women's Movements
             The 1980s: Roles and Rights

Readings: Kerber and Mathews, complete part III, documents 11-15
             Anne Moody, Coming of Age in Mississippi

Reports: The possibilities are limited only by your
             imagination. A debate might be interesting: Gloria
             Steinam, Mary Daly, Kate Millette, Phyllis Shafley....
             Data on women and education, women and unemployment,
             women and salaries over in recent years: what has been
             changing and what has not?

DUE DATES: Please note that I do not accept late papers without
             prior notification.

             Examination: February 28

             Autobiographical Assignment: March 21

             Oral Interview (perhaps conducted over spring break)
                  and due for discussion in April

             Independent Project: Oral presentation on appropriate
             date or written proposal due February 14 and final
             paper due April 16.

Cornell University

Women in American Society, Past and Present
History 326/Women's Studies 326
Spring, 1986

Professor M.B. Norton
Ms. Vivian Conger

Textbooks:

James Axtell, ed., The Indian Peoples of Eastern America
Carol Berkin and Mary Beth Norton, eds., Women of America: A History
John Demos, Entertaining Satan
Charlotte Perkins Gilman, The Yellow Wallpaper
Sherna Gluck, ed., From Parlor to Prison
Maxine Hong Kingston, The Woman Warrior
Anne Moody, Coming of Age in Mississippi
Mary Beth Norton, Liberty's Daughters
Dorothy Sterling, ed., We Are Your Sisters
Leslie W. Tentler, Wage-Earning Women
Anzia Yezierska, Bread-Givers

This course surveys women's experience in the United States
since the arrival of Europeans on the North American continent. It
is intended to introduce students to the methodology of women's
history in addition to exploring the too-often hidden and forgotten
gender dimensions of many aspects of the American past. Thus most of
the assigned readings for the course are primary sources (written by
women themselves, rather than by historians), and each student is
required to complete an original term paper (10-15 pages) based on
such primary sources. Further, participation in class discussions is
an important part of the course. Each student is expected to attend
section meetings on Fridays and to contribute actively to the
discussion of the assigned readings.

All students in the course are required to attend a special
Women's History Sources Workshop, which will be held on Friday and
Saturdy, February 21-22, co-sponsored by the Cornell University
libraries and the History Department. The workshop will explore the
primary sources available for the study of women in the Cornell
library system and will be invaluable for research on the term paper
assignment for this course. Further details will be announced in
class.

There will be a preliminary exam and a final. A paragraph
defining a term paper topic is due on Friday, March 21. Students
should consult with Prof. Norton or Ms. Conger before preparing this
paragraph. Two copies of the term paper (one will be returned with
comments) are due on Monday, May 5. Students may, if they wish,
submit a first draft for a preliminary critique (only the final draft
will be graded); if this option is selected, the draft must be
submitted on Monday, April 21.

Introduction to Women's History

Jan. 27   Berkin & Norton, Women of America, 3-47

Women in Early America

Feb. 3   Axtell, Indian Peoples, any 4 selections from each of the
               sections, plus all selections by the "Fox Woman"

Feb. 10   Berkin & Norton, Women of America, 114-136
               Demos, Entertaining Satan, introduction, chapters 3, 6, 9,
               12; and at least 3 other chapters (descriptions of
               specific incidents)

Feb. 17   Berkin & Norton, Women of America, 48-67, 92-113
               Norton, Liberty's Daughters, part 1

The Era of Domesticity

Feb. 24   Berkin & Norton, Women of America, 68-91
               Norton, Liberty's Daughters, part 2

March 3   Berkin & Norton, Women of America, 139-149, 177-269

March 10   Sterling, We Are Your Sisters

Organization and Industrialization

March 17   Yezierska, Bread-Givers

March 31   Berkin & Norton, Women of America, 150-176
               Gilman, Yellow Wallpaper

April 7   Gluck, From Parlor to Prison

The Modern Era

April 14   Berkin & Norton, Women of America, 213-417

April 21   Tentler, Wage-Earning Women

April 28   Kingston, Woman Warrior

May 5   Moody, Coming of Age in Mississippi

G8752x
Fall 1986

R. Rosenberg
410 Lehman Hall

GRADUATE COLLOQUIUM IN AMERICAN WOMEN'S HISTORY

This colloquium will survey the secondary literature in American women's history from the Revolution to the present to help students prepare for their doctoral orals in American history.

Requirements for the colloquium include two 5-7 page analytical papers (based on the assigned readings of any two weeks of the student's choice) and a final exam.

1. Women and the American Revolution

> Linda Kerber, Women of the Republic
> Articles by Cott and Norton in Nancy Cott and
> > Elizabeth Pleck, eds., A Heritage of Her Own,
> > selections 4 & 5.

> Recommended:

> > Articles by Walsh, Ulrich and Wells in Heritage
> > Laurel Thatcher Ulrich, Goodwives
> > Mary Beth Norton, Liberty's Daughters

2. The Emergence of the Victorian Family

> Mary Ryan, Cradle of the Middle Class
> Articles by Cott and Smith-Rosenberg (2) in Heritage,
> > selections 6, 8, and 14.
> Jaqueline Jones, Labor of Love, Labor of Sorrow,
> > chapter, 1.

> Recommended:

> > Articles by Lerner, Smith, Faragher/Stansell, and
> > > Glasco, in Heritage.
> > Carl Degler, At Odds, chs. 1-6.
> > Catherine Clinton, The Plantation Mistress
> > Nancy Cott, Bonds of Womanhood
> > Suzanne Lebsock, The Free Women of Petersburg
> > Jan Lewis, The Pursuit of Happiness
> > Ann Douglas, The Feminization of American Culture
> > Carroll Smith-Rosenberg, Disorderly Conduct

3. The Birth of the Woman's Rights Movement

Ellen DuBois, Feminism and Suffrage
William Leach, True Love and Perfect Union, ch. 6.
Ruth Bordin, Woman and Temperance, chs. 1-2.
Ellen DuBois, et. al., "Politics and Culture in Women's
    History: A Symposium," Feminist Studies 6 (Spring
    1980): 26-64.

Recommended:

Eleanor Flexnor, A Century of Struggle

4. Women Workers

Alice Kessler-Harris, Out to Work, chs. 4-7.
Jones, Labor of Love, chs. 2-5.
Articles by Pleck and Smith in Heritage, selections 16
    and 17.

Recommended:

Thomas Dublin, Women at Work
David Katzman, Seven Days a Week
Ruth Rosen, The Lost Sisterhood
Leslie Woodcock Tentler, Wage Earning Women
Mary Jo Buhle, Women and American Socialism

5. Education and the Professions

Rosalind Rosenberg, Beyond Separate Spheres
Margaret Rossiter, Women Scientists in America, ch. 3
Regina Morantz-Sanchez, Sympathy and Science, ch. 9.
Mary Roth Walsh, Doctors Wanted, ch. 6.
Barbara Solomon, In the Company of Educated Women, ch.9

Recommended:

Helen Horowitz, Alma Mater
Jean Strouse, Alice James

6. Settlement Houses and Suffrage

> Allen Davis, _American Heroine_, chs. 1-11.
> Article by Cook, in _Heritage_, selection 18
> Degler, _At Odds_, chs. 13-14
> William Chafe, _American Woman_, intro., chs. 1 & 5.

> Recommended:

>> Kathryn Kish Sklar, "Hull House in the 1890s: A
>> Community of Women Reformers," _Signs_ 10
>> (Summer 1985): 658-677.
>> Estelle Freedman, "Separatism as Strategy,"
>> _Feminist Studies_ (Fall 1979): 512-29.
>> Barbara Sicherman, _Alice Hamilton_
>> Anne Firor Scott, _One Half the People_

7. The Sexual Revolution

> Linda Gordon, _Woman's Body, Woman's Right_, chs. 5-12.
> William O'Neill, "Divorce in the Progressive Era,"
> _American Quarterly_, Summer 1965, 205-217.

> Recommended:

>> David Kennedy, _The Birth Control Movement_
>> James Mohr, _Abortion in America_
>> Kristin Luker, _Abortion and the Politics of
>> Motherhood_
>> Degler, _At Odds_, chs. 8-12
>> James Reed, _From Private Vice to Public Virtue_
>> Elaine May, _Great Expectations_

8. White Collar Promises

> Ruth Cowan Schwartz, _More Work for Mother_, chs. 3-6.
> Lois Scharf, _To Work and to Wed_, chs. 1-2.
> Kessler-Harris, _Out to Work_, ch. 8.
> Article by Stricker in _Heritage_, selection 20.

> Recommended:

>> Susan Strasser, _Never Done_
>> Margery Davies, _Woman's Place Is at the Typewriter_
>> Sheila Rothman, _Woman's Proper Place_

9. Women and the New Deal

Susan Ware, Holding Their Own, chs. 1-4.
Jones, Labor of Love, ch. 6.
Milkman article in Heritage, selection 22.
Lois Scharf, To Work and to Wed, chs. 3-7.
Joan Hoff Wilson and Marjorie Lightman, eds.,
Without Precedent: The Life and Career of
Eleanor Roosevelt, biographical sketch by William
Chafe, pp. 3-27.

Recommended

Winifred Wandersee, Women's Work and Family
Values, 1920-1940
Margaret Hagood, Mothers of the South
Jacquelyn Dowd Hall, The Revolt Against Chivalry

10. War and the Apotheosis of Family Life

Susan Hartmann, The Home Front and Beyond
William Chafe, The American Woman, ch. 6-9
Kessler-Harris, Out to Work, ch. 10.
Nancy P. Weiss, "Motherhood, the Invention of
Necessity,"American Quarterly 29 (Winter 1977):
519-46.
Schwartz, More Work for Mother, ch. 7.

Recommended

Leila Rupp, Mobilizing Women for War
Karen Anderson, Wartime Women
Betty Friedan, The Feminine Mystique

11. The Rebirth of Feminism

Jones, Labor of Love. chs. 7-8.
Kessler-Harris, Out the Work, 11, and "The Debate Over
Equality for Women in the Work Place: Recognizing
Differences," in Women and Work 1 (1985): 141-161.
Chafe, American Woman, ch. 10 and Epilogue.
Sylvia Hewlett, A Lesser Life, Part B.

Recommended

Sara Evans, Personal Politics
Jo Freeman, The Politics of Women's Liberation
Virginia Durr, Outside the Magic Circle
Shirley Abbott, Womenfolk: Growing Up Down South

History V57.0635   Professor Susan Ware
Women and the American Experience   Fall, 1986

    This course is an introduction to the major themes and
experiences of American women from the colonial period through
the present. Through its broad sweep, it will demonstrate both
elements of continuity and change in women's lives over the past
three centuries.

    Course requirements: the required text is Nancy Woloch,
Women and the American Experience (1984). Other assigned
readings are:
        --Nancy Cott, The Bonds of Womanhood
        --Louisa May Alcott, Work
        --Anzia Yezierska, Bread Givers
        --Charlotte Perkins Gilman, Herland
        --Mamie Garvin Fields, Lemon Swamp and Other Places
        --Betty Friedan, The Feminine Mystique
Students will be expected to write two short (3-5 pages) papers,
which will each count one-quarter of the final grade. The first
paper will be an analysis of a 19th century woman's diary; the
second will be a book review of Lemon Swamp, concentrating on
issues of class, race, and gender. The final exam will count for
half the final grade.

                CLASS MEETINGS AND ASSIGNMENTS

9/18 Introduction: Gender as a factor in historical analysis

        UNIT I: WOMEN IN COLONIAL SOCIETY, 1600-1780

    Nancy Woloch, Women and the American Experience, ch. 1-4

9/23 The Rhythms of Preindustrial Life

9/25 Witchcraft

9/30 Cultural artifacts

    Come to class with an artifact from the colonial period (up
to 1780) which helps to explain the texture of women's lives.
You might choose a poem or diary entry; a portrait; a drawing of
colonial furniture, samplers or other handicrafts, tools, or
clothing; a religious tract; town records, property lists, or
business records. Class discussion will revolved around what you
have discovered, and how this example helps us draw
generalizations about women's lives in the period.

10/2 Historians disagree: what impact did the American
Revolution have on women?

UNIT II: WOMAN'S SPHERE AND 19TH CENTURY AMERICA, 1790-1865

Woloch, <u>Women and the American Experience</u>, ch. 5-8
Nancy Cott, <u>The Bonds of Womanhood</u>
Louisa May Alcott, <u>Work</u>

10/7   The Cult of Domesticity

Discussion of Cott, <u>The Bonds of Womanhood</u>

10/9   Health and Sexuality

10/14   Lowell Mill Girls

PAPER DUE on a 19th century woman's diary

10/16   Women and Slavery

10/21   Women on the Frontier

10/23   Women writers

Assignment: read a short story from <u>Godey's Ladies Magazine</u>

10/28   The early Women's Rights Movement, 1840-1868

10/30   The 19th century female life cycle

Discussion of Alcott, <u>Work</u>

UNIT III: WOMEN IN INDUSTRIALIZING AMERICA, 1865-1920

Woloch, <u>Women and the American Experience</u>, ch. 9-14
Anzia Yezierska, <u>Bread Givers</u>
Charlotte Perkins Gilman, <u>Herland</u>

11/6   Immigrant Women and the World of Work

11/11   Discussion of Yezierska, <u>Bread Givers</u>

11/13   Women and the Labor Movement

11/18   Prostitution

11/20   The History of Higher Education for Women, with special attention to the history of women at NYU

11/25   Jane Addams and the Settlement Movement

12/2 Charlotte Perkins Gilman's feminist vision

    Discussion of Gilman, <u>Herland</u>

12/4 Women and the Professions: Medicine as a test case

12/9 The Woman Suffrage campaign

    UNIT IV: WOMEN IN MODERN AMERICA, 1920 TO THE PRESENT

    Woloch, <u>Women and the American Experience</u>, ch. 15-20
          Mamie Garvin Fields, <u>Lemon Swamp</u>
         Betty Friedan, <u>The Feminine Mystique</u>

12/11 Debate: Protective Legislation versus the ERA

12/16 Changing Attitudes towards women's friendships

    PAPER DUE: analysis of Fields, <u>Lemon Swamp</u>

12/18 The Public and Private Worlds of Eleanor Roosevelt

1/6 Popular Culture and Hollywood

    Vacation assignment: watch an old movie from the 1930s with
an eye towards its portrayal of women

1/8 Historians disagree: was World War II a watershed for
women?

1/13 Postwar America

    Discussion of Friedan, <u>The Feminine Mystique</u>

1/15 Contemporary women's lives

Brown University

AC/HI 163
Semester I, 1985

Mari Jo Buhle
82 Waterman St, Rm 206
Office Hours: W, 3:00-5:00

HISTORY OF AMERICAN WOMEN

Cott & Pleck,eds.	A Heritage of Her Own	Touchstone
Baxandall, et.al.	America's Working Women	Vintage
Friedman & Shade,eds.	Our American Sisters,3d ed	Heath
Alcott	Little Women	Modern Library
Robinson	Loom and Spindle	Press Pacifica
Lerner	Majority Finds Its Past	Oxford
Phelps	The Silent Partner	Feminist Press
Solomon, ed.	Short Fiction of Sarah Orne Jewett & Mary Wilkins Freeman	Signet
Jones	Labor of Love, Labor of Sorrow	Basic Books
Sterling, ed.	We Are Your Sisters	Norton
Dorenkamp, et.al.	Images of Women in American Popular Culture	Harcourt, Brace Jovanovich
Cott	Bonds of Womanhood	Yale

Recommended: Mary Ryan Womanhood in America, 3d Edition (Watts)

Books are available for purchase at the Dorrwar Bookstore, 107 Hope St;
and non-circulating at the Sarah Doyle Center Library.

RESERVE READING

Materials designated * are on reserve in the Rockefeller Libary.
Materials designated + are on reserve in the Sarah Doyle Library.

Mary Ryan's Womanhood in America, a valuable textbook, is on reserve in both libraries.[HQ1410/R9] This book is strongly recommended as a supplementary text, especially to students with little background in American history. The Dorrwar Bookstore carries a few copies.

Jacqueline Jones's Labor of Love, Labor of Sorrow is also on reserve. The assigned reading for this term comprises only the first two chapters. Students planning to enroll in AC164 are advised to purchase the book for use during both semesters.

WRITTEN ASSIGNMENTS

Three Short Essays dues: Monday, September 23
                        Monday, October 28
                        Wednesday, November 27

Each essay will be 6-7pp long and will cover a conceptual theme developed within one unit of the course. Topics will be assigned approximately ten days in advance. No extensions will be granted. Late papers, unless accompanied by a verified excuse from the Dean's Office or Health Service, will be downgraded a fraction of a grade for each day late. This policy is designed to ensure fairness.

During the reading period, students will work on a small resarch paper (12-15pp). This paper will be due on Monday, December 16. Directions for this project will be given after the Thanksgiving recess. There is no final examination.

SECTIONS

Sections meet on Friday as designated on the syllabus. Attendance is mandatory. Students should be prepared to discuss the assigned reading for the entire week.

SYLLABUS

I. INTRODUCTION

Sept. 4   Introductory Remarks

Sept. 6   Women's History: Old and New
          Lerner, "New Approaches to the Study of Women in American History,"
              and "Black Women in the United States," Majority Finds Its
              Past, 3-24; 63-82
          Cott & Pleck, "Introduction," A Heritage of Her Own, 9-24
          Recommended: Gordon, Buhle, and Dye, "The Problem of Women's
                      History," Berenice Carroll, ed., Liberating
                      Women's History (1976),75-92

II. PRE-INDUSTRIAL PARADIGMS

Sept. 9   The Colonial Family
          L. Ulrich, "Vertuous Women Found: New England Minsterial
              Literature, 1668-1735," A Heritage of Her Own, 58-80
          J. Demos, "Husbands and Wives," Our American Sisters,41-54
          W. Jordan, "Fruits of Passion: The Dynamics of Interracial Sex,"
              Our American Sisters,154-69
          Recommended: Edmund Morgan, The Puritan Family, (1944)

Sept.11   Work & Expectations of Colonial Women
          Carr & Walsh, "The Planter's Wife: The Experience of White Women in
              Seventeenth-Century Maryland," A Heritage of Her Own,25-57; or
              Our American Sisters,55-86
          America's Working Women,6-40
          R.V. Wells, "Quaker Marriage Patterns in Colonial Perspective,"
              A Heritage of Her Own,81-106
          Recommended: Laurel Thatcher Ulrich, Good Wives: Image and
                      Reality in the Lives of Women in Northern New
                      England, 1650-1750(1982)

Sept.13   Forms of Protest: Anne Hutchinson
<SECTION L. Koehler, "The Case of the American Jezabels: Anne Hutchinson and
              Female Agitation During the Years of Antinomian Turmoil, 1636-
              1640," Our American Sisters,17-40
          Recommended: B. Barker Benfield, "Ann Hutchinson and the Puritan
                      Attitude," Feminist Studies,I(Fall 1972),65-96*

Sept.16   Changes in Sexual Relations --the 18th Century
          N. Cott, "Divorce and the Changing Status of Women in Eighteenth-
              Century Massachusetts," Our American Sisters,87-116;
              "Eighteenth-Century Family and Social Life Revealed in
              Massachusetts Divorce Records," A Heritage of Her Own,107-35;
              and "Passionlessness: An Interpretation of Victorian Sexual
              Ideology,1790-1850," A Heritage of Her Own,162-81
          Recommended: Ellen Rothman, "Sex and Self-Control: Middle Class
                      Courtship in America, 1770-1879," Journal of
                      Social History, 15(Spring 1982),409-26*

62

Sept.18   The Revolution --A Turning Point?
            Norton,"Eighteenth-Century American Women in Peace and War: The
                Case of the Loyalists," A Heritage of Her Own,136-61
            L. Kerber, "Daughters of Columbia: Educating Women for the
                Republic, 1785-1805," Our American Sisters,137-53
            Recommended:Ann D. Gordon, "The Young Ladies Academy of
                            Philadelphia," Carol Berkin & Mary Beth Norton, eds.,
                            Women of America: A History (1979),68-91

Sept.20   Historiography and Problems of Interpretation
<SECTION   G. Lerner, "The Challenge of Women's History," Majority Finds Its
                Past, 168-80
            J. Hoff Wilson, "The Illusion of Change: Women and the American
                Revolution," Our American Sisters,117-36
            E. Kornfeld, "Women in Post-Revolutionary American
                Culture: Susanna Haswell Rowson's American Career, 1792-1824,"
                Journal of American Culture 6(Winter 1983),56-62 * +
            Recommended: Patricia Spacks, "'Ev'ry Woman Is at Heart a Rake'"
                            Eighteenth Century Studies, 8(Fall 1974) * +

III. WOMAN'S CULTURE

Sept.23   Separation of Spheres
            Cott, Bonds of Womanhood, Introduction and Chapter 1
            A. de Tocqueville, "How the Americans Understand the Equality of
                the Sexes"; T.H. Bayly, "Why Don't the Men Propose?"
                Images of Women in American Popular Culture,69-72;177-78
            Recommended: Alice Clark, Working Life of Women in the Seven-
                            teenth Century (1919)

Sept.25   Woman's Sphere: Home and Family
            Cott, Bonds of Womanhood, Chapters 2-4
            C. Beecher, "Statistics on Female Health"; Godey's Lady's Book,
                "Health and Beauty"; W.M. McGuffey, "My Mother's Grave," Images
                of Women in American Popular Culture,20-23;129-31;234-35
            Recommended: Barbara Welter, Dimity Convictions: The American
                            Woman in the Nineteenth Century (1976)

Sept.27   The Nature of Social Relations
<SECTION   Smith-Rosenberg, "The Female World of Love and Ritual: Relations
                between Women in Nineteenth-Century America," A Heritage of Her
                Own, 311-42
            Cott, Bonds of Womanhood, Chapter 5
            T.S. Arthur, "Sweethearts and Wives"; E. Dickinson, "The Letters of
                Emily Dickinson,"Images of Women in American Popular Culture,
                186-96;352-59
            Recommended: Carl N. Degler, At Odds: Women and the Family in
                            America from the Revolution to the Present(1980)
                            Chapters I, II, VII *
                            Estelle B. Freedman, "Sexuality in Nineteenth-
                            Century America: Behavior, Ideology, and
                            Politics," Reviews in American History,10(December
                            1982)

63

Sept.30   "Marry, Stitch, Die, or Do Worse"
           America's Working Women, 41-68
           C. Groneman, "Working-Class Immigrant Women in Mid-Nineteenth
             Century New York: The Irish Woman's Experience," Journal of
             Urban History,4(May 1978),255-74 * +
           Recommended: Joan M. Jensen & Sue Davidson, eds., A Needle, a
                        Bobbin, a Strike: Women Needleworkers in America
                        (1984)

Oct.2   A Community of Women: Lowell
           H. Robinson, Loom and Spindle (1898)
           Recommended: Thomas Dublin, Women at Work: The Transformation
                        of Work and Community in Lowell, Massachusetts,
                        1826-1869 (1979); and Farm to Factory: Women's
                        Letters, 1830-1860 (1982)

Oct.4   Reflections on Life at Lowell
<SECTION   H. Robinson, Loom and Spindle (1898)
           Recommended: Lucy Larcom, A New England Girlhood (1889) *

Oct. 7   The Plantation Mistress
           A.F. Scott, "Women's Perspectives on the Patriarchy in the 1850s,"
             Our American Sisters, 213-26
           Recommended: Catherine Clinton, The Plantation Mistress: Woman's
                        World in the Old South (1982)

Oct. 9   The Slave Woman
           J. Jones, Labor of Love, Labor of Sorrow, Chapter I
           E.V. Genovese, "Life in the Big House" and H. G. Gutman, "Marital
             and Sexual Norms Among Slave Women," A Heritage of Her Own, 290-310
           L.Schweninger,"A Slave Family in the Antebellum South," Our American
             Sisters,227-42
           Recommended: Herbert G. Gutman, The Black Family Under Slavery and
                        Freedom, 1750-1925 (1976)

Oct.11   Reflections on Life Under Slavery
<SECTION   D. Sterling, We Are Your Sisters, Part I
           Recommended: Charlotte Forten,The Journal of Charlotte L. Forten
                        (1953)

Oct.14   Holiday --No Class

Oct.16   "Scribbling Women"
           A.D. Wood, "The `Scribbling Women' and Fanny Fern: Why Women
             Wrote," American Quarterly, 23(Spring 1971),2-24 * +
           F. Fern, "Sober Husbands, Women and Money, Mrs. Weasel's Husband";
             A. Carey, "The Bridal Veil"; and F. Fern, "The Old Maid of the
             Period,"Images of Women in American Popular Culture,72-75;201;
             222-23
           Recommended: Nina Baym, Woman's Fiction: A Guide to Novels
                        By and about Women in America, 1820-1870(1978)
                        M. Kelley, "The Sentimentalists: Promise and
                        Betrayal in the Home," Signs, 4(Spring 1979),434-46

Oct.18   A Community of Women: A Yankee Family
<SECTION   L.M. Alcott, Little Women (1869)
            J.Fetterly, "Little Women: Alcott's Civil War,: Feminist Studies,
                5(Summer 1979), 369-84 * +
            Recommended: Sarah Elbert, A Hunger for Home: Louisa May Alcott
                    and Little Women (1984) *
                    Nina Auerbach, Communities of Women: An Idea in
                    Fiction (1978)

Oct.21   On the Frontier
            Faragher & Stansell, "Women and Their Families on the Overland Trail
                to California and Oregon, 1842-1867," A Heritage of Her Own,
                246-67
            Riley, "'Not Gainfully Employed': Women on the Iowa Frontier, 1833-
                1870," Our American Sisters, 213-26
            Recommended: Lillian Schlissel, Women's Diaries of the Westward
                    Journey (1982)
                    Polly Welts Kaufman, Women Teachers on the Frontier
                    (1984)

Oct.23   No Class

Oct. 25   Categories of Analysis: Race, Class, and Gender
<SECTION   Lerner, "The Lady and the Mill Girl: Changes in the Status of Women
                in the Age of Jackson,1800-1840," Majority Finds Its Past,
                15-30; or, A Heritage of Her Own, 182-96
            L. Glasco, "The Life Cycles of Household Structure of American
                Ethnic Groups: Irish, Germans, and Native-born White in
                Buffalo, New York, 1855," A Heritage of Her Own,268-89
            J. Kelly-Gadol, "The Social Relations of the Sexes: Methodological
                Implications of Women's History," Signs, 1(Summer 1976),800-
                24 * +
            B. Thornton Dill, "Race, Class and Gender: Prospects for an All-
                Inclusive Sisterhood," Feminist Studies,9(Spring 1983),131-
                150 * +
            Recommended:Judith Newton, Mary P. Ryan, and Judith R.
                    Walkowitz,eds. Sex and Class in Women's History
                    (1983)

IV. POLITICS

Oct.28   "The Dawning Light of New Era"
        G.Lerner, "Woman's Rights and American Feminism," Majority Finds Its
           Past, 48-62
        E. DuBois, "Women's Rights Before the Civil War," Our American
           Sisters, 291-316
        D.S. Smith, "Family Limitation, Sexual Control, and Domestic
           Feminism in Victorian America," A Heritage of Her Own,222-45
        S. Truth, "Speech at the Akron Women's Rights Convention"; F. Fern,
           "A Chapter on Housekeeping" and "Feminine Waiters at Hotels";
           Seneca Falls Convention,"Declaration of Sentiments"; J. G.
           Bennett, "Woman's Rigths Convention"; S. Truth, "Address on
           Woman's Rights"; S.J. Hale, "Editor's Table,"Images of Women in
           American Popular Culture, 11-12;289-90;305-6;409-22
        Recommended: Ellen DuBois, "The Radicalism of the Woman Suffrage
                 Movement: Notes Toward the Reconstruction of
                 Nineteenth-Century Feminism,: Feminist Studies, 3
                 (1975), 63-71

Oct.30   Her Sister's Keeper: Moral Reform and Benevolence
        S. Benson, "Business Heads and Sympathizing Hearts: The Women of
           the Providence Employment Society, 1837-1858," Journal of
           Social History, 12(Winter 1978),302-12 * +
        C. Smith-Rosenberg, "The Beauty, the Beast and the Militant Woman: A
           Case Study of Sex Roles and Social Stress in Jacksonian
           America," A Heritage of Her Own,197-221
        Recommended: Barbara J. Berg, The Remembered Gate: Origins of
                 American Feminism (1978)
                 Mary Ryan, "The Power of Women's Networks: A Case
                 Study of Female Moral Reform in Antebellum America,"
                 Feminist Studies, 5(Spring 1979),66-86 +

Nov.1   Female Anti-Slavery
<SECTION   G. Lerner, "Political Activities of Anti-Slavery Women," Majority
           Finds Its Past,112-28
        D. Sterling, We Are Your Sisters, Part II
        S.M Grimke, "The Pastoral Letter of the General Association of Con-
           gregational Ministers of Massachusetts," Images of Women in
           American Popular Culture,409-13
        Recommended: Blanche Glassman Hersh, The Slavery of Sex: Feminist
                 Abolitionists in America (1978)

Nov.4   The Civil War & the Woman's Movement
        D. Sterling, We Are Your Sisters, Part III
        J. Jones, Labor of Love, Labor of Sorrow, Chapter 2
        E. Freedman, "Separatism as Strategy: Female Institution Building
           and American Feminism, 1870-1930," Feminist Studies, 5(Fall
           1979),512-29 * +
        Recommended: Mary Livermore, The Story of My Life (1899)

Nov.6　The Woman Question & the Labor Question
America's Working Women, 85-131
D.J. Walkowitz, "Working-Class Women in the Gilded Age," Our
American Sisters, 243-66
Recommended: Helen Campbell, Prisoners of Poverty (1887)

Nov.8　Sisterhood in Sentiment
<SECTION　E.Stuart Phelps, The Silent Partner (1871)
Recommended: Christine Stansell, "Elizabeth Stuart Phelps: A Study
in Rebellion," Massachusetts Review,13(1972),239-56*+

Nov.11　Women in Higher Education
Mary Putnam Jacobi, "Female Invalidism"　　　* +
E.H. Clarke, "Sex in Education"; and M.C.Thomas, "Diary
Excerpts(1870,1871)," Images of Women in American Popular
Culture, 43-47
Helen Lefkowitz Horowitz, Alma Mater: Design and Experience in
the Women's Colleges (1984), Chapter "Acting a Manly Part"* +
Recommended: Julia Ward Howe,ed., Sex and Education: A Reply to
Dr. E.H. Clark's "Sex in Education" (1874)

Nov.13　Beyond Woman's Sphere
J. Antler, "Feminism and Life-Process: The Life and Career of Lucy
Sprague Mitchell, Feminist Studies, 7(Spring 1981),134-57 * +
S. Weir Mitchell, "Rest"; and C.P. Gilman, "The Yellow Wallpaper,"
Images of Women in American Popular Culture,24-38
G.Lerner, "Community Work of Black Club Women," Majority Finds Its
Past, 83-93
J. St. Pierre Ruffin, "Address to the First National Conference of
Colored Women," Images of Women in American Popular Culture,
400-03
Recommended: Karen J. Blair, The Club Woman as Feminist (1980)

Nov.15　Race & Class Dimensions of "Woman's Advancement"
<SECTION　D. Sterling, We Are Your Sisters, Parts IV & V
G. Lerner, "Black and White Women in Interaction and Confrontation,"
A Majority Finds Its Past, 94-111
S. Levine, "Labor's True Woman: Domesticity and Equal Rights in the
Knights of Labor," Journal of American History,70(September
1983),323-39 * +
Recommended: Sharon Harley and Rosalyn Terborg-Penn, The Afro-
American Woman: Struggles and Images (1978)

Nov.18　The Woman's Crusade
R. Bordin, "'A Baptism of Power and Liberty': The Women's Crusade
of 1873-1874," Ohio History, 87(Autumn 978),383-404 * +
J.R. Jeffrey, "Women in the Southern Farmers' Alliance: A Recon-
sideration of the Role and Status of Women in the Late Nine-
teenth-Century South," Our American Sisters,348-71
Recommended: Barbara Leslie Epstein, Politics of Domesticity(1981)
Donald B. Marti, "Sisters of the Grange: Rural
Feminism in the late Nineteenth Century," Agricultural
History, 58(July 1984)

Nov.20   Socialist Feminism & Cultural Feminism in the 19th Century
         N. Cott, Bonds of Womanhood, Conclusion
         Recommended: Mari Jo Buhle, Women and American Socialism,1870-1920
                      (1981), Chapters 1 & 2

Nov.22   Culture & Politics
<SECTION DuBois, et.al., "Politics and Culture in Women's History: A
              Symposium," Feminist Studies, 6(Spring 1980),26-64 * +

Nov.25   A Droll Perspective on Woman's Rights

V. REFLECTIONS

Dec.2   Immigrant Women, Culture, and Politics
         Carol Turbin, "We Are Nothing But Women: Irish Working Women in
              Troy"; and Lucie Cheng Hirata, "Chinese Immigrant Women in
              Nineteenth-Century California," Women of America: A History,
              Berkin and Norton, eds., 202-44 *
         "Speak Out on Domestic Service"   * +
         Recommended: Hasia R. Diner, Erin's Daughters in America: Irish
              Immigrant Women in the Nineteenth Century (1983)

Dec.4   Demise of New England
         B. Solomon,ed., Short Fiction of Sarah Orne Jewett and Mary Wilkins
              Freeman
         V. Drachman, "Female Solidarity and Professional Success: The
              Dilemma of Women Doctors in Late Nineteenth-Century America,"
              Journal of Social History,15(Summer 1982),607-20 * +
         Recommended: Gail Parker,ed., The Oven Birds: American Women and
              Womanhood, 1820-1920 (1972)

Dec.6   Local Color/Woman's Culture
<SECTION A.D. Wood, "The Literature of Impoverishment: The Women Local Color-
              ists in America, 1865-1912," Women's Studies, 1(Winter 1972)*+
         Recommended: Susan Koppelman, Old Maids: A Selection of Short
              Stories by Nineteenth-Century Women Writers (1984)*
              Josephine Donovan, New England Local Color (1983)*

Dec.9   EVALUATIONS & DISCUSSION OF FINAL PROJECT
         G. Lerner, "Placing Women in History" and "The Majority Finds Its
              Past," Majority Finds Its Past,145-67
         Recommended: Darlene R. Roth, "Review Essay: Growing Like Topsy:
              Research Guides to Women's History," Journal of
              American History, 70(June 1983),95-100 +
              Jill K. Conway, Linda Kealey, and Janet E. Schulte,
              The Female Experience in Eighteenth- and Nineteenth-
              Century America: A Guide to the History of Women
              (1982)
              Nancy Sahli, Women and Sexuality in America: A Bib-
              liography (1984)

History 173A   Professor Estelle Freedman
Winter, 1986-7   Office: Rm 7, Bldg 200
M-W-Th 11:00-12:15   Hours: Wed, 2-4 p.m.

AMERICAN WOMEN'S HISTORY, 1620-1870

History 173A is the first part of a two-quarter survey of women's historical experiences in the United States from the colonial era to the present. Each quarter is a five unit course. During the winter quarter we will cover the period up to 1870 with the following themes in mind: women's relation to the economy, to the family, and to political movements; changing ideals of womanhood; and class, race and ethnic variations in female experience. A major goal of the course is to present women's history both as an integral part of American social history and as a unique subject of historical investigation.

Although I do not require that students take both 173A and 173B, I strongly urge you to do so. The themes discussed this quarter will be explored further and brought up-to-date in spring quarter. Most of the books required for this class will be required next quarter as well.

REQUIREMENTS

Attendance at all classes and completion of all reading assignments is critical. Most class sessions will combine a lecture, your questions and discussion of the reading assignments. Therefore it is important that students complete the assigned readings by the beginning of each week. On several occasions we will devote an entire class to discussion of a particular book or set of readings.

Writing requirements consist of one take home mid-term (due Feb. 2), a take-home final exam (due Mar. 18), and one 5 page paper based on UNCLE TOM'S CABIN (due Feb. 20).

BOOKS (all paperbacks, ordered at bookstore and Meyer reserve)

> Nancy Woloch, WOMEN AND THE AMERICAN EXPERIENCE (background text)
> Nancy Cott and Elizabeth Pleck, eds., A HERITAGE OF HER OWN
> Nancy Cott, ed., ROOT OF BITTERNESS: DOCUMENTS OF THE SOCIAL HISTORY OF AMERICAN WOMEN
> Linda Kerber, WOMEN OF THE REPUBLIC: INTELLECT AND IDEOLOGY IN REVOLUTIONARY AMERICA
> Jacqueline Jones, LABOR OF LOVE, LABOR OF SORROW: BLACK WOMEN, WORK AND THE FAMILY FROM SLAVERY TO THE PRESTENT
> Harriet Beecher Stowe, UNCLE TOM'S CABIN
> COURSE READER, at Stanford University Bookstore (contains historical articles not in the above texts and primary documents about Native American, black, rural, lesbian and working class women and on the women's rights movement)

> For browsing about individual lives, see NOTABLE AMERICAN WOMEN at Green Library

History 173A, Winter 1987

SUMMARY OF TOPICS AND ASSIGNMENTS   DATES

I. INTRODUCTION TO WOMEN'S HISTORY   Jan. 7-8

   Michelle Zimbalist Rosaldo, "Woman, Culture and Society: A Theoretical
      Overview," COURSE READER #1
   Joan Kelly, "The Social Relations of the Sexes: Methodological Implications
      of Women's History" COURSE READER #2
   Gerda Lerner, "The Challenge of Women's History," COURSE READER #3

II. PRE-INDUSTRIAL AMERICA

   A. WOMEN, WORK AND FAMILY TO 1750   Jan. 12-15

   Documents from Axtell, INDIAN PEOPLES, Jensen, WITH THESE HANDS, and
      Baxandall, AMERICA'S WORKING WOMEN, in COURSE READER #4-6
   Ulrich, "Vertuous Women Found," in HERITAGE
   Carr and Walsh, "The Planter's Wife," in HERITAGE
   Cott, ROOT, pp. 34-46
   Woloch, WOMEN AND THE AMERICAN EXPERIENCE, chs. 1-2
   (We will discuss the readings on Jan. 15)

      No class Mon., Jan. 19, Martin Luther King, Jr.'s birthday observed

   B. SLAVERY, SERVITUDE AND ECONOMIC CHANGE
           IN THE EIGHTEENTH CENTURY   Jan. 21-22

   Cott, ROOT, pp. 31-33, 77-82
   Jordan, "Fruits of Passion," COURSE READER #7
   Cott, "Eighteenth Century Family Life," HERITAGE
   Woloch, WOMEN, ch. 4

   C. THE AMERICAN REVOLUTION AND ITS LEGACY   Jan. 26-29

   Cott, ROOT, 91-110
   Documents from Rossi, FEMINIST PAPERS, COURSE READER #8
   Norton, "Eighteenth-Century American Women in Peace and War," HERITAGE
   Kerber, WOMEN OF THE REPUBLIC, chs. 2-4, 7-9 (pp. 33-136, 189-288)
   (We will spend most of the class of Jan. 28 discussing these readings.)

      MID-TERM EXAM HANDED OUT JAN. 29 AND DUE FEB. 2 AT 11 A.M.

Further reading on Part II:

Mary P. Ryan, WOMANHOOD IN AMERICA, chs. 1-2; Carolyn Niethammer, DAUGHTERS OF
THE EARTH: THE LIVES AND LEGENDS OF AMERICAN INDIAN WOMEN; Edmund S. Morgan,
THE PURITAN FAMILY; John Demos, A LITTLE COMMONWEALTH and ENTERTAINING SATAN:
WITCHCRAFT AND THE CULTURE OF EARLY NEW ENGLAND; Julia Cherry Spruill, WOMEN'S
LIFE AND WORK IN THE SOUTHERN COLONIES; Lyle Koehler, A SEARCH FOR POWER: THE
°WEAKER SEX'IN SEVENTEENTH CENTURY NEW ENGLAND; Laurel Ulrich, GOODWIVES: IMAGE
AND REALITY IN THE LIVES OF WOMEN IN NORTHERN NEW ENGLAND, 1650-1750; Robert V.
Wells, "Quaker Marriage Patterns in a Colonial Perspective," in HERITAGE; Mary
Beth Norton, LIBERTY'S DAUGHTERS: THE REVOLUTIONARY EXPERIENCE OF AMERICAN
WOMEN, 1750-1800; Mary Wollstonecraft, A VINDICATION OF THE RIGHTS OF WOMAN, in
Rossi, FEMINIST PAPERS.

History 173A, Winter 1985

III. INDUSTRIALIZATION AND THE "FEMALE SPHERE"

Over the next two weeks all students should read Harriet Beecher Stowe, UNCLE TOM'S CABIN. The five page paper, due on Feb. 20, can address one of the following topics, drawing on course readings and the novel: northern women's attitudes towards race; women's health; or the meaning of domesticity for northern and southern women, both black and white. You can write on a different topic as long as it is approved by me at least a week before the paper is due.

A. DOMESTICITY AND SISTERHOOD   Feb. 2-5

Cott, ROOT, 117-125, 130-40, 157-77
Lerner, "The Lady and the Mill Girl," HERITAGE
Smith-Rosenberg, "The Female World of Love and Ritual," HERITAGE
Documents from Lerner, BLACK WOMEN, and Sterling, WE ARE YOUR SISTERS,
  COURSE READER #9   *Stansell, CITY OF WOMEN*
Woloch, WOMEN, chs. 5-6

B. WOMEN'S WORK OUTSIDE THE HOME   Feb. 9-12

Cott, ROOT, 126-41, 200-216
Documents from Axtell, Lerner and Sterling, COURSE READER #10
Jensen, "Native American Women and Agriculture," COURSE READER #11
Faragher and Stansell, "Women and Their Families on the Overland
  Trail," HERITAGE
Jones, LABOR OF LOVE, chap. 1
(We will discuss the readings on Feb. 12)

**No class Feb. 18, George Washington's birthday observed (not to
mention Abraham Lincoln and Susan B. Anthony!)**

* *

                                                        Feb. 18-19

This week we depart from the regular class routine to concentrate on cultural sources of women's history. We will have a slide review of previous topics, a guest lecture on women and American art, and we may even have time for some music. We will also discuss Uncle Tom's Cabin.

* *

C. HEALTH AND SEXUALITY   Feb. 23-26

Cott, ROOT, 263-270, 277-92, 299-303
Cott, "Passionlessness," HERITAGE
Gutman, "Marital and Sexual Norms," HERITAGE
Documents from Lerner and from Katz, GAY AMERICAN HISTORY, COURSE READER
  #12
Smith, "Family Limitation,... " HERITAGE
(We will discuss the readings on Feb. 26)

Further reading on Part III:

71

Nancy Cott, THE BONDS OF WOMANHOOD; Kathryn Kish Sklar, CATHARINE BEECHER: A
STUDY IN AMERICAN DOMESTICITY; Louisa May Alcott, LITTLE WOMEN; Carl Degler,
AT ODDS: WOMEN AND THE FAMILY IN AMERICA; Ann Firor Scott, THE SOUTHERN LADY;
Catharine Clinton, THE PLANTATION MISTRESS; Julie Roy Jeffrey, FRONTIER WOMEN;
Suzanne Lebsock, THE FREE WOMEN OF PETERSBURG; Thomas Dublin, WOMEN AT WORK;
THE TRANSFORMATION OF WORK AND COMMUNITY IN LOWELL, MASSACHUSETTS, 1826-1860;
James Mohr, ABORTION IN AMERICA; Lillian Faderman, SURPASSING THE LOVE OF MEN;
Ben Barker-Benfield, THE HORRORS OF THE HALF-KNOWN LIFE; Christine Stansell,
CITY OF WOMEN: SEX AND CLASS IN NEW YORK CITY, 1789-1860.

IV. FROM REFORM TO WOMEN'S RIGHTS

   A. WOMEN AND ANTE-BELLUM REFORM   Mar. 2-5

      Cott, ROOT, 181-85, 194-99
      Smith-Rosenberg, "Beauty, The Beast, and the Militant Woman," HERITAGE
      Documents from Rossi and Sterling, COURSE READER #13
      (We will discuss these readings on March 11)

   B. THE WOMEN'S RIGHTS MOVEMENT, 1848-1870   Mar. 9-12

      Woloch, WOMEN, chaps 7-8
      Documents from Rossi and Sterling, COURSE READER #14
      (Readings discussed March 11)

At the last class we will have a slide review and take time to evaluate the
course. The take-home final exam questions will be handed out at the end of
class and will be due at the History Department office by 4 p.m. on Wednesday,
March 18th. There will be no incompletes, except in the case of dire
emergency. Late papers will be penalized by one full grade per day; no papers
will be accepted after Thursday, March 19th.

Further reading on Part IV:

Eleanor Flexner, CENTURY OF STRUGGLE; Blanche Hersh, THE SLAVERY OF SEX:
FEMINIST ABOLITIONISTS IN AMERICA; Barbara Berg, THE REMEMBERED GATE: THE
ORIGINS OF AMERICAN FEMINISM; Mary Ryan, THE CRADLE OF THE MIDDLE CLASS; Ellen
DuBois, FEMINISM AND SUFFRAGE; Elisabeth Griffith, IN HER OWN RIGHT: THE LIFE
OF ELIZABETH CADY STANTON; Nancy Hewitt, WOMEN'S ACTIVISM AND SOCIAL CHANGE:
ROCHESTER, NEW YORK, 1822-1872; Celia Eckhardt, FANNY WRIGHT: REBEL IN AMERICA

* *

MARCH 8 IS INTERNATIONAL WOMEN'S DAY

   Watch for listings of speakers and special events during National Women's
History Week. If anyone is interested in working with the group that is
planning these events, please let me know early in the quarter.

* *

History 173A, U.S. Women's History, 1620-1879
Winter, 1987
Professor Estelle Freedman

SUMMARY OF LECTURES AND CLASS DISCUSSIONS

Jan. 7 Introductions to course, syllabus, students, teacher
  8 Why Women's History--historiography

  12 Native and English Women on the Eve of Settlement
  14 New England family life
  15 Women's Work in the Early Colonies (+readings)

  19 HOLIDAY
  21 Slaves and indentured servants
  22 Social change in the 18th Century

  26 Women in the Era of the American Revolution
  28 The Impact of the Revolution--Kerber reading discussion
  29 Slide review; hand out mid-term, due Feb. 2 in class

Feb. 2 Industrialization and the Female Sphere
  4 Domesticity--Ideal and Labor
  5 Sisterhoods: Education and Religion

  9 Wage labor--textile and urban workers
  11 Slavery
  12 The West--Pioneers and Native Americans (+readings)

  16 HOLIDAY
  18 Guest lecture by Lesley Wright on women and American art
  19 Slides and discussion of UNCLE TOM'S CABIN

  23 Fertility decline, contraception and health
  25 Sexuality and Sexual Deviance
  26 Slides and discussion of readings

Mar. 2 Women and Ante-bellum Reform, 1: Origins
  4 Women and Ante-bellum Reform, 2: Organizational change
  5 The origins of the women's rights movement

  9 Growth and Crisis in 19c women's rights, to 1870
  11 Discussion of Readings
  12 Summary, review and course evaluations; hand out exams

  18 Exams due at History Department Office by 4 p.m.

St. Olaf College

Seminar   The Origins of American Culture   Dr. Joan Gundersen

History 92/Am. Studies 99
Optional Women's Studies Credit

Students should purchase the following books:

   Thad Tate and David Ammerman, The Chesapeake in the Seventeenth Century
   Edwin Perkins, The Economy of Colonial America
   Peter Wood, Black Majority
   Paul Boyer and Stephen Nissenbaum, Salem Possessed
   Linda Kerber, Women of the Republic

A packet of primary sources should be purchased at the history office.

Course background: No field of history has expanded more rapidly in the last
   twenty years than the area of social history. Revitalized and
   reconceptualized as the "New Social History", the field relies on a
   variety of interdisciplinary approaches and has blurred any distinction
   between the approaches of history and American Studies. One measure of
   that growth is that women's history, now a separate field, began as part
   of social history. The impact of the New Social History on colonial
   studies has been revolutionary. Colonialists were among the first to
   embrace the new techniques because they freed colonial history from a
   political framework which fit poorly. This course is a reflection of the
   new scholarship, and will be organized topically so that we may compare
   and contrast the variety of experiences in Colonial America, of all
   races, classes, and both sexes.

Course format: This class will be run as a seminar. Lectures will be
   infrequent. The class will depend upon student participation and
   preparation to succeed. Students will be expected to come prepared to
   discuss assigned materials, to lead class discussions, present reports,
   and to write in several historical genres. There will be no final exam,
   rather the final draft of a substantial research paper will be due at the
   time of the exam. Students will present an earlier draft of the paper to
   the class for comments and criticism before rewriting it to submit for
   the final. To facilitate this rewriting, there will be a optional
   session on computer word processing. If a class can be said to have a
   mood, the mood of this course will be collegiality, not competitivness.
   We will be a group of scholars sharing findings and comments with each
   other.

Special credit: This course is crosslisted for history, American studies, and
   women's studies credit. In general this will make little difference.
   All students will have the same assignments and requirements. Women's
   studies students should choose a paper topic dealing with women and
   choose at least one book review and two-thirds of the article readings
   from among the works starred as appropriate for women's history.

74

American studies students, may choose to do their research papers using the approach of another discipline (for example, economic analysis).

Course assignments:

1) Research Paper of 15-25 pages in length. This paper should demonstrate the student's abilities to find appropriate documents, articles, and monographs. It should have a thesis and offer an interpretation about a topic appropriate for the course of the student's choice. 35% of grade.

2) One page abstracts on assigned books (Perkins, Wood, Boyer & Nissenbaum, and Kerber). An abstract is a summary without analysis which states the thesis, main arguments, and findings. See syllabus for dates due. 24% of grade.

3) Oral report on a topic from the accompanying list. This report should not exceed 10 minutes in length. It should draw from a variety of sources, and the presenter should have copies of a bibliography to circulate to the class at the time of the presentation. 10% of grade.

4) Discussion leading. The class will be divided into small groups. Each group will be responsible for leading the discussion on one of the assigned monographs, and for making a short presentation to the class each time an article assignment is due. Out of each set of four articles, each group will be assigned one to read. 11% of grade.

5) Two two-page typed book reviews on books drawn from the accompanying reading list. Reviews MUST include critical analysis and comments. One review is due Oct. 3 and the other Nov. 5.   20% of grade.

Assignments

Sept.   5 Th   Introduction

UNIT I   THE ECONOMY

Sept. 10 T   The Empire
                Perkins due
                Read: packet, pp. 1-4

Sept. 12 Th   Farming
                Reports on New England land and open grazing
                Read: Article from list; packet, pp. 7-10

Sept. 17 T   Trade
                Reports on currency, tobacco
                Read: one of the pamphlets on reserve; packet, pp. 5-6

75

UNIT II   THE PEOPLE

    Sept.   19 Th Red
                    Report on Iroquois
                    Read: Article from list; packet, p. 11

    Sept.   24 T   White
                    Report on Bastardy
                    Read: Tate essays 2, 7; packet, pp. 12-14

    Sept.   26 Th Black
                    Wood due
                    Read: Article from list

UNIT III   THE FAMILY

    Oct.   5   T   Marriage
                    Report on marriage contracts
                    Read: Tate essay 4; Article from list; packet, pp. 18-22

    Oct.   3   Th No Class
                    Book Review Due

    Oct.   8   T   Life and Death
                    Read: Tate essay 3; packet, pp. 15-17

    Oct.   10 Th Children and Servants
                    Reports on servants
                    Read: Tate essay 5; Article from list; packet, pp. 32-40

UNIT IV   THE COMMUNITY

    Oct.   15 T   Settlement Patterns
                    Read: Tate essay 6; packet, pp. 23-31

    Oct.   17 Th Defining Community
                    Boyer & Nissenbaum due

    Oct.   22 T   Political Community
                    Report on courts
                    Read: Tate essays 8,9; Article from list

UNIT V   RELIGION

    Oct.   24 Th Established Religions
                    Report on Jews
                    Read: packet, pp. 45-51; Article from list

    Oct.   29 T   Fall Break

    Oct.   31 Th Great Awakening
                    Read: packet, pp. 55-60; Article from list

    Nov.   5   T   Disestablishment

Book Review due
Read: packet, pp. 61-62

UNIT VI   ARTS AND SCIENCES

Nov.   7 Th   Education
              Reports on King's College, literacy, slave schools
              Read: packet, pp. 63-75

Nov.   12 T   Theater in the Colonies

Nov.   14 Th Performing Arts and Literature
              Read: packet, 76-91

Nov.   19 T   Science
              Reports on transit of Venus, childbirth
              Read: packet, pp. 92-100
              First group of papers due

UNIT VII   AN ERA ENDS

Nov.   21 Th Student Paper Presentations
              Read: copies of papers in advance

Nov.   26 T   Student Paper Presentations
              Read: copies of papers in advance

Dec.   3 Th Student Paper Presentations
              Read: copies of papers in advance

Dec.   5 Th Student Paper Presentations
              Read: copies of papers in advance

Dec.   10 T   Impact of the Revolution
              Kerber book due

Oral Report Topics

Sept. 12	How did New England towns assign land?
Sept. 12	Grazing rights and fences (or how come there are so many laws about pigs?)
Sept. 17	Currency in the colonies
Sept. 17	Who marketed tobacco?
Sept. 19	Women's roles among the Cherokee
Sept. 24	Regulation of Bastardy
Oct. 1	Pre-Nuptual Agreements
Oct. 10	Laws governing indentured servants
Oct. 10	Who were the indentured servants?
Oct. 22	Who appeared at county courts and why?
Oct. 24	Jews in the colonies
Nov. 7	The founding of Kings College
Nov. 7	Schools for slaves in Virginia

Nov. 7	How literate were colonial women?
Nov. 19	Colonial efforts during the transit of Venus
Nov. 19	Childbirth practices

Article Assignments

Sept. 12

*James Henretta, "Families and Farm: Mentalite' in Pre-Industrial America," William and Mary Quarterly, 3rd ser., XXXV(1978), 477-498.

*David Coon, "Eliza Lucas Pinckney and the Reintroduction of Indigo Culture in South Carolina," Journal of Southern History, XLII (1976), 61-76.

Russell Menard, Lois G. Carr, and Lorena Walsh, "A Small Planter's Profits: The Cole Estate and the Growth of the Early Chesapeake Economy," William and Mary Quarterly, 3rd ser., XL(1983), 171-186.

Bettye Hobbs Pruitt, "Self-Sufficiency and the Agricultural Economy of Eighteenth-Century Massachusetts," William and Mary Quarterly, 3rd ser., XLI (1984), 333-64.

Sept. 19

Calvin Martin, "The European Impact on the Culture of a Northeastern Algonquian Tribe: An Ecological Interpretation," William and Mary Quarterly, 3rd ser., XXXI(1974), 3-24.

James P. Ronda, "'We Are Well as We Are': An Indian Critique of Seventeenth-Century Christian Missions," William and Mary Quarterly, XXXIV(1977), 66-82.

James H. Merrell, "The Indians' New World: The Catawba Experience," William and Mary Quarterly, 3rd ser., XLI (1984), 537-565.

*Daniel Richter, "War and Culture: The Iroquois Experience," William and Mary Quarterly, 3rd ser., XL (1983), 528-559.

Sept. 26

*Allan Kulikoff, "The Beginnings of the Afro-American Family in Maryland, in A.C. Land, L.G. Carr, E. Papenfuse, Law, Society, and Politics in Early Maryland, Johns Hopkins University Press, 1977, pp. 171-196.

*Russell Menard, "The Maryland Slave Population, 1658 to 1730: A Demographic Profile of Blacks in Four Counties," William and Mary Quarterly, 3rd ser., XXXII (1975), 29-54.

Philip Morgan, "Work and Culture: The Task System and the World of Lowcountry Blacks, 1700 to 1800," William and Mary Quarterly, 3rd ser., XXXIX(1982), 563-599.

*Joan R. Gundersen "The Double Bonds of Race and Sex: Black and White Women in a Colonial Virginia Parish," Journal of Southern History, LII (1986), 351-372

Oct. 3

*Daniel Scott Smith, "Parental Power and Marriage Patterns: An Analysis

of Historical Trends in Hingham, Massachusetts," Journal of Marriage
and the Family, XXXV (1973), 419-428.

*James M. Gallman, "Determinants of Age at Marriage in Colonial
Perquimans County, North Carolina," William and Mary Quarterly, 3rd
ser., XXXIX (1982), 176-191.

*Nancy Cott, "Eighteenth-Century Family and Social Life Revealed in
Massachusetts Divorce Records," Journal of Social History, X (1976),
20-43.

*Robert V. Wells, "Quaker Marrriage Patterns in a Colonial Perspective,"
William and Mary Quarterly, 3rd ser., XXIX (1972), 415-442.

Oct. 10

*Karin Calvert, "Children in American Family Portraiture, 1670 to 1810,"
William and Mary Quarterly, 3rd ser., XXXIX (1982), 87-113. Note:
This comes from the same volume as the Reinier essay. A second copy
of this journal is at Carleton and another in my office.

Barry Levy, "'Tender Plants': Quaker Farmers and Children in the Delaware
Valley, 1681-1735," Journal of Family History, III(1978), 116-135.

Ross W. Beals, Jr., "In Search of the Historical Child: Minature
Adulthood and Youth in Colonial New England," American Quarterly,
XXVII (1975), 379-398.

*Jacqueline S. Reinier, Rearing the Republican Child: Attitudes and
Practices in Post-Revolutionary Philadelphia," William and Mary
Quarterly, 3rd ser., XXXIX (1982), 150-163. Note: This comes from
the same volume as the Calvert essay. A second copy of this journal
is at Carleton and another in my office.

Oct. 22

*Barbara S. Lindeman, "'To Ravish and Carnally Know': Rape in the
Eighteenth-Century Massachusetts," Signs X (1984), 63-82.

*Donna Spindel and Stuart W. Thomas, Jr., "Crime and Society in North
Carolina, 1663-1740," Journal of Southern History, XLIX (1983), 223-
244.

Rachel Klein, "Ordering the Backcountry: The South Carolina Regulation,"
William and Mary Quarterly, XXXVIII(1981), 661-680.

David Alan Williams, "The Small Farmer in Eighteenth-Century Virginia
Politics," Agricultural History, XLIII (1969), 91-101.

. 28

*Carla Gardina Pestana, "The City Upon a Hill Under Seige: The Puritan
Perception of the Quaker Threat to Massachusetts Bay, 1656-1661,"
New England Quarterly, LVI (1983), 323-353.

Patricia Bonomi and Peter Eisenstadt, "Church Adherence in the
Eighteenth-Century British American Colonies," William and Mary
Quarterly, 3rd ser., XXXIX (1982), 245-286.

*Joan R. Gundersen, "The Non-Institutional Church: The Religious Role of
Women in Eighteenth-Century Virginia," Historical Magazine of the
Protestant Episcopal Church, LI (1982), 347-357.

David Scobey, "Revising the Errand: New England's Ways and the Puritan
Sense of the Past," William and Mary Quarterly, XLI (1984), 3-31.

Oct. 31

Rhys Isacc, "Religion and Authority: Problems of the Anglican Establishment in the Ear of the Great Awakening and the Parson's Cause," William and Mary Quarterly, XXX (1973), 3-36.

*Gerald Moran, "Conditions of Religious Conversion in the First Society of Norwich, Connecticut, 1718-1744," Journal of Social History, 5 (1972), 331-43.

*Mary Beth Norton, "'My Resting Reaping Times': Sara Osborne's Defense of her Signs: A Journal of Women in Society, XI (1976).

Jon Butler, "Enthusiasm Described and Decried: The Great Awakening as Interpretive Fiction," Journal of American History, LXIX (1982), 305-325.

Book Review Reading List

*Joy and Richard Buel, The Way of Duty
*John Demos, Entertaining Satan
*Laurel Thatcher Ulrich, Goodwives
*Lyle Kohler, The Search for Power
James Lemon, The Best Poor Man's Country
*Daniel Blake Smith, Life in the Great House
Philip Greven, Four Generations
Alice Jones, The Wealth of a Nation-to-Be
Edmund Morgan, American Slavery, American Freedom
Michael Zuckerman, Peaceable Kingdoms
Louis B. Wright, The Cultural Life of the American Colonies
Gerald Mullins, Flight and Rebellion
Bernard Sheehan, Savagism and Civility
Brooke Hindle, The Pursuit of Science in Revolutionary America
Richard Shryock, Medicine and Society in Early America
Richard Bushman, From Puritan to Yankee
Frederick Mills, Bishops by Ballot
Thomas Buckley, Church and State in Revolutionary Virginia
Thomas Cronan, Changes in the Land
*Mary Beth Norton, Liberty's Daughters
*Annette Kolodny, The Land Before Her
David Stannard, The Puritan Way of Death
T.H. Breen, Puritans and Adventurers
*Charles Akers, Abigail Adams
Frederick B. Tolles, Meeting House and Counting House
*Linda Speth, Women, Family and Community in Colonial America
Robert Gross, The Minutemen and Their World
*Marylynn Salmon, Women and the Law of Property in Early America
Richard Beeman, The Evolution of the Southern Backcountry
*books and articles especially suitable for women's history

Documents Packet

Table of Contents

WOMEN IN EARLY AMERICA -- Suggested Readings
Lisa Wilson Waciega,

OVERVIEW
1) Mary Beth Norton, "The Evolution of White Women's
Experience in Early America," American Historical Review 89
(June 1984), 593-619.

FAMILY AND MARRIAGE
1) Nancy Cott, "Divorce and the Changing Status of Women in
Eighteenth-Century Massachusetts," WMQ 33 (October 1976),
586-614.
2) Lois Green Carr and Lorena S. Walsh, "The Planter's Wife:
The Experience of White Women in Seventeenth-Century
Maryland," WMQ 34 (October 1977), 542-571.
3) Carl N. Degler, At Odds: Women and the Family in America
from the Revolution to the Present (NY, 1980).
4) J. William Frost, The Quaker Family in Colonial America
(NY, 1973).
5) Alexander Keyssar, "Widowhood in Eighteenth-Century
Massachusetts: A Problem in the History of the Family,"
Perspectives in American History 8 (1974), 83-119.
6) Laurel Thatcher Ulrich, Good Wives: Image and Reality in
the Lives of Women in Northern New England, 1650-1750 (NY,
1982).
7) Jan Lewis, The Pursuit of Happiness: Family and Values in
Jefferson's Virginia (Cambridge, 1983).
8) Judith Walzer Leavitt, Brought to Bed: Childbearing in
America, 1750-1860 (NY, 1986).
9) Catherine M. Scholten, Childbearing in American Society:
1650-1850 (NY, 1985).
10) Joan M. Jensen, Loosening the Bonds: Mid-Atlantic Farm
Women, 1750-1800 (New Haven, 1986).
11) John Demos, A Little Commonwealth: Family Life in
Plymouth Colony (NY, 1970).
12) Edmund S. Morgan, The Puritan Family: Religion and
Domestic Relations in Seventeenth-Century New England (NY,
1944).
13) Lee Virginia Chambers-Schiller, Liberty, A Better
Husband: Single Women in America: The Generations of 1780-
1840 (New Haven, 1984).
14) Nancy F. Cott, The Bonds of Womanhood, "Woman's Sphere"
in New England, 1780-1835 (New Haven, 1977).
15) Terri L. Premo, "'Like A Being Who Does Not Belong:' The
Old Age of Deborah Norris Logan," PMHB (January 1983), 85-
112.
16) Lorena S. Walsh, "'Till Death Us Do Part': Marriage and
Family in 17th-Century Maryland," in The Chesapeake in the
17th Century: Essays on Anglo-American Society, 126-152.
Edited by Thad W. Tate and David L. Ammerman (NY, 1979).

WORK
1) Carr and Walsh, "The Planter's Wife."

2) Claudia Goldin, "The Economic Status of Women in the
Early Republic: Quantitative Evidence," Journal of
Interdisciplinary History 16 (Winter 1986), 375-404.
3) Alice Kessler-Harris, Out to Work: A History of Wage-
earning Women in the United States (NY, 1982).
4) Lisa Wilson Waciega, " A 'Man of Business': The Widow of
Means in Southeastern Pennsylvania, 1750-1850," WMQ 64
(January 1987), 40-64.
5) Ulrich, Good Wives.
6) Jensen, Loosening the Bonds.
7) Cott, The Bonds of Womanhood.
8) Mary Beth Norton, "A Cherished Spirit of Independence:
The Life of an Eighteenth-Century Boston Businesswoman," in
Women of America: A History, 50-67. Edited by Carol Ruth
Berkin and Mary Beth Norton (Boston, 1979).
9) Carole Shammas, "The Female Social Structure of
Philadelphia in 1775," PMHB (January 1983), 69-83.
10) Laurel Thatcher Ulrich, "' A Friendly Neighbor': Social
Dimensions of Daily Work in Northern Colonial New England,"
Feminist Studies 2 (1980): 392-405.

LAW
1) Cott, "Divorce and the Changing Status of Women."
2) Carr and Walsh, "The Planter's Wife."
3)Suzanne Lebsock, The Free Women of Petersburg: Status and
Culture in A Southern Town, 1784-1860 (NY, 1984).
4) Mary Beth Norton, "Gender and Defamation in Seventeenth-
Century Maryland," WMQ (January, 1987), 3-39.
5) Marylynn Salmon, "Equality or Submersion? Feme Covert
Status in Early Pennsylvania," in Women of America: A
History, 92-113. Edited by Carol Ruth Berkin and Mary Beth
Norton (Boston, 1979).
6)Marylynn Salmon, "Women and Property in South Carolina:
The Evidence from Marriage Settlements, 1780 to 1820," WMQ
39 (October 1982), 655-685.
7)Linda E. Speth, "More Than Her 'Thirds': Wives and Widows
in Colonial Virginia," in Women, Family and Community in
Colonial America: Two Perspectives. Introduced by Carol
Berkin (NY, 1983).
8) Marylynn Salmon, Women and the Law of Property in Early
America (Chapel Hill, 1986).
9) Joan R. Gundersen and Gwen Victor Gampel, "Married
Women's Legal Status in Eighteenth-Century New York and
Virginia," WMQ 39 (January 1982), 114-134.

RELIGION
1) Frost, The Quaker Family.
2) Carol S. Karlsen, The Devil in the Shape of a Woman:
Women in Colonial New England (forthcoming Norton, 1987).
3) Jean R. Soderlund, "Women's Authority in Colonial
Pennsylvania and New Jersey Quaker Meetings, 1680-1760," WMQ
(forthcoming October 1987).
4) Jensen, Loosening the Bonds.
5) Cott, The Bonds of Womanhood.

6) Mary Maples Dunn, "Women of Light," in _Women of America: A History_, 115-136. Edited by Carol Ruth Berkin and Mary Beth Norton (Boston, 1979).

THE REVOLUTION
1) Cott, "Divorce and the Changing Status of Women."
2) Linda K. Kerber, _Women of the Republic: Intellect and Ideology in Revolutionary America_ (Chapel Hill, 1980).
3) Mary Beth Norton, "Eighteenth-Century American Women in Peace and War: The Case of the Loyalists," _WMQ_ 33 (July 1976), 386-409.
4) Mary Beth Norton, _Liberty's Daughters: The Revolutionary Experience of American Women, 1750-1800_ (Boston, 1980).
5) Joan Hoff-Wilson, "The Illusion of Change: Women and the American Revolution," in _The American Revolution: Explorations in the History of American Radicalism_, 385-444. Edited by Alfred F. Young (Dekalb, 1976).
6)D'Ann Campbell, _Women at War with America, Private Lives in a Patriotic Era_ (Cambridge, Mass., 1984).
7)Constance B. Schulz, "Daughters of Liberty: The History of Women in the Revolutionary War Pension Records, _Prologue_, vol. 16, no. 3, 139-153.

American Civilization 164
Spring, 1986

Mari Jo Buhle
82 Waterman Street
Weds. 3:00-5:00

HISTORY OF AMERICAN WOMEN

Books available at the Dorrwar Bookstore:

Cott & Pleck, eds.	A Heritage of Her Own	Touchstone
Baxandall, et.al.,eds.	America's Working Women	Vintage
Friedman & Shade, eds.	Our American Sisters	Heath
Jones	Labor of Love, Labor of Sorrow	Basic
Showalter, ed.	These Modern Women	Feminist Press
Anderson	Wartime Women	Greenwood
Evans	Personal Politics	Vintage
Friedan	Feminine Mystique	Dell
Hooks	Ain't I A Woman	South End
Ehrenreich	Hearts of Men	Anchor
Chopin	The Awakening	Avon
Yezierska	The Breadgivers	Persea
LeSueur	Salute to Spring	International
Plath	The Bell Jar	Bantam
Walker	Meridian	Pocket Books
Dorenkamp, et.al.,eds.	Images of Women in American Popular Culture	Harcourt,Brace Jovanovich

Recommended: Lois Banner, Women in Modern America, 2d ed., which is on reserve and available in limited quanitity at the Doorwar Bookstore.

Reserve Reading: Citations marked "*" are on 3-hr reserve at the Rockefeller Library and at the Sarah Doyle Library.

Hollywood feature films will be screened weekly Feb. 26-April 2

INTRODUCTION

Jan.22   Description of Course
        Recommended: Gerda Lerner, "New Approaches to the Study of Women in
            American History," A Majority Finds Its Past(1979),3-14 *
            Bonnie Thorton Dill, "Race, Class, and Gender:
            Prospects for an All-Inclusive Sisterhood," Feminist
            Studies, 9(Spring 1983),131-50 *

Jan.24   19th-Century Legacy: Woman's Culture & Woman's Sphere
        C.Smith-Rosenberg, "The Female World of Love and Ritual: Relations
            between Women in Nineteenth-Century America," A
            Heritage of Her Own, 311-42
        E. Freedman, "Separatism as Strategy: Female Institution Building
            and American Feminism," Feminist Studies, 5(Fall
            1979),512-29 *
        Recommended: Leila J. Rupp, "Reflections on Twentieth-Century
            American Women's History," Reviews in American
            History, 9(June 1981),275-84
            Alice Echols, "The Demise of Female Intimacy in the
            Twentieth Century," University of Michigan Occasional
            Papers in Women's Studies, VI(1978)

I. THE NEW WOMAN AND THE PROGRESSIVE ERA

Jan.27   New Woman Defined
        L.A. Kryder, "Self-Assertion and Social Commitment: The
            Significance of Work to the Progressive Era's New
            Woman,"Journal of American Culture, 6(Summer 1983),
            25-30 *
        C.M. Thomas,"Address to the Students at the Opening of the Academic
            Year 1899-1900," Images of Women in American Popular
            Culture,48-52
        Recommended: Roberta Frankfort, Collegiate Women: Domesticity and
            Career in Turn-of-the-Century America (1978)
            M. Deland, "The Change in the Feminine Ideal." Atlantic
            (March 1910),289-302 *   Monthly,

Jan.29   "Restlessness" and the Middle-Class
        S. Herman, "Loving Courtship or the Marriage Market? The Ideal and
            Its Critics, 1871-1911," Our American Sisters, 329-47
        S. Weir Mitchell, "Rest"; Charlotte Perkins Gilman, "The Yellow
            Wallpaper"; "How to Get Plump," Images of Women in
            American Popular Culture, 24-38;135-39
        Recommended: Mary Armfield Hill, ed., Charlotte Perkins Gilman: The
            Making of a Radical Feminist, 1860-1896(1980);Endure:
            The Diaries of Charles Walter Stetson (1985)

Jan.31   Literary Reflections
<SECTION   K. Chopin, The Awakening (1899)
           K. Chopin, "The Dream of an Hour," Images of Women in American
                      Popular Culture, 206-08
           Recommended: Cynthia Griffin Wolff, "Thanatos and Eros: Kate
                      Chopin's The Awakening," American Quarterly,
                      25(1973),449-71

Feb.3   Wage-Earning Women
           "Migrants and Immigrants" and "The Human Cost of Industry,"
                      America's Working Women, 132-66
           J. Jones, Labor of Love, Labor of Sorrow, Chapters 3-5
           "Stenography in New York City"; M. Pinzer, "Letter to Fanny Quincy
                      Howe," Images of Women in American Popular
                      Culture,306-07;394-99
           Recommended: B. Klaczynska, "Why Women Work: A Comparison of
                      Various Groups: Philadelphia, 1910-1930," Labor
                      History, 17(Winter 1976), 73-87
                      Elizabeth Ewen, Immigrant Women in the Land of
                      Dollars: Life and Culture on the Lower East Side (1985)

Feb.5   Wage-Earning Women and their Families
           J. Smith, "Our Own Kind: Family and Community Networks in
                      Providence," A Heritage of Her Own, 393-411
           E. Pleck, "A Mother's Wages: Income Earning Among Married Italian
                      and Black Women,1896-1911," A Heritage of Her
                      Own,367-92
           Recommended: Virginia Yans-McLaughlin, Family and Community:
                      Italian Immigrants in Buffalo, 1880-1930 (1977)
                      Helen Barolini, ed., The Dream Book: An Anthology of
                      Writings by Italian American Women(1985)

Feb.7   The Jewish New Woman
<SECTION   A. Yezierska, The Breadgivers (1925); "How I Found America," Images
                      of Women in American Popular Culture,301-04
           Recommended: Charlotte Baum, et.al., The Jewish Woman in America
                      (1976)
                      Sydney Weinberg, "The World of Our Mothers: Family,
                      Work and Education in the Lifes of Jewish Immigrant
                      Women," Frontiers, 7(Fall, 1983)

Feb.10   The Women's Movement Revives
           S. Strom, "Leadership and Tactics in the American Woman Suffrage
                      Movement: A New Perspective from Massachusetts," Our
                      American Sisters, 372-92
           J.Addams, "Women,War, and Babies," Images of Women in American
                      Popular Culture, 279-80
           Recommended: Paula Baker, "The Domestication of Politics; Women and
                      American Political Society, 1880-1920," American
                      Historical Review, 89(June 1984),620-47

87

Feb.12   Women's Strikes & Trade Unions
          "Working-Class Power," "Strikes and the Tradition of Struggle," and
                    "Women's Consciousness and Class Conflict," America's
                    Working Women,167-222
          A. Kessler-Harris, "'Where Are the Organized Women Workers?'" A
                    Heritage of Her Own, 343-66
          Recommended: Susan Porter Benson, "'The Customers Ain't God': The
                    Work Culture of Department-Store Saleswomen, 1890-1940,"
                    Michael Frisch and Daniel J. Walkowitz, eds.,
                    Working-Class America (1983), 185-211
                    Ardis Cameron, "Bread and roses revisited: Women's
                    culture and working-class activism in the Lawrence
                    strike of 1912," Ruth Milkman, ed., Women's Work and
                    Protest: A Century of U.S. Women's Labor History
                    (1985),42-61 *

Feb.14   Cross-Class Alliances
<SECTION N. Schrom Dye, "Creating a Feminist Alliance: Sisterhood in the New
                    York Women's Trade Union League, 1903-1914," Our
                    American Sisters, 393-410
          Recommended: Meredith Tax, The Rising of the Women: Feminist
                    Solidarity and Class Conflict, 1880-1917 (1980)

Feb.17   No Class

Feb.19   The New Morality and Feminism
          J. McGovern, "The American Woman's Pre-World War I Freedom in
                    Manners and Morals," Our American Sisters, 479-499
          L. Gordon, "Birth Control and Social Revolution," A Heritage of Her
                    Own, 445-75
          M. Sanger, "Is Race Suicide Probable?" S. Glaspell, "Trifles: A
                    Play in One Act,"Images of Women in American Popular
                    Culture,272-74;373-90
          Recommended: Kathy Peiss, Cheap Amusements: Working Women and
                    Leisure in Turn-of-the-Century New York (1985)

Feb.21   Friendships, Networks, and Politics
<SECTION B.W. Cook, "Female Support Networks and Political Activism: Lillian
                    Wald, Crystal Eastman, Emma Goldman," A Heritage of
                    Her Own, 412-44
          J. Conway, "Women Reformers and American Culture,1870-1930," Our
                    American Sisters, 432-43
          N. Sahli, "Smashing: Women's Relationships Before the Fall,"
                    Chrysalis, 8(Summer 1979),17-29 *
          Recommended: Kathryn Kish Sklar, "Hull House in the 1890s: A
                    Community of Women Reformers," Signs, 10(Summer
                    1985),658-99

II. "THESE MODERN WOMEN"

Feb.24   Flappers and Philosophers
          L. Pruette, "The Flapper," The New Generation (1930) *
          Recommended: Paula Fass, The Damned and the Beautiful (1977)

Feb.26   The Heterosexual Main Chance
          Lindsey & Evans, The Companionate Marriage (1927), Chapter V *
          R. Hall, "The Well of Loneliness"; B. Smith, "A Tree Grows in
                    Brooklyn," Images of Women in American Popular
                    Culture, 39-42; 178--83
          Recommended: Leila Rupp, "Imagine My Surprise: Women's
                    Relationships in Historical Perspective," Frontiers,
                    5(1981)

          MOVIE: "Our Dancing Daughters" (1928)

Feb.28   Filmic Reflections
<SECTION M. Ryan, "The Projection of a New Woman: The American Movie Moderns
                    in the 1920s," Our American Sisters, 500-18
          Recommended: Molly Haskell, From Reverence to Rape: The Treatment
                    of Women in the Movies (1973)
                    Majorie Rosen, Popcorn Venus (1973)

Mar.3   Woman's Place Is . . . .
          M. Davies, "Woman's Place Is At the Typewriter" in Capitalist
                    Patriarchy and the Case for Socialist Feminism, Zillah
                    Eisenstein, ed. (1979),248-66 *
          R. Schwartz Cowan, "Two Washes in the Morning and a Bridge Party at
                    Night: The American Housewife Between the Wars," Our
                    American Sisters,519-40
          "Homemaking," America's Working Women, 223-31
          Recommended: Evelyn Nakano Glenn, "The Dialectics of Wage Work:
                    Japanese American Women and Domestic Service, 1905-
                    1940," Feminist Studies, 6(Fall, 1980)

Mar.5   Careers, Marriage, and the ERA
          C. Chambers, "The Campaign for Women's Rights in the 1920s," Our
                    American Sisters, 457-78
          F. Stricker, "Cookbooks and Law Books: The Hidden History of Career
                    Women in Twentieth Century America," A Heritage of
                    Her Own, 476-98
          Recommended: Nancy F. Cott, "Feminist Politics in the 1920s: The
                    National Woman's Party," Journal of American History,
                    71(June 1984),43-68

          MOVIE: "Wife versus Secretary" (1936)

Mar.7   Retrospective on the "Roaring Twenties"
<SECTION E. Showalter, ed., These Modern Women: Autobiographical Essays from
                    the Twenties (1978)
          E.J. McDougald, "The Double Task," Images of Women in American
                    Popular Culture, 77-83
          Recommended: Winifred Wandersee, Women's Work and Family Values,
                    1920-1940 (1981)

Mar.10   The Great Depression and Women's Status
          Robert & Helen Lynd, Middletown in Transition (1937), 167-80 *
          "The Depression," America's Working Women, 241-51
          R. Milkman, "Women's Work and the Economic Crisis: Some Lessons
                  from the Great Depression," A Heritage of Her Own,
                  507-41
          J. Jones, Labor of Love, Labor of Sorrow, Chapter 6
          Recommended: Lois Scharf, To Work and To Wed: Female Employment,
                  Feminism, and the Great Depression (1980)

Mar.12   Gastonia
          "Women in the Union Movement," America's Working Women, 252-83
          M. Frederickson, "'I know which side I'm on': Southern women in the
                  labor movement in the twentieth century," R. Milkman,
                  ed., Women's Work and Protest (1985),156-80 *
          Recommended: Fielding Burke, Call Home the Heart(1932)
                  Dolores Janiewski, Sisterhood Denied: Race, Gender,
                  and Class in a New South Community (1985)

          MOVIE: "Golddiggers of 1933" (1933)

Mar.14   Proletarian Literary Reflections
<SECTION M. LeSueur, Salute to Spring (1940)
          T.Olsen, "I Stand Here Ironing," Images of Women in American Popular
                  Culture, 257-62
          Recommended: Meridel Le Sueur, Ripening: Selected Work, 1927-1980
                  (1982)

Mar.17   World War II and Women's Work
          Film: "Rosie the Riveter"
          "War Work," America's Working Women, 284-98
          K. Anderson, Wartime Women: Sex Roles, Family Relations, and the
                  Status of Women During World War II (1981)
          Recommended: Harriet Arnow, The Dollmaker (1954)

Mar.19   Freudian Backlash
          B. Friedan, The Feminine Mystique (1963), Chapters 1-6
          F.Lundberg & M. Farnham, "Chimera; Or Modern Woman"; "The
                  Psychopathology of Feminism"; "Mother and Child";
                  A. Montagu, "The Natural Superiority of Women" ; P.
                  Wylie, "Common Women," Images of Women in American
                  Popular Culture,5-6;15-17;236-37;55-57;238-50
          Recommended: Ferdinand Lundberg and Marynia Farnham, Modern Woman:
                  The Lost Sex (1947)

          MOVIE: "Lady in the Dark" (1944)

Mar.21   Race & Class Dimensions of War Work
<SECTION Maureen Honey, "The Working Class Woman and Recruitment Propaganda
                  During World War II," Signs,8(Summer 1983),672-87*
          J. Jones, Labor of Love, Labor of Sorrow, Chapter 7
          Recommended: Karen Anderson, "Last Hired, First Fired: Black Women
                  Workers During World War II," Journal of American
                  History, 69(June 1982),82-97

III. TOWARD WOMEN'S LIBERATION

Mar.31   Work, Education, and Women's Dilemma
         "1940-1955," America's Working Women, 299-330
         J. Vanek, 'Time Spent in Housework," A Heritage of Her Own,499-506
         B. Friedan, The Feminine Mystique, Chapter 7
         A. Stevenson, "A Purpose for Modern Woman"; "Amercan Woman's
                 Dilemma," Images of Women in American Popular Culture,
                 113-17;290-94
         Recommended: Louise Kapp Howe, Pink Collar Workers: Inside the
                 World of Women's Work (1977)
                 Leila Rupp, "The Survival of American Feminism: The
                 Women's Movement in the Post-War Period," in Reshaping
                 America, edited by Robert Bremner and Richard Gard (1983)

Apr.2   Modern Romance
         B. Friedan, The Feminine Mystique, Chapters 8 & 9
         "What Every Woman Should Know About Kinsey"; A. Moody, "Coming of
                 Age in Mississippi"; H. Sekaquaptewa, "Me and Mine";
                 J.DeYonker & T.Tobin, "Your Marriage," Images of
                 Women in American Popular Culture, 18-20; 183-86; 196-
                 200;202-205
         Recommended: Brandon French, On the Verge of Revolt: Women in
                 American Films of the 1950s (1978)

         MOVIE: "Imitation of Life" (1957)

Apr.4   Cultural Contradictions: A Literary Case Study
<SECTION S. Plath, The Bell Jar
         Mirra Komarovsky, "Cultural Contradictions and Sex Roles," American
                 Journal of Sociology, 54(November 1946) *
         N. Ephron, "A Few Words About Breasts; H. Whitcomb & R. Lang, "More
                 than Skin Deep," Images of Women in American Popular
                 Culture, 143-48; 167-71
         Recommended: Lynn White, Educating Our Daughters (1950)

Apr.7   Civil Rights and the New Left
         Film "Fundi"
         S. Evans, Personal Politics: The Roots of Women's Liberation in the
                 Civil Rights Movement and the New Left (1979)
         S.Lee,"Friendship,Feminism and Betrayal," Images of Women in
                 American Popular Culture,359-63
         Recommended: Ellen Cantarow, et.al., eds., Moving the Mountain:
                 Women Working for Social Change (1980)

Apr.9   The Personal is Political
            J. Jones, Labor of Love, Labor of Sorrow, Chapter 8
            A. Walker, "Everyday Use"; J. Strouse, "Toni Morrison's Black
                 Magic"; P.Marshall, "Pastorale," Images of Women in
                 American Popular Culture,250-56;330-39;345-52
            A. Walker, "The Civil Rights Movement: What Good Was It?" in In
                 Our Mother's Garden(1983), 119-29 *
            Recommended: Rosalyn Terborg-Penn, "Survival Strategies among
                 African-American Women workers: A continuing
                 process," R. Milkman, ed., Women's Work and
                 Protest(1985),139-55 *

Apr.11   "Exploring the oppressions...."
<SECTION A. Walker, Meridian (1976)
            P. Murray, "The Liberation of Black Women," Our American
                 Sisters,579-91
            Recommended: Ann Moody, Coming of Age in Mississippi (1968)
                 Roseann P. Bell, Bettye J. Parker, Beverly Guy-
                 Shaftall, eds. Sturdy Black Bridges: Vision of Black
                 Women in Literature (1979)

Apr.14   Cultural Revolution
            Charles Reich, The Greening of America (1970), Chapters I & IX
            S. Firestone, "The Culture of Romance"; S. Brownmiller,
                 "Confessions: 'He Made Me Do It!'" "In Amerika They
                 Call Us Dykes"; G. Steinem, "What I Would Be Like If
                 Women Win"; S. Firestone, " Alternatives" Images of
                 Women in American Popular Culture, 149-54;390-93;442-
                 53
            Recommended: Theodore Roszak, The Making of a Counter Culture:
                 Reflections on the Technological Society and Its
                 Youthful Opposition (1969)

Apr.16   Women's Liberation
            C.E. Harrison,"A 'New Frontier' for Women: The Public Policy of the
                 Kennedy Administration," Our American Sisters, 541-62
            "1955-1974," America's Working Women, 336-400
            B. Friedan, The Feminine Mystique, Chapter 10
            J. Nelson, "I'm Not Your Girl"; B. Baer and G. Matthew, "The Women
                 of the Boycott"; "Controversy Over the Equal Rights
                 Amendment"; "Women of 'La Raza' Unite!" Images of
                 Women in American Popular Culture, 294-300;310-
                 319;423-28;430-32
            Recommended: Jo Freeman, The Politics of Women's Liberation (1975)

Apr.18   . . . And Men
<SECTION B. Ehrenreich, The Hearts of Men (1983)
            M. Mannes, "Deadlier Than the Male"; M. Morgan, "The Total Woman";
                 L. Wolfe, "Evaluating the Sexual Revolution";C.
                 Rivers, "Can A Woman Be Liberated and Married?"
                 R. Cohen, "Fog at the Scene of the Crime"; "Marvin V.
                 Marvin";Images of Women in American Popular Culture,
                 13-15;100-104;208-27
            Recommended: James Dittes, The Male Predicament: On Being a Man
                 Today (1985)

Apr.21   Feminism in the 1980s
          Belle Hooks. Ain't I A Woman (1981)
          J. Jones, Labor of Love, Labor of Sorrow, "Epilogue: 1984"
          N. Amdur, "Women Make Big Gains in Marathon"; D. Martin and P. Lyon,
                    "Lesbian Mothers"; E. Goodman, "Drafting Daughters";
                    K. Kenyon, "A Pink-Collar Worker's Blues"; L. Daniels,
                    "Women Coal Miners Fear Loss of Newly Won Equality"; S
                    Gordon, "The New Corporate Feminism"; Sr. M. Kane,
                    "Statement to Pope John Paul I"; V. Gornick, "Lesbians
                    and Women's Liberation," Images of Women in American
                    Popular Culture,52-54;274-78;281-83;308-09;319-26;428-
                    29;432-36
          Recommended: Zillah R. Eisenstein, Feminism and Sexual Equality:
                    Crisis in Liberal America (1984)

Apr.23   Another Voice
          W. Chafe, "The Paradox of Progress," Our American Sisters,563-78
          A. Rich, "Commencement Address at Smith College, 1979," Images of
                    Women in American Popular Culture, 117-23
          Recommended: Mirra Komarovsky, Women in College: Shaping New
                    Feminine Identities (1985)

Apr.25   Course Evaluations and Discussion of Final Paper

93

Harvard University

WOMEN IN MODERN AMERICA
History 1602B

Professor Catherine Clinton   Fall 1985
  Robinson Hall L-24/495-5146   Tu. & Th. Noon - One
  Office Hours: Tu. & Th. 11-NOON   Sever Hall 213

COURSE REQUIREMENTS:

  ATTENDANCE OF LECTURES, REQUIRED GUEST LECTURES AND SECTIONS
  TWO PAPERS & FINAL EXAM
    5-8 pgs.   ON PRIMARY RESOURCE 9(DUE NOV. 19TH)
    10-15 pgs. INDIVIDUAL TOPIC (DUE JAN. 13TH)

ALL WRITTEN WORK MUST BE TYPED. PAPERS MUST CONFORM TO REQUIRED
LENGTH (250 WORDS PER PAGE) AND SUBMITTED ON DATE DUE UNLESS
EXTENSIONS ARE SECURED ONE WEEK IN ADVANCE.

ALL REQUIRED READING IS AVAILABLE FOR PURCHASE AT THE COOP OR ON
RESERVE AT LAMONT AND HILLES LIBRARIES.
WEEKLY READING ASSIGNMENTS MUST BE COMPLETED IN ADVANCE OF YOUR WEEKLY
SECTION, BUT IT IS RECOMMENDED THAT YOU COMPLETE THE READING BEFORE
MONDAY LECTURES EACH WEEK TO FACILITATE APPRECIATION OF THE MATERIAL.

TEXTS FOR THE COURSE: (FICTION IS STARRED)

BROWN, RITA MAE/RUBYFRUIT JUNGLE*
CANTAROW, ELLEN/MOVING THE MOUNTAIN
CLINTON, CATHERINE/THE OTHER CIVIL WAR
EISENSTEIN, HESTER/CONTEMPORARY AMERICAN FEMINISM
HALL, JACQUELYN/REVOLT AGAINST CHIVALRY
HARTMAN, SUSAN/THE HOMEFRONT AND BEYOND
JONES, JACQUELINE/LABOR OF LOVE, LABOR OF SORROW
KESSLER-HARRIS, ALICE/OUT TO WORK
MCCARTHY, MARY/THE GROUP*
ROSEN, RUTH/THE LOST SISTERHOOD: PROSTITUTION IN AMERICA
ROSENBERG, ROSALIND/BEYOND SEPARATE SPHERES
SHIVERS, LOUISE/HERE TO GET MY BABY OUT OF JAIL*
SHOWALTER, ELAINE, ED./THESE MODERN WOMEN
WALKER, ALICE/THE COLOR PURPLE*
WARE, SUSAN/HOLDING THEIR OWN
WOLOCH, NANCY/WOMEN AND THE AMERICAN EXPERIENCE

ALL OF THE ABOVE (EXCEPT JONES) ARE AVAILABLE FOR PURCHASE AT THE COO

TOURS OF THE SCHLESINGER LIBRARY, RADCLIFFE YARD, WILL BE SCHEDULED
DURING OCTOBER. STUDENTS WILL FAMILIARIZE THEMSELVES WITH THIS
VALUABLE RESOURCE FOR THEIR PAPERS ON PRIMARY SOURCES. IN ADDITION,
THE TEXTS FOR THIS COURSE ARE AVAILABLE ON A RESERVE SHELF AT THE
SCHLESINGER LIBRARY, SECOND FLOOR. (THE BOOKS AT SCHLESINGER ARE NON
CIRCULATING. THE LIBRARY IS OPEN NINE TO FIVE AND TWO EVENINGS A WEE
---WEDS. & THURS.---UNTIL NINE)

```
WEEK I.        NO READING
  9/19           INTRODUCTORY

WEEK II.       CLINTON, CHAPTERS 5-10
  9/24           WHY WOMEN'S HISTORY?
  9/26           EDGING TOWARD EQUALITY

WEEK III.      ROSENBERG, CHAPTERS 3-8 (SECTION MEETINGS BEGIN)
  10/1           WOMEN AND THE VOTE
  10/3           FEMINIST FOREMOTHERS

WEEK IV.       SHOWALTER (ALL)
  10/8           CAREER VRS. FAMILY
  10/10          CAPITALISM, CONSUMERISM AND WOMEN

WEEK V.        ROSEN (ALL)
  10/15          BIRTH CONTROL, ABORTION & SEXUALITY
  10/17          SISTERHOOD AND LESBIAN IDENTITY

WEEK VI.       KESSLER HARRIS, PART II, (CHAPTERS 4-7)
               JACQUELINE JONES, CHAPTER 5 (ON RESERVE)
  10/22          WOMEN IN THE WORKFORCE
  10/24          BREAKING DOWN BARRIERS

WEEK VII.      WARE (ALL); HALL, CHAPTERS 5-9
  10/29          THE DEPRESSION DECADE
  10/31          WOMEN'S IMAGES IN POPULAR CULTURE

WEEK VIII.     HARTMANN (ALL)
               KESSLER HARRIS, CHAPTERS 8-11
  11/5           WOMEN AND WAR
  11/7           CULTURAL CONFLICTS IN THE FIFTIES

WEEK IX.       MCCARTHY (ALL)
               SHIVERS (ALL)
  11/12          VIDEO: FUNDI, THE LIFE OF ELLA BAKER
  11/14          NO LECTURE

WEEK X.        CANTAROW (ALL)
               JACQUELINE JONES, CHAPTER 7
  11/19          GUEST LECTURE
  11/21          DISSENT AND ORGANIZATION

WEEK XI.       WALKER (ALL)
  11/26          RACE AND GENDER
  11/28          THANKSGIVING

WEEK XII.      EISENSTEIN (ALL)
  12/3           RADICAL FEMINISTS IN FERMENT
  12/5           BACKLASHES AND ANTI-FEMINISM

WEEK XIII.     BROWN (ALL)
  12/10          FROM EQUAL PAY TO COMPARABLE WORTH
  12/12          WOMEN'S ISSUES EMERGING IN THE EIGHTIES
```

Oberlin College
Department of History

History 261: Turning Points in American Women's History:
The Twentieth Century

Fall 1985   Carol Lasser
MF at 2:30 with Wednesday discussions   Rice 313; X8192
            to be arranged

In the opening years of the twentieth century, the
American woman suffrage movement, already over fifty years
old, began to gain momentum. Yet the surge of activity
which culminated in the achievement of votes for women in
1920 did not persist. In subsequent decades, women
undertook no successful mass mobilization in pursuit of
gender equality in employment, in the family, or in
political life. Only in the late 1960s did widespread
feminist organization again become a factor in American
life. This movement, still evolving today after two decades
of existence, has incorporated some of the older feminist
goals, restimulated historic controversies, and introduced
new items for the public agenda of feminism and the private
agendas of American women.

This course charts the ebb and flow of feminist
activity and marks its "turning points" across the twentieth
century by looking at the ideas, dynamics and institutions
of the movement itself and by examining the relation between
organized feminism and the changes in the public and private
lives of women from different class, racial and ethnic
backgrounds. The course analyzes major shifts in women's
experiences, particularly in light of the changing economic,
demographic, social and political patterns of the nation
over the the century; it traces the developing contours of
the female labor market, the emergence of new patterns
combining paid employment, marriage and childbearing, and
the impact of wars, depression and prosperity on both the
ideals and the realities of women's lives. In the end, the
course seeks to aid students in understanding the historical
roots and the contemporary situation of women in American
society and in thinking critically about changing gender
roles and shifting feminist goals.

FORMAT, REQUIREMENTS and GRADING

Format: The course generally meets Mondays and Fridays for
lectures, and is divided into discussion sections meeting at
1:30, 2:30 and 3:30 on Wednesdays. Students are expected to
attend all classes, to prepare for discussion sections by
completing the reading assignments, and to participate in
class discussions.

Requirements: Students must write a midterm examination, a
final examination, and a project (described below). No
student will receive credit for the course without
completing all requirements.

Midterm Examination: This is an essay examination,
scheduled for October 18. Essays questions on which the
midterm examination will be based will be distributed in
advance. Students may elect to take their midterm
examination outside of class, in which case they may spend
no more than one hour in actual writing, and must return
their completed examination by class time on October 18.
Students who prefer to take their midterm examination in
class will write it during class time on October 18.

Final examination: This examination will be scheduled
during the regular examination period.

Student Projects: Students will examine popular magazines
(Life, Time, Fortune, Ladies' Home Journal, Good
Housekeeping, etc.) finding material from three time
periods--(1) the Depression (2) the World War Two years, (3)
the early 1950s--and choose a particular focus for
comparison of material by or about women in the three
periods. Papers may focus, for example, on a regular column
or feature, a particular kind of advertisement or product,
or a kind of fiction. Students will write a five to eight
page paper based on an analysis of this material. Papers
should include photocopies of the material used when
possible and appropraite. Papers should stress a single
theme, and develop a logical, historically valid argument.
Papers will be due in class November 20. THIS IS A FIRM
DEADLINE! Papers not turned in on that date will be
penalized in grading and will not receive written comments.

Grading: The midterm examination will count approximately
one-quarter of the final grade; the project will count
approximately one-quarter of the final grade; class
participation will count approximately one-fifth of the
final grade; the final examination will count approximately
two-fifths of the final grade.

Books Recommended for Purchase:
   Aileen Kraditor, The Ideas of the Woman Suffrage
      Movement
   Linda Gordon, Woman's Body, Woman's Right
   Tillie Olsen, Yonnondio
   Peggy Dennis, Autobiography of An American Communist
      (if available)
   Maya Angelou, I Know Why the Caged Bird Sings
   Barbara Ehrenreich, The Hearts of Men
   Betty Friedan, The Feminine Mystique
   Sara Evans, Personal Politics

SCHEDULE OF CLASSES

Week 1
September 9   Introduction: History, Women's History and
                Women's Studies
September 11   Women's Lives in Nineteenth-Century America
                (a slide lecture)
September 13   Woman Suffrage and Woman's Rights in
                Nineteenth-Century America (a slide lecture)

Week 2
September 16   Suffrage, Peace and Feminism in the Era of
                the First World War
September 18   DISCUSSION: The Suffrage Movement and Its
                Legacy
                READING: Kraditor, Ideas of the Woman
                Suffrage Movement, Chapters 1-3, 5-9.
September 20   Becoming "Modern": Popular Images of Women in
                the 1920s

Week 3
September 23   Black Women in the Early Twentieth Century:
                The Heritage of Slavery and the First Urban
                Migrations
September 25   READING: Gordon, Woman's Body, Woman's Right,
                pp. 1-91.
                NO CLASS DISCUSSION: YOM KIPPUR
September 27   "New Women," New Work? Women's Employment,
                1900-1930

Week 4
September 30   Working Women, Protective Legislation and the
                Equal Rights Amendment: Varieties of Female
                Activism

October 2 DISCUSSION: Birth Control and Female Activism
 READING: Gordon, Woman's Body,Woman's Right,
 pp. 95-300.

October 4 Depression and Disruption: Women and Their
 Families under Stress

Week 5
October 7 Women's Work in the Great Depression

October 9 DISCUSSION: Women's Roles in the Economic
 Crisis
 READING: Olsen, Yonnondio, entire; and
 Gordon, Woman's Body, pp. 301-340.

October 11 Survivals of Feminism in the 1930s: Networks
 and Party Work

Week 6
October 14 FILM: UNION MAIDS

October 16 DISCUSSION: Women and the American Left: How
 Radical?
 READING: Dennis, Autobiography, at least pp.
 1-158; more if you wish (if available).
    OR
 Sherna Gluck, "Socialist Feminism between the
 Two World Wars: Insights from Oral History,"
 in Lois Scharf and Joan M. Jensen, eds.,
 Decades of Discontent: The Women's Movement,
 1920-1940, pp. 279-297; and Robert Shaffer,
 "Women and the Communist Party, USA, 1930-
 1940," Socialist Review 45(May-June 1979):73-
 118.

October 18 MIDTERM EXAMINATION

BREAK

Week 7
October 28 Black and White Together? Some Aspects of
 the History of Women and Interracial
 Cooperation

October 30 DISCUSSION: Growing Up Black Between the Wars
 READING: Angelou, I Know Why the Caged Bird
 Sings, entire.

November 1 American Women and the Second World War

Week 8
November 4 FILM: The Life and Times of Rosie the Riveter

November 6 DISCUSSION: Men, Women and Families: Changing
 Relations
 READING: Gordon, Woman's Body, pp. 341-418;
 Barbara Ehrenreich, The Hearts of Men, pp.1-
 87, Friedan, Feminine Mystique, Chapter 2.

November 8 The Baby Boom, Dr. Spock and Sex in the 1950s

Week 9
November 11   The Rise of the Suburbs and the Women's
               Culture of the 1950s
November 13   DISCUSSION: Up from Housewifery
               READING: Friedan, The Feminine Mystique,
               Chapters 1,3, 5-10, 12, 14.
November 15   Working Women and the Revival of Feminism

Week 10
November 18   FILM: Nellie and Mitsuye
November 20   PROJECTS DUE
               DISCUSSION: Charting the Course of American
               Womanhood, 1930-1960: Presentations from
               Student Projects
November 22   The Radicalization of Liberal Feminism: Sex
               and Civil Rights

Week 11
November 25   Women in the Counterculture and the Antiwar
               Movement: Hippies, Feminists and Politicos
November 27   DISCUSSION: Up From the Mimeo Machine
               READING: Evans, Personal Politics, pp. 1-192
               and 233-242 (PLEASE COME TO AN EARLIER
               DISCUSSION SECTION IF NECESSARY).
November 29   The Rise of Women's Music

Week 12
December 2   From the New Left to Women's Liberation
December 4   DISCUSSION: The Tyranny of Structurelessness
               READING: Evans, Personal Politics, pp. 193-
               232; and Martha Shelley, "Notes of a Radical
               Lesbian" in Morgan, ed., Sisterhood is
               Powerful, pp. 306-311 (also photocopy on
               reserve), Marge Piercy, "The Grand Coolie
               Damn," in Morgan, Sisterhood, pp. 421-438,
               and Pat Mainardi, "The Politics of Housework"
               in Morgan, Sisterhood, pp. 447-455; "Joreen,"
               "The Tyranny of Structurelessness," in Koedt
               el. al., Radical Feminism, pp. 285-299.
December 6   The Rise of Antifeminism

Week 13
December 9   Three Varieties of Feminism
December 11   DISCUSSION: Contemporary Feminist Positions
               and Oppositions
               READING: Ehrenreich, Hearts of Men, pp. 88-
               184; Betty Friedan, "An Open Letter to the
               Women's Movement." in It Changed My Life, pp.
               473-498; "The Impasse of Socialist-Feminism,"
               Socialist Review 79(1985):93-110; Catharine

MacKinnon, "The Male Ideology of Privacy: A Feminist Perspective on Abortion," <u>Radical America</u> 17 (July-August 1983): 23-38.

December 13   Where Do We Go From Here? Continuities and Discontinuities in American Feminist Issues

Office Hours will be announced in class and posted on my office door. Please feel free to discuss the course with me; I welcome your input.

Barnard College

History 3082   Ms. Rosenberg
Fall 1986   410 Lehman

AMERICAN WOMEN IN THE TWENTIETH CENTURY

This lecture course will survey the varied experiences
of women in twentieth century America. Special attention
will be given to changes in family life, sexuality,
housework, education, the workforce, and women's
participation in politics.
Lectures and assigned readings are described below.
Requirements for this course include two midterm exams (30%
each of final grade) and a final exam (40% of final grade).

Required Books (Available at Bookforum)

Carol Berkin and M. B. Norton, eds., Women of America
William Chafe, American Woman
Nancy Cott and E. Pleck, ed., A Heritage of Her Own
Allen Davis, American Heroine
Theodore Dreiser, Sister Carrie
Barbara Ehrenreich, The Hearts of Men
David Katzman, Seven Days a Week
David Kennedy, Birth Control in America
Anne Moody, Coming of Age in Mississippi

Schedule of Lectures and Readings

Week 1: The American Woman in 1900

        Theodore Dreiser, Sister Carrie
        Carroll Smith-Rosenberg, "The Female World of Love
            and Ritual," in Cott and Pleck, Heritage.

    2. The Feminization of Public Life

        Allen Davis, American Heroine, pp. 3-134.
        Blanche Cook, "Female Activism," in Heritage.
        Rosalind Rosenberg, "The Academic Prism," in
            Carol Berkin and Mary Beth Norton, eds.,
            Women of America.

    3. The Shirtwaist Revolution

        David Katzman, Seven Days a Week
        Alice Kessler-Harris, "Where Are the Organized
        Women Workers?" in Heritage.

102

4. Winning the Vote

    Davis, American Heroine, 135-231.
    Chafe, The American Woman, 3-47, 112-132.

5. Review Session and MIDTERM EXAM

6. Making Sex Modern

    David Kennedy, Birth Control in America.
    Linda Gordon, "Birth Control and Social
        Revolution," in Heritage.

7. Feminists - New Style

    Chafe, American Woman, pp. 48-111.
    Stricker, "Cookbooks and Lawbooks," in Heritage.
    Joann Vanek, "Time Spent in Housework," in
        Heritage.

8. Crisis Years

    Chafe, American Woman, pp. 135-198.
    Ruth Milkman, "Women's Work and the Economic
        Crisis," in Heritage
    Leila Rupp, "Woman's Place is in the War," in
        Women of America.

9. The Apotheosis of the Family

    Chafe, American Woman, pp. 199-225.

10. Review Session and SECOND MIDTERM EXAM

11. Black Women in White America

    Anne Moody, Coming of Age in Mississippi.
    Jaquelyn Hall, "'A Truly Subversive Affair,' Women
        Against Lynching in the Twentieth Century
        South," in Women of America.
    Carol Stack, "The Kindred of Viola Jackson,"
        in Heritage.

12. The Rebirth of Feminism

    Chafe, American Women, pp. 226-254.
    Barbara Ehrenreich, The Hearts of Men, chs. 1-5.

13. Current Realities

    Ehrenreich, Hearts of Men, chs. 8-10.

University of California, Los Angeles

History 156D

Political and Social History of American Women, 1820-1920

Winter, 1987
Tu.Thurs. 11:00-12:15   Prof. K. K. Sklar
Kinsey 141   5337 Bunche (825-4508)
                               Office Hrs.
                                   Tu.Thurs. 12:30-2

COURSE GOALS:

This is the second of a three-quarter sequence on the
history of women in the United States. The focus this
quarter is on the emergence of women as a political force,
and the experience of women during the development of modern
industrial society. The purpose of the course is to provide
students with knowledge of the major themes in U.S. women's
history and to acquaint them with examples of the major
works of scholarship on women. Important themes in the
course are: 1) the transformation of women's place in
family life; 2) the transformation of women's work;
3) the transformation of women's political culture;
4) a comparison of the experience of women from different
class, racial, and ethnic backgrounds.

REQUIRED READING:

Nancy Cott and Elizabeth Pleck, eds., A Heritage of Her Own
Kathryn Kish Sklar, Catharine Beecher
Harriet Beecher Stowe, Uncle Tom's Cabin
Miriam Schneir, ed., Feminism: The Essential Writings
Alice Kessler-Harris, Out to Work
Florence Kelley, The Autobiography of Florence Kelley
Anzia Yezierska, Bread Givers
Nancy Woloch, Women and the American Experience

COURSE REQUIREMENTS:

Attendance is required at lectures. There will be a midterm
examination worth 40% of the final grade. The final exam
comprises 60% of the course grade. Both exams will consist
of essay and identification questions.

WEEK ONE

Jan. 6: Women and Fertility Reduction, 1800-1860

Jan. 8: The Transformation of 19th Century Family Values

> Reading:
>   Cott & Pleck, Heritage, Cott,
>   "Passionlessness;" & Smith, "Family
>   Limitation;" & Smith-Rosenberg, "Beauty,
>   the Beast, and the Militant Woman;" &
>   "Female World of Love and Ritual"
>   Woloch, Women and the American Experience,
>   Chapters 5 & 6

WEEK TWO

Jan. 13: Women and Education, 1800-1860

Jan. 15: Women's Political Culture: Domestic Feminism

> Reading:
>   Sklar, Catharine Beecher

WEEK THREE

Jan. 20: Black Women: Slave and Free, 1820-1860

Jan. 22: Women and the Anti-Slavery Movement, 1820-1860

> Reading:
>   Woloch, Chapters 7 & 8
>   Schneir, Feminism, "Sarah Grimke," pp. 35-48
>   Harriet Beecher Stowe, Uncle Tom's Cabin
>   Heritage, Genovese, "Life in the Big House,"
>   & Gutman, ""Marital and Sexual Norms"

WEEK FOUR

Jan. 27: Women's Work & Westward Migration

Jan. 29: Textile Mills: Oppression or Opportunity?
          Guest Lecturer, Prof. Thomas Dublin, UCSD

> Reading:
>   Kessler-Harris, Out to Work, Cpts. 2 & 3.
>   Heritage, Lerner, "Lady & the Mill Girl;" &
>   Stansell & Faragher, "Women and their
>   Families on the Overland Trail;" & Glasco,
>   "The Life Cycles and Household Structure of
>   American Ethnic Groups"
>   Schneir, Feminism, pp. 49-61.

WEEK FIVE

    Feb. 3: The Emergence of the Women's Rights Movement

    Feb. 10: Women's Rights and American Political Processes, 1848-1869

           <u>Reading</u>:
           Schneir, <u>Feminism</u>, pp. 62-159

WEEK SIX

    Feb. 10: MIDTERM EXAM

    Feb. 12: The Women's Christian Temperance Union and the Transformation of Women's Political Culture, 1873-1893

           <u>Reading</u>:
           Review reading for weeks 1-5

WEEK SEVEN

    Feb. 17: Women's Work during Rapid Industrialization

    Feb. 19: Trade Union Organizing among Women, 1860-1920

           <u>Reading</u>:

           <u>Heritage</u>, Kessler-Harris, "Where are the Organized Women Workers?"
           <u>Out to Work</u>, Cpts. 4-6
           Schneir, "Senate Report," pp. 254-267
           Woloch, Cpts. 9 & 10

WEEK EIGHT

    Feb. 24: Racial & Ethnic Differences among Women Workers

    Feb. 26: Chinese and Japanese Women in California

           <u>Reading</u>:
           <u>Heritage</u>, Pleck, "A Mother's Wages;" & Smith, "Our Own Kind"
           Yezierska, <u>Bread Givers</u>

WEEK NINE

March 3: Women Reformers in the Progressive Era

March 5: The Black Women's Club Movement

> Reading:
> Florence Kelley, <u>Autobiography</u>
> <u>Heritage</u>, Cook, "Female Support Networks"
> <u>Feminism</u>, C.P. Gilman, 230-246.
> Woloch, Chps. 11 & 12
> <u>Out to Work</u>, Chp. 7

WEEK TEN

March 10: Margaret Sanger & the Birth Control Movement

March 12: Winning Suffrage

> Reading:
> <u>Heritage</u>, Gordon, "Birth Control"
> Woloch, chp. 13-16

University of Pennsylvania

Dr. Carroll Smith-Rosenberg   Fall 1983

THE NEW WOMEN AND THE TROUBLED MAN
SOCIAL CHANGE AND THE ASSERTION OR ORDER
IN AMERICA 1870 - 1930

1. <u>Social Change Disorder and the Loss of Control, 1870-1920</u>.
   The Male World Out of Which the New Women Sprang.

   Reading: Robert H. Wiebe, <u>The Search for Order</u>

2. <u>Disorder, Liminality and Power</u>
   Two Anthropologists View Social Disorder and the Defense
   of Structure.

   Readings: M. Douglas - <u>Natural Symbols</u>, Intro, Ch 4, 56.
              V. Turner - <u>Ritual Process</u>, Ch 3, 4, 5.

3. <u>The New Women: Working Class, 1870-1930</u>:
   Jewish Women, Trade Unions and the New Cities

   Readings: M. Tax - <u>Revington Street</u>

4. <u>Prostitution and the Working Women: Real Life and Sexual Symbols</u>
        (class will divide for readings)

   Readings: Ruth Rosen - <u>The Maime Papers</u>
              Theodore Dreiser - <u>Sister Carrie</u>

GENERAL HONORS 16
Carroll Smith-Rosenberg

5. The New Women: Bourgeois. The First Generation

    Readings: Marjorie Dobken - The Making of a Feminist
               Carroll Smith-Rosenberg - "The Female World of Love
                    and Ritual"
               Roberta Wein - "Women's College and Domesticity,
                    1870 -1918"
               Harvard Eduction Q, 14 (197)

6. The New Women As Sexual Deviant, I: Education 1870-1900

    Readings: Edward Clark - Sex and Education

7. The New Women as Sexual Deviant, II: Abortion 1860s-1890s

    Reading: H.R. Storer - Is It I?

8. The First Generation of New Women Responds: The New Women's
View of Marriage

    Readings: Kate Chopen - The Awakening
               Edith Wharton - House of Mirth

A Water Shed: The Second Generation of New Women 1890s-1930s

9. The New Women Becomes Political, 1890s - 1920s

    Readings: (all) Blanche Weissen Cook - <u>Women and Support Network</u>

                (all) Mari Jo Buhle - <u>Women and Socialism</u> (selected
                                              chs.)

                (1/2 Class) Chystal Eastman - <u>Women and Revolutions</u>

             . 1/2 Class) <u>The Young Rebecca: Writings of Rebecca
                       West, 1911-1917 (Viking Press, 1982)</u>

10. The New Women as Sexual Deviant III: The Sexologists Responds.
Order Becomes Genital

    Readings: R. Krafft-Ebing - <u>Psychopathologia Sexualis</u>
              Haverlock Ellis - 2   articles

11. Female Responses: Society as Deviant or the Inversion of
Male Bougeois Mythology

    Readings: Sandra Gilbert - "Costumes of the Mind"
                Susan Gubar - "Blessings in Disguise"
       R. Barthes "Myth Today" in R. Barthes, <u>Mythologies</u>

12. Does Sexual Deviance Become Internalized?

    Readings: (1/2 class) Radcliffe Hall - <u>The Unlit Lamp</u>
           (1/2 class) Radcliffe Hall - <u>The Well of Lonliness</u>

13. Or Is This A Symbolic Debate?

    Readings: (1/2 class) Dyena Barnes - <u>Nightwood</u>
           (1/2 class) Virginia Woolf - <u>Orlando</u>

New York University

G57.1789
Topics in American Women's History: Women in the 20th Century
Professor Susan Ware
Spring, 1987

Feb. 9   Introduction: An agenda for 20th century women's history

Feb. 16   Holiday—no class

Feb. 23   Separatism and Political Activism

    Rosalind Rosenberg, BEYOND SEPARATE SPHERES (1982)
    Estelle Freedman, "Separatism as Strategy: Female
Institution Building and American Feminism, 1870-1930," FEMINIST
STUDIES (Fall, 1979), 512-529.
    Paula Baker, "The Domestication of Politics," AMERICAN
HISTORICAL REVIEW (June, 1984), 620-647.

March 2   Woman Suffrage and Birth Control

    Sherna Gluck, FROM PARLOR TO PRISON (1976) [read any three
of the oral histories]
    Linda Gordon, WOMAN'S BODY, WOMAN'S RIGHT (1976), pp. 186-
390.

March 9   Debate: Protective Legislation versus the ERA in the
1920s

March 16   Women and Professional Identity

    Joan Jacobs Brumberg and Nancy Tomes, "Women in the
Professions," in REVIEWS IN AMERICAN HISTORY (1982)
    Barbara Melosh, THE PHYSICIAN'S HAND (1982), introduction
and Chapter One
    Regina Morantz-Sanchez, SYMPATHY AND SCIENCE (1985), pp.
232-361.
    Margaret Rossiter, WOMEN SCIENTISTS IN AMERICA (1982),
selections

March 30   Women and the Labor Movement

    Ruth Milkman, ed., WOMEN, WORK, AND PROTEST (1985)

April 6   Women Face the Depression

    Meridel LeSueur, "Women on the Breadlines"
    Tillie Olsen, YONNONDIO (1974)
    Margaret Hagood, MOTHERS OF THE SOUTH (1939),
chapters 1, 6-14.
    Alice Kessler-Harris, OUT TO WORK (1982), pp. 250-272.

111

April 13 Women and World War II

   William Chafe, THE AMERICAN WOMAN (1972), pp. 135-195

          and one of the following books:

   Karen Anderson, WARTIME WOMEN (1981)
   Susan Hartmann, THE HOME FRONT AND BEYOND (1982)
   Maureen Honey, CREATING ROSIE THE RIVETER (1984)

April 20 The postwar Feminine Mystique: Image and Reality

   Betty Friedan, THE FEMININE MYSTIQUE (1963), chapters 1-3,
8-10, 14
   Eugenia Kaledin, MOTHERS AND MORE (1984), chapter 2
   Leila Rupp, "The Survival of American Feminism: The Women's
Movement in the Postwar Period," in Robert Bremner and Gary
Reichard, RESHAPING AMERICA: SOCIETY AND INSTITUTIONS, 1945-1960
(1982), pp. 33-65.
   Amy Swerdlow, "Ladies' Day at the Capitol: Women's Strike
for Peace versus HUAC," FEMINIST STUDIES (Fall 1982)

April 27 Presentation of Oral History Reports

May 4 Black Women in White America

   Jacqueline Jones, LABOR OF LOVE, LABOR OF SORROW (1985), pp.
79-330.
   Paula Giddings, WHEN AND WHERE I ENTER (1984), pp. 261-357.

May 11 Two perspectives on the Revival of Feminism

   Ethel Klein, GENDER POLITICS (1984)
   Sara Evans, PERSONAL POLITICS (1979)

May 18 The Sears Case

   Ruth Milkman, "Women's History and the Sears Case," FEMINIST
STUDIES (Summer, 1986)
   "Women's History Goes to Trial: EEOC v. Sears, Roebuck, and
Company," SIGNS (Summer, 1986), pp. 751-779.

COURSE REQUIREMENTS: There will be two required papers of
approximately 8-10 pages each, one of which will discuss an oral
history interview with a woman about her experiences in the 1950s
and early 1960s. There will also be a take-home final exam.

UNIVERSITY OF PENNSYLVANIA
DEPARTMENT OF HISTORY

HIST 475
Dr. Evelyn Brooks

THE BLACK WOMAN IN AMERICA

Office Hours: TTh 10-12:00, Rm. 212 College Hall
Phone: 898-5024

Course Description:

This course examines and analyzes the myriad experiences of
black women from slavery to the present. The first half
of the course reflects a historical perspective and examines
family life, work patterns, and organizational activities from
slavery through the 1930s. The second portion will draw
upon other disciplines--literature, sociology, political
science, and theology--in a thematic coverage of the
myths and realities of black womanhood in America since
World War II.

Course Requirements:

Class participation
Two examinations
Research paper based on primary sources (18 to 25 pages in length)

Required Readings to be Purchased:

Jones, Jacqueline. Labor of Love, Labor of Sorrow
Washington, Mary Helen. Black-Eyed Susans
Sterling, Dorothy. We Are Your Sisters

Readings on Library Reserve:

Baxter, S. and Lansing, M. Women and Politics
Christian, Barbara. Black Feminist Criticism
Cone, James and Wilmore, Gayraud, eds. Black Theology
Du Bois, W.E.B. Darkwater
Foner, Philip S. Frederick Douglass on Women's Rights
Harley, Sharon and Terborg-Penn, Rosalyn, eds. The Afro-American
     Woman
Hine, Darlene Clark, ed. The State of Afro-American History
Hooks, Bell. Feminist Theory: From Margin to Center
Lerner, Gerda, ed. Black Women in White America
Lerner, Gerda, ed. The Majority Finds its Past
Rodger-Rose, LaFrances, ed. The Black Woman
Scott, Joan. "Gender: A Useful Category of Historical Analysis."
     American Historical Review (December 1986)
Stack, Carol. All Our Kin
Steady, Filomina C., ed. The Black Woman Cross-Culturally

Lectures and Readings:

Week 1 (Sept. 4). Introduction: The Problem of Race in Women's
        History
        Required: Du Bois, ch. 7
        Suggested: Hine, ch. 9

Week 2 (Sept. 11). Theory and Method
        Required: Lerner, The Majority, ch.5
                  Scott, all
                  Steady, pp. 7-42
        Suggested: Rodgers-Rose

Week 3 (Sept. 18). Black Woman in Slavery
        Required: Jones, ch. 1
                  Sterling, Part I
        Suggested: Robertson, Claire C. and Klein, Martin A.
                   Women and Slavery in Africa, ch. 1-2
                   White, Deborah G. Ar'n't I A Woman

Week 4 (Sept. 25). The Woman Question and Black Liberation
        in the Nineteenth Century: Abolitionism and Post-Civil
        War Feminism
        Required: Foner, all
                  Harley and Terborg-Penn, 17-42
                  Sterling, Part II, Part V
        Suggested: Lerner, The Majority, ch. 8

Week 5 (October 2). Work and Family in the Nineteenth-Century
        Rural South
        Jones, ch. 2-3
        Sterling, Part III-IV

Week 6 (October 9). Urban Life Patterns
        Jones, ch. 4-6
        Harley and Terborg-Penn, pp. 43-57
        Lerner, Black Women, pp. 440-458
        Suggested: Mamie Garvin Fields and Karen Fields. Lemon Swamp

Week 7 (October 16) ***Mid-term Examination***

Week 8 (October 23). Literary Images
        Required: Washington, all
              .. Christian, pp. 1-30
        Suggested: Zora Neale Hurston, Their Eyes Were Watching God
                   Gloria Wade-Gayles. No Crystal Stair

Week 9 (October 30). Black Women and Religion
        Cone and Wilmore, pp. 363-433

Week 10 (Nov. 6). Black Women and Politics
        Baxter and Lansing, ch. 5-6

Week 11 (Nov. 13). The Feminization of Poverty
      Stack, all
      Suggested: Simms, Margaret and Malveaux, Julianne. Slipping
                 Through the Cracks

Week 12 (Nov. 20). Black Women and the Civil Rights Movement
      Jones, ch. 7-8
      Suggested: Sara Evans, Personal Politics, ch. 4-5

Week 13 (Nov. 27). Feminism Today
      Hooks, all

Week 14 (Dec. 4). Presentation of Research Findings to Class

Final Examination--check schedule

University of Pennsylvania

BLACK WOMEN AND RELIGION IN AMERICA
Evelyn Brooks

This is an interdisciplinary study of religion in America from the vantage point of black women. Their religious experiences will be examined in relation to changing family and work patterns beginning with the African past and moving through to the present. By placing black women's religious experiences at the center of our inquiry we hope to illuminate the dynamic interplay between religious institutions, socio-economic forces, and the subjective perceptions of individual women.

A variety of primary and secondary sources will be used, including letters, diaries, autobiography, poetry, and fiction. The syllabus is divided into required reading, recommended background readings, and suggested texts for the instructor. The syllabus includes a large bibliography which provides readings for both lower and upper level courses. An extensive list of required readings has been provided so that the individual instructor may decide on the most suitable combination.

Lectures and Reading Assignments

I. Introduction--Perspectives on the study of black women

Required:
Gloria Hull, et. al., But Some of Us Are Brave, Intro.
W.E.B. DuBois, "The Damnation of Women" in DuBois, Darkwater,
pp. 163-186.

Recommended:
Darlene Clark Hine, "Black Women" in The State of Afro-American History, ch. 10.

II. African Backgrounds

Required:
Benjamin Ray, African Religions: Symbol, Ritual, and Community (1976).
Edna Bay and Nancy J. Hafkin, Women in Africa: Studies in Social Change (1976)--articles by L. Mullin or C. Obbo.
A.C. Jordan, Tales from Southern Africa, forward and selected tales.

Recommended:
Geoffrey Parrinder, African Traditional Religion (1976)
J. Omosade Awolalu, Yoruba Beliefs and Sacrificial Rites (1983)
William Bascom, The Yoruba of Southwestern Nigeria
Roger Abrahams, African Folktales (good intro. on oral traditions).
Zahan, Dominique, African Traditional Religion and Spirituality
Zuesse, Edmund, Ritual Cosmos

116

Albert Raboteau, Slave Religion, pp. 1-16.
Niara Sudarkasa, "Interpreting the African Heritage
in Afro-American Family Organization," in Harriett
Pipes McAdoo, The Black Family, Ch. 1.

Instructor:
John S. Mbiti, African Religions and Philosophy (omit
discussion of Zamani and Sasa).

III. The Slave Trade

Required:
Raboteau, Slave Religion, pp. 16-92.
Sidney Mintz, "Economic Role and Cultural Tradition" in
Filomina Steady, The Black Woman Cross-Culturally,
ch. 6.
Harold Courlander, A Treasury of Afro-American Folklore

Recommended:
Marion Kilson, "West African Society and the Atlantic
Slave Trade, 1441-1865" in Nathan Huggins, et. al.,
Key Issues in the Afro-American Experience, vol 1, ch. 3.
Philip Curtin, "The Slave Trade and the Atlantic Basis:
Intercontinental Perspectives" in Huggins, 1, ch. 5.
Herbert S. Klein, "Patterns of Settlement of the Afro-
American Population in the New World" in Huggins, vol 1,
ch. 6.
Harold Courlander, A Treasury of African Folklore
Vincent Harding, There Is a River, ch. 1-2.
Ira Berlin, "Time, Space, and the Evolution of Afro-American
Society on British Mainland North America" in AHR (1980):44-70.

IV. Slavery in the U.S.

Required:
Raboteau, Slave Religion, pp. 213-321.
Deborah White, Arn't I A Woman?.
Jacqueline Jones, "My Mother Was Much of a Woman" in Jones,
Labor of Love, Labor of Sorrow, ch. 1.
Dorothy Sterling, We Are Your Sisters, part I.
Harriet Jacobs, Incidents in the Life of a Slave Girl
William Wells Brown, Clotel
Erlene Stetson, Black Sister
William Wells Brown, The Anti-Slavery Harp

Recommended:
Margaret Washington Creel, forthcoming work on Gullah
slave religion

V. Antebellum Free Blacks

Required:
William L. Andrews, Sisters of the Spirit
Jean M. Humez, "Visionary Experience and Power: The Career
of Rebecca Cox Jackson" in D. Wills and R. Newman, eds.
Black Apostles, pp. 105-145.

Sr. Frances Jerome Woods, "Congregations of Women Religious
in the Old South," in Randall M. Miller and Jon L.
Wakelyn, Catholics in the Old South, pp. 99-123.
Dorothy Sterling, We Are Your Sisters, part II.
Harriet Wilson, Our Nig
Bert James Lowenberg and Ruth Bogin, Black Women in Nine-
teenth Century America, Part II and relevant sections of
Part III.

Recommended:
Carol George, "Widening the Circle: The Black Church and
the Abolitionist Crusade" in Lewis Perry and Michael
Fellman, Antislavery Reconsidered, pp. 75-95.
Suzanne Lebsock, The Free Women of Petersburg, Ch. 4.

Instructor:
Ira Berlin, Slaves Without Masters
Leon Litwack, North of Slavery

VI. Postbellum Black Life

Required:
Jones, Labor of Love, Labor of Sorrow, ch. 2-3.
Sterling, We Are Your Sisters, pp. 261-305, 318-322, 377-394,
397-417, 479-495.
Lowenberg and Bogin, Parts 3 and 4.
Fannie Barrier Williams, "The Club Movement Among Colored
Women of America," in Booker T. Washington, A New Negro
For a New Century, ch. 18.
Ida B. Wells, Crusade for Justice, pp. 83-86, 115-124, 201-
212, 225-232, 345-353.
Charles Chesnutt, "Conjure Woman" in Conjure Woman.

Recommended:
Rosalyn Terborg-Penn, "Discrimination Against Afro-American
Women in the Women's Movement, 1830-1920" in Afro-American
Women
Wilson J. Moses, "Black Bourgeois Feminism versus Peasant
Values" in The Golden Age of Black Nationalism, 1850-1925,
ch. 5.
Lawrence Levine, Black Culture and Black Consciousness, ch. 3.

Instructor:
Vincent Harding, There is a River, ch. 13-16.
Leon Litwack, Been In the Storm So Long, pp. 450-471.

VII. The Postbellum Church, North and South, 1880-1915

Required:
David Wills, "Womanhood and Domesticity in the A.M.E.
Tradition: The Influence of Daniel Alexander Payne" in
D. Wills and R. Newman, Black Apostles, pp.
Evelyn Brooks, "The Feminist Theology of the Black Baptist
Church" in Amy Swerdlow and Hanna Lessinger, eds.,
Class, Race, and Sex, pp. 31-59.
Jualynne Dodson, "Nineteenth Century A.M.E. Preaching Women,"
in Hilah Thomas and Rosemary Skinner Keller, Women in
New Worlds, pp. 276-89.

Anna J. Cooper, A Voice From the South, ch.1.
Lowenberg and Bogin, "Amanda Smith," pp.
J.P. Campbell, "The Ordination of Women: What the Authority
   for It," A.M.E. Church Review (Apr. 1886):351-361.
Frances Harper, Iola Leroy (excerpts)
Stetson, Black Sister

VIII.   From Farm to Factory, 1915-1954

   Required:
   Jones, Labor of Love, Labor of Sorrow, ch. 5-7.
   Cherly Gilkes, "Together and In Harness: Women's Traditions
      in the Sanctified Church" Signs (Summer 1985).
   _____, "The Role of Women in the Sanctified Church:
      Institutions, Community, and the Person," Journal of
      Religious Thought (forthcoming)
   _____ and Jualyanne Dodson, "Something Within: Social
      Change and Collective Endurance in the Sacred World of
      Black Christian Women," in Rosemary Skinner Keller and
      Rosemary Reuther, Women and Religion in America, vol 3:80-130.
   Randall Burkett, Black Redemption, "Emily Christmas Kinch",
      pp. 43-49.
   Zora Neal Hurston, Sanctified Church
   _____, Their Eyes Were Watching God
   Paule Marshall, Brown Girl, Brownstones

   Recommended:
   Mamie Garvin Fields with Karen Fields, Lemon Swamp
   Rosalyn Terborg-Penn, "Discontented Black Feminists, 1920-
      1940" in Lois Scharf and Joan Jensen, eds. Decades of
      Discontent

IX.   Civil Rights and Black Power, 1955-1970

   Required:
   Jones, Labor of Love, Labor of Sorrow, ch.8
   Anne Moody, Growing Up in Mississippi
   Sara Evans, Personal Politics, ch. 2-4.
   Alice Walker, Meridian
   _____, "Advancing Lune/For Ida B. Wells" in You Can't
      Keep a Good Woman Down
   Stetson, Black Sister
   Mahalia Jackson, "Singing of Good Tidings and Freedom" in
      Milton Sernett, Afro-American Religious History, pp.
      446-457.
   Paule Marshall, Praisesong For the Widow
   Audre Lorde, Black Unicorn or Zami: A Mythobiography

Recommended:
Aldon Morris, _Origins of the Civil Rights Movement_, pp. 1-16,
  30-50, 76-99.
Martin Luther King, Jr., "Letter From Birmingham Jail--April
  16, 1963" in Sernett, pp. 430-445.
Audre Lorde, "Uses of the Erotic" in _Sister Outsider_

University of Cincinnati

WOMEN IN JEWISH CIVILIZATION

Dr. E. Sue Levi Elwell

MWF 2:00-2:50 P.M.

McMicken 007

Course description:

This course examines images of women in Jewish literature, law and
liturgy from rabbinic times to the present and contrasts those
images with the realities of Jewish women's lives as reflected in
their writings and in contemporary social and historical accounts.
During the quarter students will analyze the roles and activities
of Jewish women as a discrete group within Jewish populations
throughout the ages and consider the achievements and influence of
several notable Jewish women.

Course Requirements:

This course is conducted as a lecture-seminar, and students should
be prepared to participate actively in discussions. Grades are
based on class participation and on two written projects. The first
project, 3-5 pages long, is a written response to a question on some
aspect of women in/and Jewish law. The final project involves an
in-class presentation and a written research report prepared in
consultation with the instructor.

Texts:

Course readings are divided into two categories: basic (required)
readings and additional (recommended) readings. All basic readings
are drawn from the REQUIRED texts:

Baum, Hyman and Michel, The Jewish Woman in America. (NY: Plume,1976)
Elizabeth Koltun, ed. The Jewish Woman: New Perspectives (Philadelphia:
    Jewish Publication Society, 1976).

In addition to the required texts, the following books are recommended:

Jacob Neusner, The Way of Torah: An Introduction to Judaism (third
edition) (Belmont: CA, Duxbury). Particularly recommended for those
who are new to the discipline of Judaic Studies.

Sondra Henry and Emily Taitz; Written Out of History (N.Y.; Bloch, 1979)
Aviva Cantor, The Jewish Woman Bibliography, (N.Y. Biblio, 1980)
Blu Greenberg, On Women and Judaism. (Philadelphia: Jewish Publication
    Society, 1981) A traditionalist's view.
Julia Mazow, ed. The Woman Who Lost Her Names, (N.Y.; Harper & Row, 1980)
    Jewish women's writings.

SYLLABUS (by weeks, more or less)

1. <u>Jewish Women in Jewish Law.</u>

Basic Readings:

Selections from the Mishnah.
Judith Hauptman, "Images of Women in the Talmud," <u>Religion and Sexism</u>, Rosemary R. Ruether, ed. (NY: Simon and Schuster, 1974), pp. 184-212.
Saul Berman, "The Status of Women in Halakhic Judaism," in Koltun.
Paula Hyman, "The Other Half: Women in the Jewish Tradition," in Koltun.
Anne Goldfeld, "Women as Sources of Torah in the Rabbinic Tradition," in Koltun.

Additional Readings:

Neusner, Chapters 14 and 15
Blu Greenberg, <u>On Women and Judaism</u> (Philadelphia: Jewish Publication Society, 1980)
Leonard Swidler, <u>Women in Judaism: The Status of Women in Formative Judaism</u> (Philadelphia: Scarecrow Press, 1978)
David Feldman, <u>Marital Relations, Birth Control and Abortion in Jewish Law</u> (N.Y. Schocken Books, 1974)

II. <u>Jewish Women in the Premodern World</u>

Basic Readings:

Jacob R. Marcus, <u>The Jew in the Medieval World</u> (NY: Atheneum, 1974), Sections 60, 79, 90 and 94
Gluckel, <u>The Memoirs of Gluckel of Hameln</u>, Marvin Lowenthal, trans. (NY: Schocken Books, 1977), pp. 1-5; 23-38; 95-99; 222-230

Additional Readings:

Henry and Taitz, Chapters 5-10
Shlomo Goitein, <u>A Mediterranean Society: The Jewish Communities of the Arab World as Portrayed in the Documents of the Cairo Geniza</u>. Vol. III: The Family (Berkeley: U of California, 1978), pp. 160-359
Neusner, Chapter 18
Cecil Roth, <u>Dona Gracia and the House of Nasi</u> (Philadelphia: Jewish Publication Society, 1977)
Baum, Hyman and Michel, Chapter 1

III. <u>Ghetto and Emancipation: The Western European Experience.</u>

Basic Readings:

Michael Meyer, <u>The Origins of the Modern Jew</u> (Detroit: Wayne State University Press, 1967), pp. 85-114

Marion Kaplan, "Women's Strategies in the Jewish Community in
    Germany," New German Critique 14 (Spring 1978), 109-118
Marion Kaplan, "Bertha Pappenheim: Founder of German-Jewish
    Feminism," in Koltun

Additional Readings:

Marion Kaplan, The Jewish Feminist Movement in Germany: The
    Campaigns of the Judischer Frauenbund, 1904-1938. (Westport,
    CN: Greenwood Press, 1979).
Hannah Arendt, Rahel Varnhagen: The Life of a Jewish Woman
    (New York: Harcourt Brace Jovanovitch, 1974).
Henry and Taitz, pp. 195-206
Jacob Katz, "Family, Kinship, and Marraige Among Ashkenazim in
    the Sixteenth to Eighteenth Centuries," Jewish Journal of
    Sociology I (1959), 4-22.

IV.   Ghetto and Emancipation: The Eastern European Experience

Basic Readings:

The following selections from Lucy Davidowicz, ed., The Golden
    Tradition: Jewish Life and Thought in Eastern Europe
    (Boston: Beacon Press, 1967):
            Pauline Wengeroff, "Memoirs of a Grandmother," pp. 160-168
            Sarah Schenirer, "Mother of the Beth Jacob Schools,"
                pp. 206-209
            Puah Rakowski, "A Mind of My Own," pp. 388-393
Deborah Weissman, "Bais Yaakov: A Historical Model for Jewish
    Feminists," in Koltun
"Voices From the Heart: Women's Devotional Prayers", Chava
    Weissler, The Jewish Almanac (N.Y., Bantam, 1980)
Baum, Hyman and Michel, Chapter 3

Additional Readings:

Henry & Taitz, chapter 13
V. Jewish Women in America: The Uptown Ladies

Basic Readings:

Baum, Hyman and Michel, Chapter 2
Susan Dworkin, "Henrietta Szold: Liberated Woman," in Koltun
Hannah G. Solomon, A sheaf of Leaves (Chicago: Privately Printed,
    1911), pp. 103-127

Additional Readings:

Joan Dash, Summoned to Jerusalem: The Life of Henrietta Szold
    (New York: Harper and Row, 1979)
Rudolf Glanz, The Jewish Woman in America: Two Female Immigrant
    Generations (Vol. II: The German Jewish Woman) N.Y. Ktav,
    1977)

Anita Libman Lebeson, Recall to Life: The Jewish Woman in
America (South Brunswick, NJ: Thomas Yoseloff, 1970)
Rebekah Kohut, My Portion (NY: Albert and Charles Boni, 1925)
or More Yesterdays (NY: Bloch Publishing Co., 1950)
Hannah Solomon, Fabric of My Life (NY: Bloch Publishing Co.
1974)

VI. Jewish Women in America: The Downtown Women

Basic Readings:

Baum, Hyman and Michel, Chapters 4 and 5
Anzia Yezierska, "The Lord Giveth", The Open Cage: An Anzia
Yezierska collection ed. Alice Kessler-Harris (NY: Persea,
1979)

Additional Readings:

Hutchins Hapgood, "The Old and New Woman," in The Spirit of the
Ghetto (NY: Funk and Wagnalls, 1902).
Sydelle Kramer and Jenny Masur, eds., Jewish Grandmothers
(Boston: Beacon Press, 1976).
Rudolph Glanz, The Jewish Woman in America (Vol. I: The Eastern
European Jewish Woman) (NY: Ktav, 1976).
Any of the novels of Mary Antin and/or Anzia Yezierska.
Elizabeth Stern, I Am A Woman and A Jew (NT: J.H. Sears, 1926)

VII. Jewish Women in America: The Second and Third Generation: 1950-
1970

Basic Readings:

Baum, Hyman and Michel, Chapters 6 and 7.
Zena Smith Blau, "In Defense of the Jewish Mother," The Ghetto and
Beyond, Peter I. Rose, ed. (N.Y. Random House, 1969) pp. 57-68.
Pauline Bart, "Portnoy's Mother's Complaint," in Koltun.
Articles and excerpts on volunteerism from Lilith 5 (1978), pp. 16-2

XII. Placing Women in Modern Jewish History: the Holocaust.

Each student will read all or selections from one of the following:

Helena Birenbaum, Hope is the Last to Die (NY: Twayne
Publishers, 1977)
Charlotte Delbo, None of Us Will Return (Boston: Beacon
Press, 1978)
Fania Fenelon, Playing for Time (NY: Berkeley Publishing
Co., 1977)
Livia Jackson, Elli: Coming of Age in the Holocaust (NY:
New York Times Books, 1980)
Gerda Klein, All But My Life (NY: Hill and Wang, 1957)

Ella Lingens-Reiner, Prisoners of Fear (London: Gollancz, 1948)
Vladka Meed, On Both Sides of the Wall: Memoirs of the Warsaw Ghetto (Tel Aviv: Lohamei ha Ghettaot, 1972)
Judith Sternberg-Newman, In the Hell of Auschwitz (NY: Exposition Press, 1963)

Placing Women in Modern Jewish History: Israel.

Basic Readings:

Shulamit Aloni, "The Status of the Women in Israel," Judaism 22:2 (Spring 1973), 248-256
Marcia Freedman, "Israel: What's a Radical Feminist doing in a Place like this?" Psychology of Women Quarterly 2:4 (Spring 1978), 355-362
Roundtable Discussion on Women in Jewish Law, Israel Today, 24 August 1979, 10-14
Carol Clapsaddle, "Flight from Feminism: The Case of the Israeli Woman," in Koltun
Rachel Janait, "Stages," in Koltun

Additional Readings:

Rachel K. Shazar, The Plough Woman: Memoirs of the Pioneer Women of Palestine (NY: Herzl Press, 1975)
Lesley Hazelton, Israeli Women: The Reality Behind the Myths (NY: Simon and Schuster, 1977)
Neusner, Chapter 9

IX. **Issues of the 1970's: Women in Jewish Life**

Basic Readings:

Blu Greenberg, "Judaism and Feminism," in Koltun
Steven M. Cohen et al, "The Changing (?) Role of Women in Jewish Communal Affairs," in Koltun
Laura Geller and Elizabeth Koltun, "Single and Jewish," in Koltun
Cherie Koller-Fox, "Women and Jewish Education: A New Look at Bat Matzvah," in Koltun
Evelyn Torton Beck, "Why is this Book different from all other Books?" from Nice Jewish Girls: a Lesbian Anthology (Watertown, Ma: Persephone Press, 1982)

Additional Readings:

Anne Lapidus Lerner, "Who Hast Not Made Me a Man: The Movement for Equal Rights for Women in American Jewry," American Jewish Yearbook 77 (1977), 3-28
Amy Stone, "The Jewish Establishment is not an equal opportunity Employer," Lilith 1:4 (Fall/Winter 77/78), 25-26
Shirley Frank, "The Population Panic: Why Jewish Leaders want Jewish Women to be Fruitful and Multiply," Lilith 1:4 (Fall/Winter 77/78), 12-17

X. **Issues of the 1980's: Women in Jewish Ritual**

Basic Readings:

Esther Ticktin, "A Modent Beginning," in Koltun
Rachel Adler, "Tumah and Taharah: Ends and Beginnings," in Koltun
Myra and Daniel Leifer, "On the Birth of a Daughter," in Koltun
Arlene Agus, "This Month is for You," in Koltun
Aviva Cantor Zuckoff, "Jewish Women's Haggadah," in Koltun
Daniel Leifer, "On Writing New Ketubot," in Koltun
Judith Plaskow, "God and Feminism" Menorah 3:2 (Feb. 1882), and
    responses in Menorah 3:3
"How to get what we want by the year 2000", Lilith 7 (1980)

Additional Reading:

Susannah Heschel, "No Doors, No Guards: From Jewish Feminism to
                  A New Judaism" Menorah 4:1-2 (March 1983)

Nessa Rapoport, Preparing for Sabbath (NY: Wm. Morrow, 1982)

American University

Dr. Nadell
Spring 1987

34.320 TOPICS IN JEWISH CULTURE

WOMEN AND SEX IN JEWISH TRADITION

Images of Jewish women include the bewitchingly beautiful dark-eyed Jewess,
the serene mother kindling the Sabbath lights, and the spoiled Jewish American
Princess. This course examines these stereotypes as well as the traditional
view of the responsibilities incumbent upon Jewish women. We will also
consider how recent events such as the founding of the State of Israel and the
growth of feminism have redefined the roles of modern Jewish women.

Required Texts:

1. Charlotte Baum, Paula Hyman, & Sonya Michel, The Jewish Woman in
   America
2. The Memoirs of Gluckel of Hameln edited by Marvin Lowenthal
3. Susannah Heschel, On Being a Jewish Feminist
4. Isabella Leitner, Fragments of Isabella
5. Anzia Yezierska, The Bread Givers

Student Responsibilities:

1. Class attendance and participation, 10% of final grade.
2. One mid-term examination, tentatively scheduled for Monday, March 2, 25%
of the final grade.
3. One paper, 30% of the final grade. The paper is due Thursday, April 9.
Paper assignment to follow.
4. Final examination, 35% of the final grade, scheduled for Thursday, May 7,
11:20-1:50 p.m.

Office Hours:

Office: 202 Gray Hall.
Hours: Mondays 11:30-12:30, 2:00-4:30
       Thursdays 9:15-9:45
Phone: 885-2423

The Jewish Studies Program is located in 206 Gray Hall. Please stop by to
meet the Director, Dr. Benjamin Kahn; to use the library; to find information
about study opportunities in Israel; to read the Washington Jewish Week; or
just to say hello.

General Sources:

American Jewish History, Vol. 70, September 1980
Rachel Biale, Women and Jewish Law
Blu Greenberg, On Women and Judaism
Lesley Hazelton, Israeli Women
Sonia Henry and Emily Taitz, Written Out of History
Lilith: The Jewish Women's Magazine (15 issues to date)
Jacob Marcus, The American Jewish Woman: A Documentary History
Jacob Marcus, The American Jewish Woman
Julia Wolf Mazow (ed.), The Woman Who Lost Her Names
Susan Weidman Schneider, Jewish and Female

Jan. 22   Introduction

Jan. 26   I.   Creating and Living within the Tradition

                 A.   Biblical Women: Eve, Lilith, and the Matriarchs
                       Eve and Lilith: Genesis ch. 1:26-3:24; Aviva Cantor,
                       "The Lilith Question," In Susannah Heschel's
                       On Being a Jewish Feminist, pp. 40-50
                       Sarah: Genesis ch. 11:27-12-:20, 16:1-18:15, 21:1-14
                       Rebecca, Leah, and Rachel: Genesis ch. 24-31

Feb. 2   B.   Biblical Women: Of Independent Means
                       Miriam: Exodus 2:1-10; 15:19-21; Numbers 12
                       Deborah: Judges ch. 4-5
                       Ruth: The Book of Ruth
                       Esther: The Book of Esther

Feb. 9   C.   Tradition in the Making: Women and the Jewish Laws
                       of Marriage
                       Rachel Adler, "The Jew Who Wasn't There," in Heschel,
                       pp. 12-19
                       Charlotte Baum, Paula Hyman, and Sonya Michel, The Jewish
                         Woman in America, ch. 1
                       Blu Greenberg, On Women and Judaism, pp. 105-23 (reserve)

Feb. 16   D.   Medieval Jewish Women: Political, Social and Economic
                       Realities
                       The Memoirs of Gluckel of Hameln, all
                       Lynn Gottlieb, "The Secret Jew," in Heschel, pp. 273-77

Feb. 23   E.   Accommodators and Resisters: Jewish Women in Eastern Europe
                       Baum, Hyman & Michel, ch. 3
                       Mark Zborowski & Elizabeth Herzog, Life is With People,
                         pp. 124-41 (reserve)

Mar. 2   MIDTERM

II. Recreating the Tradition: America and the Contemporary World

Mar. 5
A. Jewish Women in America (1654-1881)
Baum, Hyman, & Michel, ch. 2
Jacob Marcus, The American Jewish Woman: A Documentary History, pp. 135-43, 170-77, 292-98, 380-83 (Reserve)

Mar. 12
B. Jewish Women in America: The East European Experience
Anzia Yezierska, The Bread Givers, all
Baum, Hyman, & Michel, ch. 4-5
Film: Hester Street (90 mins., to be viewed during class in non-print media center 12:20-2:00)

Mar. 23
C. Organization Women: Jewish Women's Organizations
Baum, Hyman, & Michel, ch. 6

Mar. 30
D. Debunking American Jewish Mythology: The J.A.P. and the Jewish Mother
Baum, Hyman, and Michel, ch. 7-8
Mimi Scarf, "Marriages Made In Heaven," in Heschel, pp. 51-64
Pamela S. Nadell, "Second Thoughts on the Jewish American Princess," Midstream Feb. 1986, pp. 28-31 (reserve)

Apr. 6
E. The Jewish Feminist Movement: The Issues
Susannah Heschel, "Introduction," to On Being a Jewish Feminist, pp. xii-xxxvi
Cynthia Ozick, "Notes Toward Finding the Right Question," in Heschel, pp. 120-51
Rachel Biale, Women and Jewish Law, ch. 1 (reserve)
Aviva Cantor with Reena Sigman Friedman, "Power Plays," in Lilith, No. 14 (Fall/Winter 1985-86), pp. 7-13
Deborah Lipstadt, "Women and Power in the Federation," in Heschel, pp. 152-66

Apr. 13
NO CLASS (Passover begins at sundown on April 13.)

Apr. 16
F. The Jewish Feminist Movement: Proponents and Opponents
Sara Reguer, "Kaddish from the Wrong Side of the Mechitzah, in Heschel, pp. 177-81
Arleen Stern, "Learning to Chant Torah," in Heschel, pp. 182-85
Deborah Lipstadt, "And Deborah Made Ten," in Heschel, pp. 207-09
Lis Harris, Holy Days: The World of a Hasidic Family, pp. 242-59 (reserve)

Apr. 20
D. Elsewhere in the Twentieth Century: Women in the Holocaust and Women in Israel
Isabella Leitner, Fragments of Isabella all

Lesley Hazelton, "Israeli Women: Three Myths," in Heschel pp. 65-87

129

University of Texas at El Paso

SYLLABUS

LA CHICANA

Tues./Thurs. 12:30 - 2:00   Office Hours: 12:00 - 12:30
                                                             2:00 - 2:30

Instructor: Dr. Vicki L. Ruiz

APRIL 7   Introduction

APRIL 9   The Aztec Heritage/Colonial México

             Martha Cotera, Diosa y Hembra, pp. 12-40

             Adelaida R. Castillo, "Malintzin Tenepal: A Preliminary Look into
             a New Perspective," in Essays on la Mujer.

APRIL 14   The Frontier Period/Conquest and Transition

             Fabiola Cabeza de Baca, "The Pioneer Women," in Aztlan: An
             Anthology of Mexican American Literature

             David Weber, Foreigners In Their Native Land, pp. 13-50; 52-86;
             88-100; 140-168.

APRIL 16   The Chicano Family: The Late 19th Century

             Richard Griswold del Castillo, "A Preliminary Comparison of Chicano,
             Immigrant and Native Born Family Structure," Aztlan (Spring 1975)

             Albert Camarillo, Chicanos in a Changing Society, pp. 101-141

APRIL 21   Introduction to Oral History

             Devra Weber, "The Organization of Mexicano Agricultural Workers,
             the Imperial Valley and Los Angeles, 1934-1938, an Oral History
             Approach," Aztlan (Fall 1972)

APRIL 23   Occupational Mobility, 1880-1950

             Mario Barrera, Race and Class in the Southwest, pp. 58-156

APRIL 28   Immigration and the Chicano Family

             Mario García, "The Chicana in American History: The Mexican
             Women of El Paso, 1880-1920 A Case Study," Pacific Historical
             Review

130

Manuel Gamino, <u>The Life Story of the Mexican Immigrant</u>, pp. 10-11;
53-55; 61-64; 75-86; 159-167; 229-232; 237-257; 263-267; 271-278.

APRIL 30   Chicanas in Literature

-Option 1: Select one book or three short stories and prepare a
short critique.

José Antonio Villarreal, <u>Pocho</u>

Helen Hunt Jackson, <u>Ramona</u>

Rodolfo Anaya, Bless <u>Me Ultima</u>

John Steinbeck, <u>Tortilla Flat</u>

Raymond Barrio, <u>Plum, Plum Pickers</u>

Edmund Villaseñor, <u>Macho</u>

Richard Vásquez, <u>Chicano</u>

Mario Suárez, "Las Comadres," in Aztlan: <u>An Anthology of Mexican-
American Literature</u>

J. L. Navarro, <u>A Blue Day on Main Street</u>

Amado Muro, "Cecilia Rosas," in <u>The Chicano: From Caricature to
Self-Portrait</u>

Guadalupe Valdés-Follis, "Recuerdo," <u>De Colores</u> (2) (1975)

Rosalie Otero Peralta, "Las dos hermanas," <u>De Colores</u> (2) (1975)

-Option 2: Write a short story or poem dealing with the Chicana
experience.

MAY 7   Chicanas in Folklore

Richard Rodríguez and Gloria Rodríguez, "Teresa Urrea, Her Life,
As It Affected the Mexican-U.S. Frontier," <u>El Grito</u> (Summer 1972)

Irene Blea, "Brujería," in 1979 NACS Conference Proceedings

Irine Macklin, "All the Good and Bad in this World," in <u>Twice
a Minority</u>

MAY 12   MID-TERM

MAY 14   The New Generation: 1920-1950

Beatrice Griffith, American Me

MAY 19   Chicanas in the Labor Movement

Laurie Coyle, Gail Hershatter, & Emily Honig, "Women at Farah: Unfinished Story," in Mexican Women in the United States

Lisa Schlein, "Los Angeles Garment District Sews A Cloak of Shame," in Mexican Women in the United States

MAY 21   Political Activism/Chicana Feminism

Adaljiza Sosa Riddell, "Chicanas and El Movimiento," Aztlan (1974)

Sonia López, "The Role of the Chicana Within the Student Movement," in Essays on la Mujer

Terry Maron, "Symbolic Strategies for Change: A discussion of the Chicana women's movement," in Twice a Minority

Martha Cotera, "Feminism: The Chicana and the Anglo versions, a historical analysis in Twice a Minority

MAY 26/
MAY 28   The Chicano Family and its Future

Maxine Baca Zinn, "Political Familialism: Toward Sex Role Equality in Chicano Families," Aztlan (1975)

Adelaida R. Castillo, "Sterilization: An Overview," in Mexican Women in the United States

Carlos Vélez-I, "Se Me Acaba La Canción: An Ethnography of Non-Consenting Sterilization Among Mexican Women in Los Angeles," in Mexican Women in the United States

Matrescence (Part I) in Twice a Minority

JUNE 2   Chicanas in the Workforce

Rosaura Sánchez, "The Chicana Labor Force," in Essays on la Mujer

Laura E. Arroyo, "Industrial and Occupational Distribution of Chicana Workers," in Essays on la Mujer

JUNE 4   Chicanas in Higher Education

JUNE 9   <u>Media Images</u>

"Chicana Gangs," Ms. (July 1978)

JUNE 11   <u>Discussion of Oral History Projects</u>

GRADES BASED ON: CLASS PARTICIPATION
                    MID-TERM
                    ORAL HISTORY PROJECT
                    BOOK REVIEW

<u>Required Books</u>:

1. Rosaura Sánchez, <u>Essays on la Mujer</u>

2. Magdalena Mora & Adelaida R. Del Castillo, <u>Struggles Past & Present
   Mexican Women in the United States</u>

3. Margarita Melville, <u>Twice a Minority</u>

Brooklyn College, CUNY

WOMEN IN PUERTO RICAN AND LATIN AMERICAN SOCIETY

Department of Puerto Rican Studies

Professor Virginia Sanchez Korrol

Course Description:

Roles of women in different historical periods. Biographies and
documents. Literary works by women who broke with traditions and
social constraints. Current research, issues and problems of
contemporary Latin women in education, government, politics and
the labor force.

Required and/or Recommended Reading:

Edna Acosta Belen. (ed.) The Puerto Rican Woman. New York:
Praeger, 1986.

Elisabeth Burgos Debray. (ed.) I...Rigoberta Menchu. London:
Verso Press, 1985.

Asuncion Lavrin. (ed.) Latin American Women: Historical
Perspectives. Westport, Connecticut: Greenwood Press, 1978.

Doris Meyer and Margarite Fernandez Olmos. (eds.) Contemporary
Women Authors of Latin America. Volumes I and II. New York:
Brooklyn College Press, 1983.

Virginia Sanchez Korrol. From Colonia to Community: The History
of Puerto Ricans in New York City, 1917-1947. Westport,
Connecticut: Greenwood Press, 1983.

Marjorie Wall Bingham and Susan Hill Gross. (eds.) Women in Latin
America. Volumes I and II. St. Louis: Glenhurst Publications,
Inc., 1985.

TOPICS

I. Women in Traditional and Religious Roles

(a) Women and religion in Colonial Spanish America.
(b) The Feminine Orders in Mexico and Brazil.
(c) The Indian Nuns of Mexico City.
(d) Women in 19th Century Puerto Rico.
(e) Tradition and the Puerto Rican woman.

II. Feminism and Education

(a) Women's rights and the 19th c. Feminist Press.
(b) Feminist world view and values.

(c) Feminism, education and philanthrophy.
(d) Women's struggle for equality in Puerto Rico.
(e) Feminism and women's organizations in Puerto Rico.
(f) Educational and professional status of women.

III Work and Labor Force Participation

(a) Development of capitalism in Puerto Rico.
(b) Effects of migration on labor force participation.
(c) Latinas in the U.S. labor market.
(d) Workers' movements and organizations.
(e) Exploitation and accomodations.

IV. Struggle for Social Change

(a) Women and the 19th c. struggles for independence.
(b) The Mexican Revolution.
(c) The Cuban Revolution.
(d) Central America.
(e) The Puerto Rican experience.

FILMS

Two Worlds of Angelita

When the Mountains Tremble

El Norte

The Operation

135

University of California, Davis

MEXICAN WOMEN IN THE UNITED STATES; A BIBLIOGRAPHY

Compiled by Vicki L. Ruiz

Año Nuevo Kerr, Louise. "The Chicano Experience in Chicago: 1920-1970." Ph.D. dissertation, University of Illinois. Chicago Circle, 1976.

Baca Zinn, Maxine. "Mexican-American Women in the Social Sciences." Signs: Journal of Women in Culture and Society Vol. 8 (1982), 269-272.

Baca Zinn, Maxine. "Political Familism: Toward Sex Role Equality in Chicano Families." Aztlan 8 (1975), 13-26.

Baer, Barbara and Matthews, Glenna. "The Women of the Boycott,: in America's Working Women: A Documentary History - 1600 to the Present, Edited by Rosalyn Baxandall, Linda Gordon, and Susan Reverly. New York: Vintage Books, 1976, 363-372.

Barrera, Mario. Race and Class in the Southwest: A Theory of Racial Inequality. Notre Dame: University of Notre Dame, 1979.

Blackwelder, Julia Kirk. Women of the Depression: Caste and Culture in San Antonio, 1929-1939. College Station: Texas A&M Press, 1984.

Blea, Irene Isabel. "Bessemer: A Sociological Perspective of a Chicano Barrio."Ph.D. dissertation, University of Colorado, Boulder, 1980.

Cabeza de Baca, Fabiola. We Fed Them Cacus. Albuquerque: University of New Mexico Press, 1954.

Camarillo, Albert. Chicanos in a Changing Society: From Mexican Pueblos to American Barrios in Santa Barbara and Southern California, 1848-1930. Cambridge: Harvard University Press, 1979.

Camarillo, Albert. Chicanos in California. San Francisco: Boyd and Fraser, 1984.

Cantarow, Ellen, "Jessie Lopez de la Cruz." In Moving the Mountain: Women Working For Social Change, 94-151. Edited by Ellen Cantarow. Old Westbury: Feminist Press, 1980.

Castañeda, Antonia: Ybarra-Frausto, Tomas; and Somers, Joseph. Literatura Chicana. Englewood Cliffs: Prentice-Hall, 1972.

Cotera, Marta. The Chicana Feminist. Austin: Information Systems Development, 1977.

Cotera, Marta. Diosa y Hembra: The History and Heritage of Chicanas in the U.S. Austin: Information Systems Development 1976.

Craver, Rebecca McDowell. The Impact of Intimacy: Mexican Anglo Intermarriage in New Mexico, 1821-1846. El Paso: Texas Western Press, 1982.

Elasasser, Nan; MacKenzie, Kyle; and Tixier y Vigil, Yvonne, Las Mujeres: Conversations with the Hispanic Community. Old Westbury: Feminist Press. 1980.

Gamio, Manuel. The Life Story of the Mexican Immigrant. Chicago: University of Chicago Press, 1931; reprint ed., New York: Dover Publications, 1971.

García, Ignacio and Goldsmith, Raquel Rubio eds., La Mexicana/Chicana. The Renato Rosaldo Lecture Series Monograph Vol I. Tucson: University of Arizona Mexican American Studies Research Center, 1985.

García, Mario T. "The Chicana in American History: The Mexican Women of El Paso, 1880-1920: A Case Study." Pacific Historical Review 49 (May 1980), 315-337.

García, Mario T. Desert Immigrants: The Mexicans of El Paso, 1890-1920. New Haven: Yale University Press, 1981.

González, Deena. "Spanish-Mexican Women on the Santa Fe Frontier: Patterns of Their Resistance and Accommodation, 1820-1880." Ph.D. dissertation, University of California, Berkeley, 1985.

González, Rosalinda M. "Chicanas and Mexican Immigrant Families 1920-1940: Women's Subordination and Family Exploitation." In Decades of Discontent: The Women's Movement, 1920-1940, 59-83. Edited by Lois Scharf and Joan Jensen. Westport: Greenwood Press, 1983.

Griswold del Castillo, Richard. La Familia: The Mexican-American Family in The Urban Southwest. Notre Dame: University of Notre Dame Press, 1984.

Gutiérrez, Ramón. Sex, Marriage, and the Family in Colonial New Mexico. Stanford: Stanford University Press, 1987.

Horowitz, Ruth. Honor and the American Dream. New Brunswick: Rutgers University Press, 1983.

Jensen, Joan and Miller, Darlis. New Mexico Women: Intercultural Perspectives. Albuquerque: University of New Mexico Press, 1986.

Loeb, Catherine. "La Chicana: A bibliographic Survey." Frontiers 5 (Summer 1980), 59-74.

Melville, Margarita B., ed. Twice A Minority: Mexican-American Women. St. Louis: C.V. Mosby Co., 1980.

Mirandé. Alfredo and Enríquez, Evangelina. La Chicana: The Mexican-American Woman. Chicago: University of Chicago Press, 1979.

Monroy, Douglas Guy. "Mexicanos in Los Angeles, 1930-1941: An Ethnic Group in Relation To Class Forces.: Ph.D. dissertation, University of California, Los Angeles, 1978.

Mora, Magdalena and Del Castillo, Adelaida R., eds. Mexican Women in the United States: Struggles Past and Present. Los Angeles: University of California, Chicano Studies Publications, 1980.

Moraga, Cherrie and Anzaldua, Gloria, eds. This Bridge Called My Back: Writings by Radical Women of Color. Watertown, MA: Persephone Press, 1981.

National Association For Chicano Studies, Voces de la Mujer Austin: University of Texas Mexican American Studies Center, 1986.

Nieto, Consuelo. "The Chicana and the Women's Rights Movement: A Perspective." Civil Rights Digest 6 (Spring 1974), 36-42.

Preciado Martin, Patricia and Bernal, Louis C. Images and Conversations: Mexican-Americans Recall A Southwestern Past. Tucson: University of Arizona Press, 1983.

Rodríguez, Richard and Gloria L. Rodríguez, "Teresa Urrea, Her Life as It Affected the Mexican-U.S. Frontier." El Grito 5 (Summer 1972), 48-68.

Romano, Octavio I. "The Anthropology and Sociology of Mexican Americans: The Distortion of Mexican American History." El Grito 2 (Fall 1968), 13-26.

Ruiz, Vicki L., Building Bridges: Mexican Women, Unionization, and the California Food Processing Industry, 1939-1950. Albuquerque: University of New Mexico Press, 1987.

Ruiz, Vicki L. and Susan Tiano, eds. Women on the United States - Mexico Border: Responses to Change. Boston: Allen and Unwin, 1987.

Sanchez, George, "Go After the Women: Americanization and the Mexican Immigrant Woman, 1915-1929," Stanford Center For Chicano Research Working Paper No. 6 (1985).

Sanchez, Rosaura and Martinez Cruz, Rosa, eds., Essays on La Mujer. Los Angeles: University of California Chicano Studies Publications, 1977.

Segura, Denise. "Labor Market Stratification: The Chicana Experience, "Berkeley Journal of Sociology 29 (1984), (1974).

Sosa Riddell, Adaljiza. "Chicanas y El Movimiento." Aztlan (1974).

Valdez, Armando; Camarillo, Albert; and Almaguer, Tomás; eds. The State of Chicano Research in Family, Labor and Migration Studies. Stanford: Stanford Center For Chicano Research, 1983.

Vargas, Zaragosa. "A History of Mexican Auto Workers at Ford Motor Company, 1918-1933." Ph.D. dissertation, University of Michigan, 1984.

Wilson, Michael. Salt of the Earth. Commentary by Deborah Silverton Rosenfelt. Old Westbury: The Feminist Press, 1978.

Ybarra, Lea. "Conjugal Role Relationships in the Chicano Family." Ph.D. dissertation, University of California, Berkeley, 1977.

Ybarra, Lea. "When Wives Work: The Impact on the Chicano Family." Journal of Marriage and the Family 44 (February 1982), 169-178.

Zavella, Patricia. "'Abnormal Intimacy': The Varying Work Networks of Chicana Cannery Workers," Feminist Studies 11 (Fall 1985), 541-557.

Zavella, Patricia. Women's Work and Chicano Families: Cannery Workers of the Santa Clara Valley. Ithaca: Cornell University Press, 1987.

University of California, Davis

V. Ruiz
358 Voorhies
Office Hours TTh 11-12
or by appointment
752-1638/0776

HISTORY 102M(2) MINORITY WOMEN IN THE UNITED STATES

This course examines from a historical perspective the experiences of women of color in the United States. Although overlooked in most U.S. History texts, Native American, Latino, Black, and Asian women have left a rich, intricate heritage. Stepping beyond the great person approach, the course emphasizes the everyday lives and patterns of minority women. I have selected monographs which I hope engage students to the extent that they feel they are "curling up with a good book" rather than drudging through the required readings.

I believe in an atmosphere of discovery. This course should be akin to an archeological dig where teacher and students together excavate a forgotten, buried past. In addition to dispelling prevalent myths and misconseptions concerning women of color and their history, I attempt to establish an environment for critical thinking, challenging students to grapple with the complexities of history.

REQUIRED READINGS:

Ruth Underhill, Papago Woman
Dexter Fisher, ed., The Third Woman: Minority Women Writers of the United States
Anne Moody, Coming of Age in Mississippi
Ellen Cantarow, ed., Moving the Mountain
Raquel Rubio Godsmith, ed., La Mexicana/Chicana, Renato Rosaldo Lecture Series
Monograph, Vol. I
Virginia Sanchez Korrol, "On the Other Side of the Ocean: The Work Experiences of Early
Puerto Rican Migrant Women"
Lourdes Miranda King, "Puertorriquenas in the U.S."
Akemi Kikumura, Through Harsh Winters

The monographs are available at the book store and the articles on Puerto Rican women will be on reserve at Shields Library.

COURSE SYLLABUS

Week 1
1/6   Documenting the Experiences of Women of Color

Week 2
1/13   Native American Women
               Instructions for Research Paper
               Film: Hopi: Songs of the Fourth World
               Reading assignment: Underhill, 1-96;
                                          Fisher, 5-16, 26-37

Week 3
1/20   Birthday of Martin Luther King, Jr. No Class

Week 4
1/27   Afro American Women: The Legacy
               Paper Topic and Preliminary Bibliography Due
               Film: Black History: Lost, Stolen, or Strayed, Part I.
               Reading assignment: Cantarow, 52-93
                                          Fisher, 139-149, 159-166, 208-213

Week 5
2/3   Afro American Women: Change and Continuity
               Instructions for Media Project
               Reading assignment: Moody, 11-384

Week 6
2/10   The Chicana Experience
               Reading assignment: Goldsmith, 5-67
                                          Cantarow, 94-151
                                          Fisher, 307-313, 324-340

Week 7
2/18   Film: Salt of the Earth
               Place and Time TBA
               Preliminary Outline Due

Week 8
2/24   Puertorriquenas y Otras Latinas
               Films: Nostras Trabajamos en la Costura
               The Life and Poetry of Julia de Burgos
               Reading assignment: Sanchez Korrol and Miranda King articles

Week 9
3/3   Asian American Women
               Film: Jade Snow Wong
               Reading assignment: Kikumura, 1-149
                                          Fisher, 433-452, 460-469

Week 10
3/11   Race, Class, and Gender
               Media Project Due
               Reading assignment: Select any 3 bibliography entries from
                                          the reading lists

Week 11
3/17   Race, Class, Gender, and Feminism
            Discussion of Research Papers
            Research Papers Due
            Reading assignment: Select any 3 bibliography entries
                                         dealing with minority women & feminism from
the reading lists

COURSE MECHANICS

I will not grade on the curve. Each assignment will be evaluated on its own merits, using
the scale outlined below:

90-100	A
80-89	B
70-79	C
60-69	D
0-59	F

The final course grade will be based on the following:

70%   Research Paper
15%   Media Project
15%   Class Participation   (includes in-class discussions and writing
exercises)

RESEARCH PAPER

Seventy percent of the class grade will be based on a research paper dealing with a segment
of minority women's experiences. It may focus on a particular group, event, person, or
historical period, or it may offer a cross-cultural examiantion of lifestyles and attitudes.
As guides for research and further reading, bibliographies detailing some of the more
significant secondary works will be distributed on the first day of class. The use of primary
documents is particularly encouraged. To avoid the problem of an incomplete essay, the
paper topic and preliminary bibliography will be due on January 27th and a rough outline on
February 18th. The length of the essay should be from 20-25 pages (excluding footnotes)
typed, doubled spaced. I will gladly critique rough drafts. The paper in its final form will
be due on March 17th, along with a xerox copy which I retain for my files.

MEDIA PROJECT

For this assignment will be short "think" pieces in which students have the opportunity to
form their own interpretations of the materials presented. It is very important to complete
the assigned readings before coming to class.

ATTENDANCE POLICY

Regular attendance is mandatory. Fifteen percent of the final grade will be based on class
participation determined, in part, by the student's attendance record.

Duke University

HISTORY 170S

THE SOCIAL HISTORY OF AMERICAN WOMEN

Professor William Chafe
08E West Duke
Office Hours: Tu, 2-4

Office Phone: 684-5267
684-3626
Home Phone: 1-942-8245

History 170S represents an effort to understand the social history of American women from the early 19th century through the present. Over the past two decades, no field of scholarship has proven more challenging or productive than that of women's history. Yet what is perhaps most exciting is the number of critical questions and issues that remain topics of debate and controversy: whether there is now, or has been a separate and distinctive women's culture; to what extent differences of class and race and region sharply divide women's experience; how social movements are born and sustained; and the degree to which the history of women is tied to and determined by such phenomena as capitalism, industrialism, patriarchy, or demography. Some of these issues we will address directly, others indirectly. Everyone is encouraged to join in the quest for answers, and I hope that controversy will be seen as a positive feature of good discussion.

There are three requirements for the seminar. First, everyone will take a final exam at the end of the semester (a take-home). Second, everyone will write a 5-7 page essay (one essay) presenting an interpretive assessment of one week's reading. Finally, everyone will write either a term paper which discusses one's own family history over three generations, focusing on the women in your family; or a research paper of 20 pages on a topic to be chosen through mutual consultation.

Eight books have been ordered for purchase and are available at The Regulator Bookshop on 9th St. In addition, there will be two other books available for optional purchase later in the semester. The required books, now available, are:

> Gerda Lerner, The Majority Finds Its Past
> Rosalind Rosenberg, Beyond Separate Spheres
> Jane Mathews and Linda Kerber, Women's America
> Anne and Andrew Scott, One Half the People
> William Chafe, The American Woman
> Alice Walker, Meridian
> Carol Gilligan, A Different Voice
> Sara Evans, Personal Politics

August 30:   Introduction

September 6:   What Is Women's History

      Gerda Lerner, The Majority Finds Its Past

September 13:   Early Feminism

      Kerber and Mathews, Women's America, pp. 190-209, 431-435
      Ellen DuBois, Feminism and Suffrage, pp. 15-53, 162-203
      Eleanor Flexner, Century of Struggle, ch's 1-6, 10

September 20:   The Intellectual Context

      Rosalind Rosenberg, Beyond Separate Spheres

September 27:   The Issues of Social Class and Culture

      Kerber and Mathews, 156-179, 257-260, 436-439
      Charlotte Perkins Gilman, The Yellow Wallpaper
      Nancy Dye, "Feminism or Unionism," Xerox 4548 on reserve
      Ruth Rosen, ed. The Maimie Papers , Introduction and Part I
      Dorothy Richardson, "The Long Day: The Story of a New
          York Working Girl," in William O'Neill, ed. Women at
          Work (skim)
      Kerber and Mathews, 214-242

October 4:   Reproductive Freedom and the Family

      Kerber and Mathews, 179-190, 310-319
      Linda Gordon, Woman's Body, Woman's Right, pp. 3-25,
          72-135, 186-248.
      Carl Degler, At Odds, pages to be assigned.

October 11:   Suffrage and Reform

      Flexner, Century of Struggle, ch's 15, 17-19, 21,-24
      Aileen Kraditor, The Ideas of the Woman Suffrage Movement,
          ch's 5-7, 9
      Kerber and Mathews, 263-295, 440-442
      Anne F. and Andrew M. Scott, One Half the People
      Jane Addams, "The Subjective Necessity of the Settlement
          House," in Addams, Twenty Years at Hull House

October 18: After Suffrage -- Reaction or Progress

    William Chafe, The American Woman, ch's 1, 3-5
    J. Stanley Lemons, The Woman Citizen, ch's to be assigned
    Kerber and Mathews, pp. 319-353, 443

October 25: No Class

November 1: World War II and Its Impact

    Chafe, The American Woman, ch's 6-8
    Karen Anderson, Wartime Women, ch. 1 and Conclusion
    Kerber and Mathews, pp. 354-374

November 8: The Postwar Years and the Feminine Mystique

    Chafe, The American Woman, ch. 9
    Marilyn French, The Woman's Room, pages to be assigned
    Betty Friedan, The Feminine Mystique, ch's 1-4, 6, 7, 12, 14

November 15: The Civil Rights Movement and Black Women

    Alice Walker, Meridian
    Kerber and Mathews, 374-94

November 29: The Rise of Women's Liberation

    Sara Evans, Personal Politics
    Kerber and Mathews, pp. 397-426, 446-452

December 6: Ongoing Issues

    Carol Gilligan, A Different Voice
    Barbara Ehrenreich, "Le Nouveau Poor", Ms. on reserve.

Sarah Lawrence College

**THE FEMALE VISION: WOMEN AND
SOCIAL CHANGE IN AMERICA,
Part I**

Fall 1986

Judith Papachristou

The books and articles for this course are on reserve in the
library. Since we'll be reading all or almost all of the
following works, you may want to buy them at the bookstore.
Some are not available in paperback, and the list may be too
expensive. If so, talk with me about priorities.

Blair, Karen, <u>The Clubwoman as Feminist, 1868-1914</u>
Bordin, Ruth, <u>From Temperance to Reform: The Quest for Power
     and Liberty, 1873-1900</u>
Dubois, Ellen, <u>Feminism and Suffrage: The Emergence of an
     Independent Women's Movement in America</u>
Giddings, Paula, <u>When and Where I Enter: The Impact of Black
     Women on Race and Sex in America</u>
Gilman, Charlotte Perkins, <u>The Yellow Wallpaper</u>
Hersh, Blache, <u>The Slavery of Sex: Feminist Abolitionists in
     America</u>
Norton, Mary Beth, <u>Liberty's Daughters: The Revolutionary Ex-
     perience of American Women, 1750-1800</u>
Sklar, Kathryn Kish, <u>Catharine Beecher: A Study in American
     Domesticity</u>

Reading assignments are due on the dates listed below:

September 11   The Religious Heritage of American Women: One
                      Woman's Protest

                      <u>Holy Bible</u> (King James version)
                          Genesis 1,2, and 3
                          Levitivus 12: 1-8 and 15:19-30
                          Deuteronomy 22:13-30
                          Matthew 19:4-9
                          Mark 5:25-34
                          Luke 10:38-42
                          John 4:1-30 and 8:1-11
                          Corinthians I, 11:1-15 and 14:34-35
                          Galatians 3:28
                          Ephesians 5:22-23
                          Timothy I 2:8-15

Lyle Koehler, "The Case of the American Jezebels" in Friedman and Shade, <u>Our American Sisters</u>, 3rd edition, pp. 17-40

(Optional reading
Mary Maples Dunn, "Women of Light," in Berkin and Norton, <u>Women of America: A History</u>, pp. 115-133

Demos, John, <u>A little Commonwealth: Family Life in Plymouth Colony,</u> chapter 5 and conclusion

Barbara Epstein, <u>Politics of Domesticity</u> chapter 1)

September 18: The Revolution and Its Impact on Women

Mary Beth Norton, <u>Liberty's Daughters: The Revolutionary Experience of American Women, 1750-1800</u>

(Optional reading:
Linda Kerber, <u>Women of the Republic</u>, especially chapters 4,5, and 9)

September 25: Social Change and the Origins of the Women's Movement

Nancy Cott, "Young Women in the Second Great Awakening in New England," <u>Feminist Studies</u>, Fall 1975

Barbara Welter, "The Cult of True Womanhood" in Welter, <u>Dimity Convictions</u> or Michael Gordon, <u>The American Family in Socio-Historical Perspective</u>

Carroll Smith Rosenberg, <u>Disorderly Conduct,</u> "Beauty, the Beast and the Militant Woman."

Mary Ryan, "The Power of Woman's Networks," <u>Feminist Studies</u>, Spring 1979

(Optional reading:
Nancy Cott, <u>Bonds of Womanhood</u>, read as much possible, especially chapter 5 and conclusion

Epstein, <u>Politics of Domesticity</u>, chapter 2
Gerda Lerner, <u>Signs</u>, spring 1979)

October 2   Origins of the Women's Movement: Abolition
and the Slavery of Sex

Blanche Hersh, <u>The Slavery of Sex</u>
Judy Papachristou, <u>Women Together</u>, chapter 1

        and

Alternatives to the Women's Movement

Charlotte Perkins Gilman, <u>The Yellow Wall-
paper</u>

(Optional reading:
Keith Melder, <u>Beginnings of Sisterhood</u> and
Gerda Lerner, <u>The Grimke Sisters</u>)

October 9:   Alternatives to the Women's Movement: Power
Behind the Throne

Kathryn Kish Sklar, <u>Catharine Beecher</u>

October 16:   On the Move: Middle and Working Class Women
before the Civil War

Papachristou, chapter 2
Suzanne Lebsock, <u>The Free Women of Peters-
burg</u>, chapter 7

Philip S. Foner, <u>Women and the American Labor
Movement</u>, chapters 1 and 2

(Optional reading:
Eleanor Flexner, <u>Century
of Struggle</u>, chapter VI

Ellen Dubois,ed. <u>Stanton/Anthony
Correspondence</u>, Part 1

Thomas Dublin, <u>Women at Work </u>, chap. 1,2,&3

October 23   Dissension and Schism: Feminist Abolitionists
after the Civil War

Papachristou, chapter 3 and 4

Ellen Dubois, _Feminism and Suffrage_, chapters 2,3,4,5 and 6

(Optional reading: Dubois, _Stanton/Anthony Correspondence_, Part 2) ·

October 30:   Suffrage: "Key to Women's Emancipation"

Ellen Dubois, ed., _Stanton/Anthony Correspondence_, Part 3

Papachristou, chapter 6

(Optional reading:
Angela Davis, _Women, Race and Class_, chapter 9 pp. 137-142

William O'Neill, _Everyone was Brave_, chapter 2)

November 6:   From Temperance to Reform: Frances Willard and the WCTU

Ruth Bordin, _Women and Temperance_

see documents in Papachristou, chapter 5

(Optional reading:
Barbara Epstein, _Politics of Domesticity_, chapters 3,4, and 5)

November 13:   Marriage and Sex: Changing Relations between Men and Women

William Leach, _True Love and Perfect Union_, pp. 3-157

Linda Gordon, _Women's Body: Women's Right,_ chapter 5

Linda Gordon and Ellen Dubois, "Seeking Ecstacy on the Battlefield: Danger and Pleasure in Nineteenth Century Feminist Sexual Thought," _Feminist Studies, Spring_

1983, pp. 7-25

(Optional reading:
Gordon, chapters 6 and 7

Daniel Scott Smith, "Family Limitation, Sexual Control and Domestic Feminism in Nictorian America," in Hartman and Banner, Clio's Consciousness Raised, pp. 119-133

James Mohr, Abortion in America)

November 20:   Changing the Conditions of Women's Work

Papachristou, chapter 8

Philip S. Foner, Women and the American Labor Movement, chapters 3 and 4

Meredith Tax, Rising of the Women, chapter 4

(Optional reading

Thomas Dublin, Women at Work, ch. 6 and 7

Jeffrey, "Women in the Southern Farmers' Alliance," in Friedman and Shade, Our American Sisters, 3rd edition)

December 4:   Towards Radical Change: The cooperative Ideal

Mari Jo Buhle, Women and American Socialism, chapters 1 and 2

Dolores Hayden, The Grand Domestic Revolution chapters 1-4

(Optional reading:
Edward Bellamy, Looking Backward

December 11:   Domestic Feminism?   The Club Movement

Karen Blair, Clubwoman as Feminist

Anne F. Scott, "On Seeing and Not Seeing: A

Case of Historical Invisibility," _Journal of American History_, June 1984, pp. 7-21

December 18:   Race and the Women's Movement Black Women Fight for Justice

Paula Giddings, _When and Where I Enter: The Impact of Black Women on Race and Sex in America_, chapters 1-6

Angela Davis, _Women, Race and Class_, chap. 11

(Optional reading:
Gerda Lerner, _Black Women in White America_ pp. 435-447)

Sarah Lawrence College

THE FEMALE VISION: WOMEN AND SOCIAL CHANGE IN AMERICA,
Part II

Spring 1987

Judith Papachristou

The following books are in the bookstore and are recommended for
purchase:

David, Allen, <u>American Heroine</u>
Evans, Sara, <u>Personal Politics</u>
Flynn, Elizabeth Gurley, <u>The Rebel Girl</u>
Friedan, Betty, <u>The Feminist Mystique</u>
Gilman, Charlotte Perkins, <u>Herland</u>
Goldman, Emma, <u>The Traffic in Women and Other Essays</u>
Schwarz, Judith, <u>Radical Feminists of Heterodoxy</u>

Rosenberg, Rosalind, <u>Beyond Separate Spheres</u> (optional purchase)

These books and all assigned reading are on library reserve.

January 22:
The Progressive Reformer: The Example of Jane Addams
What vision of social change guided Addams and others in the
settlement house movement?   What was the role of social service
in the lives of educated women at the turn of the century? What
influence did Addams have upon the lives of more ordinary
American women?

David, <u>American Heroine</u>, read to page 211
Papachristou, <u>Women Together</u>. chapter 7

(optional reading: Cook, Blanche, "Female Support Networks and
Political Activism," in Cott and Pleck, <u>A Heritage of Her own</u> and
David, Allen, <u>Spearheads for Reform</u> [familiarize yourself with
this book; skim around])

January 29:
The Radical Woman
How did radicals differ from reformers like Addams?   What was the
relation between Flynn's radicalism and feminism? What was the
significance of radical women in American history?

Flynn, Elizabeth Gurley, <u>The Rebel Girl</u>
Goldman, Emma, "The Traffic in Women"
Tax, <u>The Rising of the Women</u>, chapter 6

(optional reading: Cook, Blanche, <u>Crystal Eastman: On Women and
Revolution</u>, read iintroduction and look over the rest)

152

February 5:
Change and the Working Woman
Which women worked for wages and what did they do? What was
protective labor legislation and how did it affect working women?
What organized efforts were made to help working women during the
Progressive Era?

Kessler-Harris, Alice, Out to Work. chapters 5,6, and 7
Giddings, When and Where I Enter, chapter VIII
Tax, chapters 5,8 and 9

(optional reading: Buhle, Mari Jo, Women and American Socialism,
chapters 4 and 5 and Rosen, Ruth, The Lost Sisterhood:
Prostitution in America, 1900-1918, skim around)

February 12:
Suffrage - At Last!
Why did women get the vote in 1920? Who supported woman
suffrage? Why?

Papachristou, Women Together, chapter 9, pp. 142-146 and chapter
10
Terborg-Penn, Rosalyn, "Discontented Black Feminists...." in
Scharf, Lois and Joan M. Jensen, Decades of Discontent, pp. 261-
267
Giddings, When and Where I Enter, pp. 159-170
Inez Hayes Irwin, Angels and Amazons, chapter VI
Stevens, Doris, Jailed for Freedom

(optional reading: Tax, chapter 7 and Buhle, chapter 6)

February 19:
Women and Peace- a Feminist Vision
What was the ideology of the Woman's Peace Party? How were these
ideas reflected in Herland? Do you agree with Gilman's view of
the relation between women and peace?

Davis, American Heroine, pp. 212-281
Steinson, Barbara J., "The Mother Half of Humanity: American
Women in the Peace and Preparedness Movements in World War I," in
Berkin and Lovett, Women, War and Revolution, pp. 259-276

February 26:
Birth Control and Sexuality as Public Issues
What was the relation between birth control and sexuality? What
groups and interests worked for the legalization of birth
control? Why? What ideas about female sexuality emerged during
the Progressive Era? How do you account for the change from the
19th century?

Gordon, Linda, Women's Body, Women's Right, chapters 9 and 10

Papachristou, _Women Together_, pp. 191-196
Buhle, _Women and American Socialism_, chapter 7
Rosalind Rosenberg, _Beyond Separate Spheres_, chapter 7
Davis, Angela, chapter 12

(optional reading: Gordon, Linda, finish book and Fee, Elizabeth and Michael Wallace, "The History and Politics of Birth Control: A Review Essay," _Feminist Studies_, Spring 1979, pp. 201-115

March 5:
A New Ideology for a New Woman
What was the ideology of the New Woman? Why were ideas about women's nature changing at this time?

Schwarz, Judith, _Radical Feminists of Heterodoxy_
Rosenberg, Rosalind, _Beyond Separate Spheres_, chapters 4,5, and 6
Giddings, _When and Where I Enter_, chapter XI

(optional reading: McGovern, James, "The American Woman's Pre-World War I Freedom in Manners and Morals," Friedman and Shade, _Our American Sisters_, 2nd edition.)

March 10: Group Conferences: Group A, 3:30 p.m.

March 12:
The Twenties
What political alternatives did women have after suffrage? What issues divided the NWP from other social reformers? Why did women fail to achieve their goals by the end of the '20s?

Lemons, Stanley, _The Woman Citizen_, chapters 4-9
Cotts, Nancy, "Feminist Politics in the 1920s: The National Woman's Party," _Journal of American History_, June, 1984, pp. 43-68

(optional reading: Freedman, Estelle, "Seaparatism as Strategy," _Feminist Studies_, Fall 1979.)

March 31: Group Conferences: Group B, 3;30 p.m.

April 2:
Depression, War and the Aftermath: The Impact of Class and Color
How did the depression affect women economically and socially? Which women were most affected by World War II? What was the Feminine Mystique and where did it come from?

Ware, Susan, _Holding Their Own: American Women in the 1930s_, chapters 4 and 5
Hartman, Susan, _The Home Front and Beyond_, chapters 8 and 11
Anderson, Karen, _Wartime Women_, chapter 5
Giddings, _When and Where I Enter_, chapters XIII, XIV

Freidan, Betty, <u>The Feminine Mystique</u>, chapters 1-3 and 7-13
also look at <u>Life Magazine</u>, December 1956

April 9:
The Revival of Feminist Activism

How can you explain the revival of the women's movement by the
1970s? What events led to renewed feminist activism?

Evans, Sara, <u>Personal Politics</u>
Friedan, Betty, <u>It Changed My Life</u>, pp. 75-86
Giddings, <u>When and Where I Enter</u>, XV and XVI
(if you have time,read Shulman, Alix, <u>Burning Questions</u>, Part IV)

April 16:
Changing Laws and Changing Consciousness: Female Activism

Freeman, Jo, <u>The Politics of Women's Liberation</u>, chapters 4 and 5
Feree and Hess, <u>Controversy and Coalition</u>, chapter 4 and 5
Papachristou, <u>Women Together</u>, chapter 13
<u>Herstory</u> — look at some of the early feminist magazines

April 23:
The Emergence of Alternate Feminisms
In what way was Koedt's essay a political statement?   Do you
agree with Rich's idea of "compulsory heterosexuality?"

Feree and Hess, Controversy and Coalition, pp. 149-166
Anne Koedt, "The Myth of the Vaginal Orgasm,"
Marotta, Toby, <u>The Politics of Homosexuality</u>, chapter 4
Rich, Adrienne,   "Compulsory Heterosexuality and the Lesbian
Experience," <u>Signs, Summer 1980, pp. 631-66.</u>

<u>April 30:</u>
Socialist Feminists and the Women's Movement
Can you have a feminist revolution in a capitalist society? What
was the impact of the revival of feminism on Marxist women?
According to Hartman, what does housework tell us about the
nature of the family?

Eisenstein,   Zilah,   <u>Capitalist Patriarchy and the Case for</u>
<u>Socialist Feminism</u>, pp. 5-26, 41-55, 355=356
Hartman, Mary, "The Family as the Locus of Gender, Class and
Political Struggle: The Example of Housework," <u>Signs</u> Spring 1981,
pp. 366-94

May 5: Group Conference: Group A, 3:30 p.m.

155

May 7:
Minority Women and the Movement
How did racism affect the women's movement? In what ways were
the interests of minority and white women similar? Different?

Giddings, _How and Where I Enter_, chapters XVII-XIX
Murray, Pauli, "The Liberation of Black Women," Thompson, Mary
Lou,_The Voices of the New Feminism_, pp. 87-102
Moraga, Cherrie and Gloria Anzaldua, _This Bridge Called My Back_,
pp. 61-93, 113-120, 210-218
Joseph, Gloria and Jill Lewis, _Common Differences_, introduction
and chapters 1 and 2

May 12: Group Conference: Group B, 3:30 p.m.

May 14:
Where Do We go From Here?
Papachristou, "Hostage to Civilization"
Stacey, Judith,   "The New   Conservative Feminism," _Feminist
Studies_, Fall 1983, pp. 559-578

History 72A
Tuesdays and Thursdays - 9:30-11:00
Fall Quarter 1986

Professor Ruth Rosen
Office: 168 Voorhies
Office Hours: Tuesday
and Thursdays - 1:30-3:00
and by appointment on
Mondays.

SOCIAL HISTORY OF WOMEN AND THE FAMILY IN THE

UNITED STATES 1630-1870

History 72A will deal thematically with significant topics in the social history of women and the family, with the aim of exploring what changes have occurred as the United States changed from a pre-industrial agrarian society into a modern industrial nation.

This is not a course about "exceptional" noteworthy women in history, although we will discuss many of their achievements, but rather about the way in which the meaning and experience of gender, the social definition of sexual biological identity, has changed over time.   The course is also not aimed at the study of "images" of women, but rather at the dynamic interchange between myth and reality; the prescriptive images which society held of women and the ways in which women accepted, challenged, or transformed their social, cultural, and economic conditions.

All students are required to enroll in a section.   This is critical. Since the teaching assistants will be working with you and grading your material, it is in your interest to take advantage of the writing, reading and research skills which will be taught in the section, along with discussions which will constitute a major part of the sections' time.

In addition, there are the following requirements:

1.   A midterm essay exam. In class on October 23. 30% of grade.

2.   A final exam. The exam will consist of two essays, each one hour long. Study questions will be given out one week before the exam. 40% of grade.

3.   Five page paper on Jubilee due Nov. 18th. Question to be handed out. 30% of grade.

Note: Any student who wishes to write a substantive term paper instead of taking the final exam, may do so. In order to do this, the student must discuss the project with the teaching assistant by October 14 and prepare a written proposal, preliminary outline, and bibliography for approval. All research topics require prior approval to assure that you have chosen a topic that is possible to pursue within the quarter.   We enthusiastically encourage students to pursue this option, which entails more individual work and self discipline and a closer working relationship with the instructor and teaching assistants. In addition, there is the reward and satisfaction of completing a research project which you have designed, and initiated yourself.

History 72A besides fulfilling the General Education requirement, is also a requirement for the women's studies major. Any student who wishes to pursue a minor or major in women's studies should see the instructor or seek advice in the women's studies office located in the women's center on campus.

Finally, this course will require some serious commitment from students and it is deeply hoped that such involvement will result in both accelerated personal and intellectual growth. Lectures will raise important issues and perspectives in the history of women and the family while discussion sections will complement the lectures by offering a forum for debate and collective problem solving. From experience, however, the real learning goes on when a student takes him or herself seriously, does the work and spends time with other students outside the class discussing the issues brought up by the course.

Please feel free to come see the teaching assistants or the instructor to discuss any aspects of the course. Have a good quarter!

Required Reading

Nancy Woloch, Women and the American Experience

Nancy Cott, Roots of Bitterness - documents.

Tom Dublin - Farm to Factory - collection of writings by early women workers.

Margaret Walker, Jubilee - novel about black life in the South.

Ann Scott - One Half The People - the Suffrage Movement

Lillian Schlissel, Women's Diaries of the Westward Journey

Schedule of Lectures and Readings

Sept. 25	Introduction to Women's History
Sept. 30	Debates, Integration: Gender and History Reading: Introduction to Cott
Oct. 2	Pre-Industrial America - Family Work to 1750 Reading: Cott: Parts I and II Woloch: Chapter 1 and 2
Oct. 7	Women and Religious Heresy Continue reading
Oct. 9	The Colonial World - Slide Presentation
Oct. 14	The American Revolution and Its Legacy Reading: Woloch, Chapters 3 and 4
Oct. 16	Industrialization: The Mill Girl Reading: Dublin, Farm and Factory
Oct. 21	Industrialization: "The Female Sphere" Reading: Cott, Part III Woloch, Chapters 5-6
Oct. 23	MIDTERM - In class

Oct. 28   The Medical Metaphor: Health and Sexuality
               Reading: Cott, Part VI

Oct. 30   Women and Slavery: Black Women
               Reading: Margaret Walker, Jubilee
                           Cott: In Part IV, Narratives
                                     Mary Boykin Chestnut

Nov. 4   Women and Slavery II: Southern White Womanhood
               Reading continued

Nov. 6   Women in the West
               Reading: Women's Diaries of the Westward Journey by Lillian
                           Schlissel
                           Cott: Farnham in Part V
                                     Noble

Nov. 11   Rebellion and Utopianism
               Reading: Cott: The rest of Part V

Nov. 13   From Reform to Women's Rights
               Reading: Woloch, Chapters 7 and 8
                           Cott: Part IV
                                     Angelina Grimké
                                     Sarah Grimké

Nov. 18   The Early Women's Rights Movement

Nov. 20   The Suffrage Movement I
               Reading: Ann Scott, One Half the People (specific documents to be
                           announced)
                           Woloch, Chapters 13 and 14

Nov. 25   The Suffrage Movement II
               "Recovering Our Past" - oral interviews with suffragists - slide
               presentation. Invite friends if you wish.

Dec. 2   The Legacy of Suffrage and The Victorian World - Slide Presentation
               and Class Discussion

Dec. 4   Last Lecture

Women, Work and Society

Dr. Marion Roydhouse   Am. Civ. 677
College Hall 321B   Graduate Colloquium
Office Phone 898-5125   Fall 1986

Office hours: Wednesday 1-2.30pm
              Thursday 1-2.30pm
or by appointment

This colloquium will be a reading and discussion seminar
aimed at exploring the writings on women in the labor force and
the impact of that participation in the work force upon women
themselves, upon the immediate family, and upon the wider society
as a whole. We will begin our joint investigation at the point
when general industrialization coincides with the sizeable
movement of women into the paid work force in the 1880s and 1890s
and we will continue to the present.

As far as possible this course will be run as a joint
endeavor; the more we all participate, the more successful the
course will be. One of the aims of women's history has been just
this; the shared process of discovery. This is what is best about
this part of the wider discipline. Nor are we bounded by the
limits of one discipline; the colloquium will be as
interdisciplinary as required in our search for answers.

Each member of the colloquium will lead discussion on the topic
they have chosen from the weekly topics list. You will be
responsible for drawing up a list of questions which will be the
basis for the start of our discussion. One week after the class
meeting you will hand in a two page summary of the issues and
questions raised by your reading and the class discussion.

You will also be asked to produce a bibliography on a topic of
special interest to you. This bibliography should be divided
into two sections, primary and secondary sources, and should be
introduced by a short discussion of the kinds of questions
addressed by your bibliography and the general answers currently
put forward by other authors. You might ask, for example, what
have researchers not looked at? What questions have not been
explored? What seems weak about current work? In this way you
should, at the end of the semester, have the basis for a future
article. We will share the results of our endeavors by bringing
together the bibliographies so that the colloquium as a whole

will produce an extended bibliography of resources in the area
under study.

In order to make your task easier, I advise you to work out
a system of note-taking and bibliographical note-cards, if you do
not already have one. If you have access to a word processor/PC
then use that. If not, the most used system is that of index
cards and you can work out your own subject/index system. The
following two books are useful in this regard:
Jacques Barzun and Henry Graff, The Modern Researcher
Frank Freidel, ed.,The Harvard Guide to American History,
rev. ed., 1974. See pages 3-136.

WEEKLY TOPICS

September 4/9:   Women and Work: Questions and Introductions

September 16: Industrial Work and its Impact - 1880-1920

Reading:
Muller v. Oregon (1908) in Linda Kerber and Jane De Hart Mathews,
Women's America(1982):440-442.
Elizabeth Beardsley Butler, "Women and the Trades"in Kerber &
Mathews, Women's America:216-222
Pauline Newman,"The Triangle Shirtwaist Factory",
in Kerber & Mathews, Women's America:222-224.
Philip Foner, Women in the American Labor
Movement: From Colonial Times to the Eve of World War I:324-392.
Susan J. Kleinberg, "Technology and Women's Work:
The Lives of Working Class Women in Pittsburgh, 1870-1900," in
Labor History 17(Winter 1976)
and read 50pp in one of the following: Mrs John Van Vorst and
Marie Van Vorst, The Woman Who Toils (1904)
Dorothy Richardson, The Long Day(1905) in O'Neill,
Women At Work

read in this so that you understand the thesis:
Leslie Woodcock Tentler, Wage-Earning Women:
Industrial Work and Family Life in the United States, 1900-1930
(1979)

September 23: Textiles, Tobacco, and Southern Women: A regional
case study

Reading:
see xerox packet of autobiographies and material on a series of
strikes in 1929.

Dolores Janiewski, <u>Sisterhood Denied</u> ,pp.3-7,152-178.
Margaret Jarman Hagood, <u>Mothers of the South</u> (1939)pp.63-182.
Valerie Quinney, "Farm to Mill: The First Generation", in Marc
Miller ed.,<u>Working Lives</u>:19-21
Bertha Hendrix, "I Was in the Gastonia Strike" in <u>Working
Lives</u>:169-171.

September 30: **Progressives, Settlements and Labor Reform**

                Reading:
 Anne Firor Scott, "Jane Addams" and "Heroines and Hero Worship"
in Scott, <u>Making the Invisible Woman Visible</u>(1984):107-148.
Marlene Stein Wortman, "Domesticating the Nineteenth Century
City," in <u>Prospects: An Annual of American Culture Studies</u>, III
(1967):531-572.
John P. Rousmaniere, "Cultural Hybrid in the Slums: The College
Woman and the Settlement House, 1889-1894," <u>American
Quarterly</u>,XXII (Spring 1970): 45-66.
Estelle Freedman,<u>Their Sister's Keepers: Women's Prison Reform in
America, 1830-1930</u> (1981):22-66.
read 50 pp. in Ruth Rosen, <u>The Maimie Papers</u> (1977).
Ruth Rosen, <u>The Lost Sisterhood: Prostitution in America, 1900-
1918</u>.
Robert H. Walker, <u>Reform in America</u>,pp.163-210
Ellen Condliffe Langemann, <u>A Generation of Women: Education in
the Lives of Progressive Reformers</u>pp.9-88.

and skim one of the following on the settlement house movement,
Lillian Wald, <u>The House on Henry Street</u>; Jane Addams, <u>Twenty
Years at Hull House</u>, or Mary Kingsbury Simkhovitch,
<u>Neighborhood: My Story of Greenwich House</u>

October 7:   **Some Further Responses: Women's Organizations and
                Working Women**

                Reading:
Ruth Milkman, ed., <u>Women, Work and Protest</u>,pp.22-41.
Robin Miller Jacoby, "The Women's Trade Union League and American
Feminism," 203-224;
Nancy Schrom Dye, "Creating A Feminist Alliance: Sisterhood and
Class Conflict in teh New York Women's Trade Union League, 1903-
1914," :225-246 both in Cantor, ed., <u>Class, Sex, and the Woman
Worker.</u> (you might want to read the longer monograph, Nancy
Schrom Dye, <u>As Equals and as Sisters</u>)
Mary Frederickson, "A Place to Speak Their Minds" in Marc Miller,
ed., <u>Working Lives</u>
Mary Frederickson and Joyce Kornbluh, eds.,<u>Sisterhood and
Solidarity</u> read three chapters of your choice.

Notable American Women - The Modern Period - read the biographies
of Elisabeth Christman, Freida Miller, Theresa Wolfson, Mary
Barker, Louise Leonard McLaren, Lucy Randolph Mason, Mary Dreier,
Mary Anderson, Grace Coyle.

October 14:   Women, Labor and the Left: 1890-1950

                 Reading:
Ruth Milkman, ed., Women, Work and Protest: A Century of Women's
Labor History,pp.42-61, 86-205,235-279.
Ellen Lagemann,A Generation of Women,pp.89-137.
Susan Ware, Holding Their Own,chapter 5.
Maxine Seller, Immigrant Women,pp.81-113, 241-278.
Alice Kessler-Harris, "Where are the Organized Women Workers?" in
Nancy F. Cott, and Elizabeth H. Pleck,eds.,A Heritage of Her
Own,pp.343-366.
Elizabeth H. Pleck, "A Mother's Wages: Income Earnings Among
Married Italian and Black Women, 1896-1911," in Cott and Pleck, A
Heritage of Her Own,pp.367-392.
Alice Kessler-Harris, Out To Work,pp.217-319.
Milton Cantor, ed.,Class, Sex, and the Woman Worker,pp.101-202.
Vera Buch Weisbord, A Radical Life read sections on Lawrence,
Passaic and Gastonia.
Ann Washington Craton, "The A.F.L. and Women," in Rosalyn
Baxandall, Linda Gordon and Susan Reverby, eds., America's
Working Women, pp.255-259, and pp.265-284.
Mari Jo Buhle, Women and American Socialism, chapter 5.
Lenora O'Reilly, Rose Schneideman in Notable American Women

FAll BREAK: October 20,21.

October 28:   Paid and Unpaid :Housework, Domestic Workers, and
                 Technological Change

                 Reading:
Hasia R. Diner, Erin's Daughters in America,pp.70-105.
David Katzman,Seven Days a Weekpp.3-43,184-222,266-297.
Ruth Schwartz Cowan,More Work for Mother, pp.69-219.
Susan Strasser, Never Done: A History of American Housework,
pp180-312
Faye Dudden,Serving Women: Household Service in Nineteenth
Century America
Daniel E. Sutherland, Americans and Their Servants: Domestic
Service in the United States From 1800-1920 - skim only.

November 4: The New Woman: Posing Alternatives

                 Reading:
Charlotte Perkins Gilman Women and Economics, chapters V,X-XIV.
June Sochen, The New Woman in Greenwich Village, 1910-1920

Dolores Hayden,The Grand Domestic Revolution,pp.1-29,150-179,
268-305.
Elaine Showalter, These Modern Women
Crystal Eastman, On Women and Revolution pp.371-375, and then 74-
123.
Carroll Smith-Rosenberg,Disorderly Conduct,pp.245-296 ("The New
Woman as Androgyne: Social Disorder and Gender Crisis, 1870-
1936")
Blanche Wiesen Cook, "Female Support Networks and Political
Activism: Lillian Wald, Crystal Eastman, Emma Goldman," in Cott
and Pleck, A Heritage of Her Own,pp.412-444.

November 11: **The Professions: No Women Need Apply**

        Reading:
Choose two of the following:
Mary Roth Walsh, Doctors Wanted, No Women Need Apply: Sexual
Barriers in the Medical Profession, 1835-1975
Barbara Melosh, The Physicans Hand: Work Culture and Conflict in
American Nursing
Charlotte Conable, Women at Cornell: The Myth of Equal Education
Margaret Rossiter, Women Scientists in America: Struggles and
Strategies to 1940
Roberta Frankfort, Collegiate Women: Domesticity and Career in
Turn of the Century America
Cynthia Fuchs Epstein,Women and Law
Rosabeth Cantor, Men and Women of the Corporation
and read:

Margery Davies, "A Woman's Place is at the Typewriter: The
Feminization of the Clerical Labor Force," in America's Working
Women,pp.232-235.
Dee Garrison, "The Tender Technicians: The Feminization of Public
Librarianship, 1876-1905," Journal of Social History VI (1972):
or
Cindy Aron, "To Barter Their Souls for Gold: Female Clerks in
Federal Government Offices, 1862-1890," Journal of American
History 67(March 1981)
Joyce Antler, "After College What? New Graduates and the Family
Claim," American Quarterly XXXII: 4 (Fall, 1980)
F. Stricker, "Cookbooks and Lawbooks: The Hidden History of
Career Women in Twentieth Century America," in Cott and Pleck, A
Heritage of Her Own,pp.476-98.

Selections in Notable American Women on law/business/medicine -
read four biographies.

November 18:   **Wars, Depressions and New Deals: The Impact on**
                 Women

          Reading: read two from each section

a/Jean Westin, <u>Making Do: How Women Survived the 1930s</u> read a
selection only.
Ruth Milkman, "Women's Work and the Economic Crisis: Some Lessons
from the Great Depression," in Cott and Pleck, <u>A Heritage of Her</u>
<u>Own</u>,pp.507-541.
Winifred Wandersee, <u>Women's Work and Family Values, 1920-1940</u>
Robert and Helen Lynd, <u>Middletown in Transition</u> -for impact of
the depression on families

b/Susan Ware, <u>Holding Their Own: American Women in the 1930s</u>,
chaps. 1-3.
Susan Ware, <u>Beyond Suffrage: Women in the New Deal</u>
William Chafe, "Eleanor Roosevelt" in DeHart Mathews and Kerber,
<u>Women's America</u>pp.344-354.
Lela B. Costin, <u>Two Sisters for Social Justice: A Biography of</u>
<u>Grace and Edith Abbott</u>,pp.125-238.
Richard Lowitt and Maurine Beasley,<u>One Third of a Nation</u>, read
the preface and introduction and then skim in the reports.
see <u>Notable American Women</u> for the following: Frances Perkins,
Susan Kingsbury, Julia Lathrop, Mary Dewson.

c/Karen Anderson, <u>Wartime Women: Sex Roles, Family Relations and</u>
<u>the Status of Women During World War II</u>
Susan M. Hartmann, <u>The Home Front and Beyond: American Women in</u>
<u>the 1940s</u>, chaps. 2-5.
Sheila Tobias and Lisa Anderson, "What Really Happened to Rosie
the Riveter? Demobilization and the Female Labor Force, 1944-
1947," in DeHart Mathews and Kerber, <u>Women's America</u>,pp.354-373.
<u>America's Working Women</u>,pp.284-298.

November 25:   **Two jobs: work and family in the working**
                 class: the post war period

          Reading:
Lillian Breslow Rubin, <u>Worlds of Pain</u>
Louise Kapp Howe, <u>Pink Collar Workers: Inside the World of</u>
<u>Women's Work</u>
Documents in <u>Women's America</u>,pp.374-394.
<u>America's Working Women</u>,pp.341-345,359-400.

Joyce Ladner, <u>Tomorrow's Tommorrow</u>, skim.
Carol Stack, "The Kindred of Viola Jackson: Residence and Family
Organization of an Urban Black American Family," in Cott and
Pleck, <u>A Heritage of Her Own</u>,pp.542-554.
Lee Rainwater et al, <u>Workingman's Wife</u>,introduction and chaps.
2,3.

Jacqueline Jones, Labor of Love, Labor of Sorrow,pp.232-330.
Kathy Kahn, Hillbilly Women,pp.49-100.

and one of these:
Deborah E. Bell, "Unionized Women in State and Local Government,"
in Milkman, Women, Work and Protest,pp.280-299.
Ruth Milkman, "Women Workers, Feminism, and the Labor Movement
since the 1960s," in Milkman, ed., Women, Work and
Protest,pp.300-322.

December 2:   "Career and Home": work and family in the middle
                class: the post war period.

        Reading:
Betty Freidan,The Feminine Mystique, read as much as you need.
Marynia Farnham and Ferdinand Lundberg, Modern Woman: The Lost
Sex skim
America's Working Women,pp.299-308, 336-340.

Sara Ruddick and Pamela Daniels, eds.,Working It Out,pp.3-24 and
choose 3 other autobiographies.
Constance M. Carroll, "Three's A Crowd: The Dilemma of the Black
Woman in Higher Education," in Gloria T. Hull et al,eds., But
Some of Us Are Brave,pp.115-128.
Naomi Weiss, "Mother, the invention of Necessity: Dr Benjamin
Spock's Baby and Child Care," American Quarterly 29 (Winter
1977):519-546 and skim one advice book on child care or day care
for children.

and select two:
Ann Crittenden Scott, "The Value of Housework," MS I:I(July
1972):56-59.
William Chafe, "Where Do We Go From Here? Reflections on Equality
Between the Sexes," in Women and Equality,pp.143-168.
Lenore Weitzman, "The Impact of the 1971 Divorce Law in
California"
Barbara Ehrenreich and Karin Stallard,"The Nouveau Poor" MS
July/August 1982

December 9:   The Sears EEOC Discrimination Case: Historians as
                Expert Witnesses and the Woman Worker

        Reading:
xerox packet and;
Rosalind Rosenberg, Beyond Separate Spheres introduction and
pp.28-53, 178-246.
Alice Kessler-Harris, Out To Work,pp.217-319.
and,
Food and Food For Thought: Discussion of the
Joint Bibliographies and end of the year celebration

University of California, Los Angeles

History 171C

THE SOCIAL HISTORY OF AMERICAN WOMEN: FAMILY, WORK, AND COLLECTIVITIES, 1600-1820

Fall, 1980
T/Th 11-12:15
(plus one section time from
those listed below)

K.K. Sklar
Bunche 5377
825-4508
Office Hours: Th.
12:45-2:45 & by
appointment

Course goals: to provide students with a working knowledge of the history of American women in the colonial and early nation periods; and to increase students' understanding of and skill in historical analysis.

***Course requirements: 1) attendance at lectures 2) attendance at section 3) midterm examination in class, October 26 4) two class reports in section 5) final examination as scheduled in the Fall Schedule of Classes.

A note on the Course Reader: Although all the books listed below are highly recommended for purchase, the first on the list is required. The Course Reader is a collection of recent scholarly articles and original primary sources. All items in it require more than one reading, and several require multiple readings. Both the midterm and final examination will assume some degree of mastery of these materials.

Books recommended for purchase:

1. K.K. Sklar, ed., Readings in the Social History of American Women, 1600-1820. (purchase required)
2. M. Kay Martin and Barbara Voorhis, Female of the Species
3. John Demos, Remarkable Providences
4. Nancy Cott, Root of Bitterness: Documents in the Social History of American Women
5. Mary P. Ryan, Womanhood in America from Colonial Times to the Present
6. Patricia Mainnardi, "Quilts: The Great American Art," Radical America, Vol. 7, no. 1
7. Alice Rossi, ed., The Feminist Papers
8. Mary Wollstonecraft, Maria, or the Wrongs of Women

Times of section meetings:

a.	R 1	f.	F 11
b.	T 1	g.	F 1
c.	W 9	h.	T 2
d.	W 11	i	W 1
e.	F 9	j	R 9

***Regarding Course Requirements: Percentage of each course requirement as it contributes toward the final grade: 1) attendance at lectures (10%), 2) attendance and participation in section (10%), 3) midterm examination (25%), 4) two class reports in section (10% each), 5) final examination (35%).

Teaching Assistants

Dian Degnan
Patricia Wilson
Jesse Battan
Cynthia Shelton
Peter Singer

Lecture Schedule
History 171C

THE SOCIAL HISTORY OF AMERICAN WOMEN: FAMILY, WORK, AND COLLECTIVITIES, 1600-1820

PART I: 1600-1775

1. Sept. 28: Female as a category of historical analysis.
2. Sept. 30: Family, work, and collective boundaries for women in three Reformation groups: Puritan, Quaker, and Hutterite.
3. Oct. 5: Preindustrial family life-cycles and female life-cycles in New England: the relationship between production and re-production.
4. Oct. 7: Anne Hutchinson within New England structures of family, work, and collectivities: the relationship between class and gender conflict.
5. Oct. 12: Family, work, and collective structures among accusers and accused in the Salem witch trials.
6. Oct. 14: Preindustrial slave women and the evolution of Afro-American family structures.
7. Oct. 19: Indentured servants and planters' wives in 17th-century Mary-land.
8. Oct. 21: Transient poor women in 18th-century Massachusetts.
9. Oct. 26: MIDTERM EXAMINATION

PART II: 1775-1820

10. Oct. 28: Women and the War for Independence: Portraits of conflict.
11. Nov. 2: Native American women and the "reform" of Iroquois family life.
12. Nov. 4: Quaker women and the demographic transition.
13. Nov. 9: New England women and the demographic transition.
14. Nov. 11: Markets, technology, and female labor.
15. Nov. 16: Degrees of freedom and unfreedom among black women in Virginia.
16. Nov. 18: White women in family, work, and collectivities on the early frontier.
17. Nov. 23: Female leadership and participation in the Second Great Awaken-ing.
    Nov. 25: Thanksgiving Holiday
18. Nov. 30: Female education: the transition to modernity.
19. Dec. 2: Enlightenment and Romantic feminism: from salon to grass roots.

History 171C
Required Reading

I.   SEPT. 28: FEMALE AS A CATEGORY OF HISTORICAL ANALYSIS

   1. Judith Brown, "Economic Organization and the Position of Women Among
   the Iroquois" (course reader)

   2. M. Kay Martin and Barbara Voorhies, Female of the Species, pp. 212-332
   (purchased paperback)

II. SEPT. 30: FAMILY, WORK, AND COLLECTIVE BOUNDARIES

   1. The Old Testament, "Genesis," chapters 2 and 3 (course reader)

   2. The New Testament, "The First Letter of Paul to the Corinthians,"
   11:1-16 (course reader)

   3. The New Testament, "The Letter of Paul to the Ephesians," chapters 5 and
   6 (course reader)

   4. Jean Calvin, Commentaries on the Epistles of Paul the Apostle to the
   Corinthians, chapter 11, verses 3-12 (course reader)

   5. Dedham Town Records excerpt 1776 (course reader)

   6. John Demos, Remarkable Providences (New York, 1972), pp. 37-42, 53-56,
   168-174, 192-193, 213-220. (purchased paperback)

   7. Quaker "Rules of Discipline" excerpts (course reader)

III. OCT. 3: PREINDUSTRIAL FAMILY LIFE-CYCLES

   1. Laurel Ulrich, "Vertuous Women Found," (course reader)

   2. Demos, pp. 128-150, 162-168, 174-178.

   3. Anne Bradstreet poems (course reader)

   4. Robert Schnucker, "Elizabethan Birth Control and Puritan Attitudes"
   (course reader)

   5. Mary Ryan, Womanhood in America from Colonial Times to the Present,
   "Adam's Rib: Women in Agrarian Society," pp. 19-82. (purchased paperback)

IV. OCT. 7: ANNE HUTCHINSON

1. "Examination of Mrs. Anne Hutchinson," "Ordinary Dealings at Suffolk
County Court," and "Church Trial of Mistress Ann Hibbens," in Nancy Cott,
Root of Bitterness, pp. 34-65, (purchased paperback)

2. Lyle Koehler, "The Case of the American Jezebels" (course reader)

V. OCT. 12: SALEM

1. Paul Boyer and Stephen Nissenbaum, Salem Possessed:The Social Origins
of Witchcraft, pp. 82-150 (Powell reserve)

2. Cott, Root, "Mercy Short, Bewitched," pp. 65-69; and Susanna Martin, on
"Trial for Witchcraft," pp. 70-75.

3. "Why more women than men are ministers of the devil," Fray Martin de
Castanega, Tratado de las Supersticiones y Hechicherias (Logroño, Spain,
1529), (course reader)

4. Demos, pp. 349-380

VI. OCT. 14: PREINDUSTRIAL SLAVE WOMEN

1. Reread relevant portions from Ryan

2. John Locke, The Second Treatise of Government, "Of Political or Civil
Society," Paragraphs 77-88 and 128-131, (course reader)

3. Allan Kulikoff, "The Beginnings of the Afro-American Family in Maryland,"
(course reader)

VII. OCT. 19: INDENTURED SERVANTS AND PLANTERS' WIVES

1. Alice Clark, The Working Life of Women in the Seventeenth Century,
(London, 1919), "Agriculture" (course reader)

2. Cott, Root. "The Trappan'd Maiden," pp. 31-33, and "Letter from an
Indentured Servant," pp. 89-90.

3. Reread relevant portions in Ryan.

VIII.OCT. 21: TRANSIENT POOR WOMEN IN 18TH CENTURY MASSACHUSETTS

1. Edith Abbott, Women in Industry: A Study in American Economic History,
"The Colonial Period," (course reader)

2. Douglas Jones, "The Strolling Poor: Transiency in Eighteenth Century
Massachusetts," Journal of Social History, Spring 1975, V. 8, (Reserve
Reading Room, Powell Library)

IX. OCT. 26: EXAM

X.   OCT. 28: WOMEN AND THE WAR FOR INDEPENDENCE: PORTRAITS OF CONFLICT

1. Mary Beth Norton, "Eighteenth-Century American Women," (course reader)

2. Galloway, Gannett, and Wister diaries in Elizabeth Evans, ed., <u>Weathering the Storm, Women of the American Revolution,</u> (N.Y., 1974), pp. 185-244, 303-334, 110-151. (Powell reserve)

XI.   NOV. 2: NATIVE AMERICAN WOMEN AND THE "REFORM" OF IROQUOIS FAMILY LIFE

1. Joan Jensen, "Native American Women and Agriculture, A Seneca Case Study," (course reader)

2. Demos, 257-313.

3. Review reading in <u>Female of the Species</u>, pp. 212-332

XII. NOV. 4: QUAKER WOMEN AND THE DEMOGRAPHIC TRANSITION

1. Coale, "The Demographic Transition," (course reader)

2. Quaker "Rules of Discipline, 1806", (course reader)

3. Janis Calvo, "Quaker Women Ministers in Nineteenth Century America," (course reader)

XIII. NOV. 9: NEW ENGLAND WOMEN AND THE DEMOGRAPHIC TRANSITION

1. Daniel Smith and Michael Hindus, "Premarital Pregnancy in America, 1640-1971" (course reader)

2. Daniel Smith, "Parental Power and Marriage Patterns" (course reader)

3. Susanna Rowson, <u>Charlotte Temple: A Tale of Truth</u>, originally published 1791, London and New York, (Excerpts, course reader)

XIV. NOV. 11: MARKETS, TECHNOLOGY AND FEMALE LABOR

1. Edith Abbott, "The Period of Transition," from <u>Women in Industry</u>, (course reader)

2. Mary Ryan, <u>Womanhood in America</u>, "Changing Roles, New Risks: Women in Commerical America," pp. 83-136.

3. Bessie (1861 Memoir regarding weaving c. 1800), (course reader)

XV.   NOV. 16: DEGREES OF FREEDOM AND UNFREEDOM AMONG BLACK WOMEN IN VIRGINIA

1. Robert Bremner, et al., <u>Children and Youth in America: A Documentary History</u> (Cambridge: Harvard University Press, 1970), Vol. I, pp. 324-339. (Reserve Reading Room, Powell Library)

171

XVI. NOV. 18: FRONTIER

1. Kercheval, A History of the Valley of Virginia, (excerpts, course reader)

2. Henry Glassie, 3 maps from Pattern in the Material Folk Culture of the Eastern United States, (course reader)

3. John Modell, "The Family and Fertility on the Indiana Frontier, 1820," (course reader)

4. Patricia Mainardi, "Quilts: The Great American Art," Radical America, Vol. 7, no. 1 (1973), 36-68. (purchased pamphlet)

XVII. NOV. 23: FEMALE LEADERSHIP AND PARTICIPATION IN THE SECOND GREAT AWAKENING

1. "Sarah Osborn's Religious Conversion," in Cott, Root, pp. 83-88.

2. Nancy Cott, "Young Women in the Second Great Awakening in New England," (course reader)

3. Keith Melder, "Ladies Bountiful," (course reader)

4. Mary Beth Norton, "My Resting, Reaping Times", (course reader)

XVIII. NOV. 30: FEMALE EDUCATION

1. Bessie memoir, chapter on keeping school, c. 1800, (course reader)

2. Abigail Foote, diary excerpt regarding teaching dame school, 1775, (course reader)

3. "Letters from Eliza Southgate to Her Cousin Moses Porter," (c. 1800), Cott, Root, pp. 103-110,

XIX. DEC. 2: ENLIGHTENMENT AND ROMANTIC FEMINISM

1. Alice Rossi, ed., The Feminist Papers (New York, 1969), pp. 1-117: (Introduction, Adams, Murray, Wollstonecraft, and Wright). (purchased paperback)

2. Mary Wollstonecraft, Maria, or the Wrongs of Women, (originally published 1788), (purchased paperback)

University of California, Los Angeles

American Women and Social Movements, 1830-1940

Prof. K. K. Sklar   History 201 -- graduate level
Bunche 5377   Winter 1987
Office Hours
   Tu.Th. 12:30-2pm
825-4508

<u>Course Goals</u>: This seminar seeks to introduce students to writings on the history of women's participation in social movements in the nineteenth and early twentieth centuries. Methodological and historiographic issues will be emphasized.

<u>Requirements</u>: Two short papers (7-10pages) are required, one on readings for weeks 2-4, one on readings for weeks 5-10. One long paper (15-20 pages) is also required. This paper should compare women in social movements before and after the Civil War, and may be a rewriting of the two short papers. The first two papers are due the week of the readings they discuss. The long paper is due Monday, March 16.

<u>Books Available for Purchase</u>:

Cott & Pleck, <u>A Heritage of Her Own: Toward a Social History of American Women</u> (1979) (for History 156D)

Kathryn Kish Sklar, <u>Catharine Beecher: A Study in American Domesticity</u> (1973)

Ellen DuBois, <u>Feminism & Suffrage: The Emergence of an Independent Women's Movement, 1848-1869</u> (1978)

Thomas Dublin, <u>Women at Work: The Transformation of Work and Community in Lowell, Massachusetts, 1826-1860</u> (1979)

Ruth Bordin, <u>Woman and Temperance: The Quest for Power and Liberty, 1873-1900</u> (1981)

Alice Kessler-Harris, <u>Out to Work: A History of Wage-Earning Women in the United States</u> (1982)

<u>PART I. 1820-1869</u>

WEEK ONE: INTRODUCTION TO GENDER AS A CATEGORY OF
(Jan. 8)   HISTORICAL ANALYSIS
           <u>Reading</u>: Joan W. Scott, "Gender: A Useful Category of Historical Analysis," <u>American Historical Review</u>, Dec., 1986.

WEEK TWO: "DOMESTIC FEMINISM"
(Jan.15)

Required Reading

(1)   Daniel Scott Smith, "Family Limitation, Sexual Control and Domestic Feminism in Victorian America," in Cott & Pleck, eds., A Heritage of Her Own.

(2)   Carroll Smith-Rosenberg, "Beauty, the Beast, and the Militant Woman," in Heritage of Her Own.

(3)   Kathryn Kish Sklar, Catharine Beecher: A Study in American Domesticity (1973), chapters 11 & 12.

(4)   K. K. Sklar, "The Founding of Mount Holyoke," in Carol Berkin & Mary Beth Norton, eds., Women of America.

(5)   Nancy F. Cott, The Bonds of Womanhood, "Women's Sphere" in New England, 1780-1835 (1977), chapter 5 & conclusion.

Also Recommended:

Nancy F. Cott, "Passionlessness," in Heritage.

Mary P. Ryan, Cradle of the Middle Class: The Family in Oneida County, New York, 1790-1865 (1981), chapter 3.

Suzanne Lebsock, The Free Women of Petersburg: Status and Culture in a Southern Town, 1784-1860 (1984), chapter 7 & epilogue.

WEEK THREE: THE ANTI-SLAVERY AND WOMEN'S RIGHTS MOVEMENTS
(Jan. 22)
                 Required Reading:

              (1) Gerda Lerner, "The Political Activities of
Anti-slavery Women," in The Majority Finds its Past.

              (2) Ellen DuBois, Feminism and Suffrage: The
Emergence of an Independent Women's Movement in America,
1848-1869 (1978)

              (3) Biographies of Black Women in Notable
American Women: Mary Ann Shadd Cary
                 Ellen Craft
                 Sarah Mapps Douglass Douglass
                 Charlotte L. Forten Grimke
                 Sarah Parker Remond
                 Maria W. Miller Stewart
                 Sojourner Truth
                 Harriet Tubman

Also Recommended:

Nancy A. Hewitt, Women's Activism and Social Change,
Rochester, New York, 1822-1872 (1984), chapters 4 & 7.

Joan M. Jensen, Loosening the Bonds: Mid-Atlantic Farm
Women, 1750-1850 (1986), chapter 11.

Jean E. Friedman, The Enclosed Garden: Women and Community
in the Evangelical South, 1830-1900 (1985), chapter 4.

Gerda Lerner, The Grimke Sisters from South Carolina:
Pioneers for Woman's Rights and Abolition (1967)

Jacqueline Jones, Soldiers of Light and Love: Northern
Teachers and Georgia Blacks, 1865-1873 (1980)

Bert James Loewenberg and Ruth Bogin, eds., Black Women in
Nineteenth-Century American Life (1976)

Linda Perkins, "The Black Female Missionary Educator During
and After the Civil War," in History of Blacks in North
Caroline and the South, (1984).

Jacqueline Jones, Labor of Love, Labor of Sorrow: Black
Women in America (1986)

Alice Rossi, The Feminist Papers, pp. 239-322, 378-470

WEEK FOUR: WOMEN AND ANTEBELLUM LABOR MOVEMENTS
(Jan. 29)
Required Reading:

(1) Thomas Dublin, Women at Work: The
Transformation of Work and Community in Lowell,
Massachusetts, 1826-1860 (1979).

(2) Christine Stansell, City of Women: Sex and
Class in New York, 1790-1860 (1986), chapters 6 & 7.

(3) Alice Kessler-Harris, Out to Work: A
History of Wage-Earning Women in the United States (1982),
chapter 3.

PART II: 1870-1940

WEEK FIVE: THE WOMEN'S CHRISTIAN TEMPERANCE UNION
(Feb. 5)
Required Reading:

(1) Ruth Bordin, Woman and Temperance: The
Quest for Power and Liberty, 1873-1900 (1981)

(2) Estelle Freedman, "Separatism as Strategy:
Female Institution Building and American Feminism, 1870-
1930," Feminist Studies, Vol. 5, No. 3 (Fall 1979).

(3) Biographies of Black Women in Notable
American Women: Frances Ellen Watkins Harper
Amanda Berry Smith

Also Recommended:

Ruth Bordin, Frances Willard: A Biography (1986)

Carroll Smith-Rosenberg, "The Female World of Love and
Ritual: Relations between Women in 19th-Century America,"
in Heritage.

Blanche Wiesen Cook, "Female Support Networks and Political
Activism: Lillian Wald, Crystal Eastman, Emma Goldman," in
Heritage.

Biographies of Black Women in NAW who were active in the
YWCA: Eva del Vakia Bowles
Addie D. Waites Hunton

Friedman, The Enclosed Garden, chapter 6.

176

WEEK SIX: THE SOCIAL SETTLEMENT AND WOMEN'S CLUB MOVEMENTS
(Feb.12)
Required Reading:

(1) Kathryn Kish Sklar, "Hull House as a Community of Women Reformers in the 1890's," SIGNS, (Summer 1985)

(2) Karen Blair, The Clubwoman as Feminist: True Womanhood Redefined, 1868-1914 (1980), chapters 5 & 6.

(3) Gerda Lerner, "The Community Work of Black Club Women," in The Majority Finds Its Past.

(4) Biographies of Black Women in Notable American Women: Janie Porter Barrett
    Victoria Earle Matthews
    Josephine St. Pierre Ruffin
    Ida Bell Wells-Barnett
    Fannie Barrier Williams

Also Recommended:

Ellen Sue Levi Elwell, "The Founding and Early Programs of the National Council of Jewish Women: Study and Practice as Jewish Women's Religious Expression," Unpub. PhD. Diss., Indiana University, 1982.

Sara Essa Gallaway, "Pioneering the Woman's Club Movement: The Stody of Caroline Maria Severance in Los Angeles," Unpub. PhD diss., Carnegie-Mellon University, 1985.

Rebecca Louise Sherrick, "Private Visions, Public Lives: The Hull House Women in the Progressive Era," Unpub. PhD. Diss. (Northwestern University, 1980)

Martha Elizabeth May,"Home Life: Progressive Social Reformers' Prescriptions for Social Stability, 1890-1920," Unpub. PhD. Diss. (SUNY, Binghamton, 1984)

WEEK SEVEN: WOMEN AND THE SOCIALIST AND LABOR MOVEMENTS,
 (Feb. 19)   1880-1930

Required Reading:

(1) Nancy Schrom Dye, As Equals and As Sisters:
Feminism, Unionism, and the Women's Trade Union League of
New York (1980)

(2) Alice Kessler-Harris, Out to Work, ch. 6-7.

(3) Alice Kessler-Harris, "Where are the
Organized Women Workers?" in Heritage.

(4) Mari Jo Buhle, Women and American
Socialism, 1870-1920 (1981)

Also Recommended:

Meredith Tax, The Rising of the Women: Feminist Solidarity
and Class Conflict, 1880-1917 (1980)

Ruth Milkman, Ed., Women, Work & Protest: A Century of U.S.
WOmen's Labor History (1985), chapters 1-8.

Martha Jane Soltow and Mary K. Wery, American Women and the
Labor Movement, 1825-1974: An Annotated Bibliography (1976)

James J. Kenneally, Women and American Trade Unions (1978)

Mari Jo Buhle, Women and the American Left: A Guide to
Sources (1983)

WEEK EIGHT: THE WOMAN SUFFRAGE MOVEMENT
(Feb. 26)
<u>Required Reading</u>:

(1) Elinor Lerner, "Immigrant and Working Class Involvement in the New York City Woman Suffrage Movement, 1905-1917: A Study in Progressive Era Politics," Unpub. PhD Diss., UC, Berkeley, 1981.

(2) Paula Baker, "The Domestication of Politics: Women and American Political Society, 1780-1920," <u>American Historical Review</u>, Vol. 89, #3 (1984).

(3) Sharon Hartman Strom, "Leadership and Tactics in the American Woman Suffrage Movement: A New Perspective from Massachusetts," <u>Journal of Amer. History</u>, Vol. 62, No. 2, (Sept. 1975).

(4) Rosalyn Terborg-Penn, "Black women in the Woman Suffrage Movement," in Sharon Harley & Rosalyn Terborg Penn, eds., <u>The Afro-American Woman: Struggles and Images</u> (1978)

(5) William O'Neill, <u>Everyone Was Brave: A History of Feminism in America</u> (1969), chapters 3-5.

Also Recommended:

Eleanor Flexner, <u>Century of Struggle: The Woman's Rights Movement in the United States</u> (1959), chapters 16, 17, 19-24

Aileen Kraditor, <u>The Ideas of the Woman Suffrage Movement, 1890-1920</u> (1965), chapters 5-9.

Linda Claire Steiner, "The Women's Suffrage Press, 1850-1900: A Cultural Analysis," Unpub. PhD. Diss., U. of Ill, Urbana, 1979.

Frances Sizemore Hensley, "Change and Continuity in the American Women's Movement, 1848-1930: A National and State Perspective," Unpub. PhD. Diss, Ohio State U., 1981.

Linda G. Ford, "American Militants: An Analysis of the National Woman's Party, 1913-1919," Unpub. PhD. diss. Syracuse University, (1984.)

WEEK NINE: AFTER SUFFRAGE
(Mar. 5)
            Required Reading:

            (1) J. Stanley Lemons, <u>The Woman Citizen:</u>
<u>Social Feminism in the 1920's</u> (1973)

            (2) O'Neill, <u>Everyone Was Brave</u>, chapter 8.

            (3) Nancy F. Cott, "Feminist Politics in the
1920's: The National Woman's Party," <u>Journal of American</u>
<u>History</u>, Vol. 71, #1 (June 1984).

            (4) Kathryn Kish Sklar, "Why Were Most
Politically-Active Women Opposed to the ERA in the 1920's?"
Joan Hoff Wilson, ed., <u>Rights of Passage: The Past and</u>
<u>Future of the ERA</u> (1986).

<u>Also Recommended</u>:

Felice D. Gordon, <u>After Winning: The Legacy of the New</u>
<u>Jersey Suffragists, 1920-1947</u> (1986)

Willie Mae Coleman, "Keeping the Faith and Disturbing the
Peace: Black Women from Anti-Slavery to Women's Suffrage,"
Unpub. PhD Diss., UC Irvine, (1982)

WEEK TEN: THE 1930'S
(Mar. 12)
            Required Reading:

            (1) Susan Ware: <u>Beyond Suffrage: Women in the</u>
<u>New Deal</u> (1981)

            (2) Jacqueline Dowd Hall, <u>Revolt Against</u>
<u>Chivary: Jessie Daniel Ames and the Women's Campaign</u>
<u>Against Lynching</u> (1979).

180

Cornell University

Spring, 1987
Women's Studies 238/HDFS 258
The Historical Development of Women as Professionals, 1800-1985
Professor Joan Jacobs Brumberg
Vivian Bruce Conger, Teaching Assistant

Required Texts: One copy of each of the required texts is available on Reserve in Uris Library.

Charlotte Conable, Women At Cornell:The Myth of Equal Education (Cornell)
Ruth Schwartz Cowan, More Work For Mother:The Ironies of Household Technology from the Open Hearth to the Microwave (Basic Books)
Faye E. Dudden, Serving Women: Household Service in 19th Century America (Wesleyan)
Barbara Melosh, The Physician's Hand: Work Culture and Conflict in America Nursing (Temple)
Margaret Rossiter, American Women in Science to 1940 (John Hopkins)
Katherine Sklar, Catherine Beecher: A Study in American Domesticity (W.W.Norton)

Additional Required Reading: On reserve in Mann and Uris

Joan Jacobs Brumberg and Nancy Tomes, "Women in the Professions: A Research Agenda for American Historians," Reviews in American History (June, 1982).

Virginia Drachman, "Female Solidarity and Professional Success: The Dilemma of Women Doctors in Late 19th Century America," Journal of Social History (Summer 1982), 607-619.

Darlene Clark Hine, "Mable K. Staupers and the Integration of Black Nurses into the Armed Forces," from August Meier and John Hope Franklin, eds. Black Leaders of the Twentieth Century (Illinois)

Regina Markell Morantz, "Feminism, Professionalism, and Germs: The Throught of Mary Putnam Jacobi and Elizabeth Blackwell," American Quarterly 34 (Winter 1982), 459-478.

Kathryn Kish Sklar, "Hull House in the 1890s: A Community of Women Reformers", SIGNS 10:41(1985), 658-677.

Virginia Woolf,"Shakespeare's Sister" from A Room of One's Own and "Professions for Women"

Schedule of Lectures, Readings, Discussion

FOR SCHEDULED DISCUSSIONS, STUDENTS ARE EXPECTED TO COMPLETE
READING ASSIGNMENTS DUE FOR THAT DAY. STUDY GUIDES WILL BE
PROVIDED FOR EACH OF THE ASSIGNED BOOKS EXCEPT COWAN. INTELLIGENT
CLASS PARTICIPATION IS A COMPONENT OF YOUR GRADE.

January 27: Historical Issues in Female Professionalization: A Road Map

29: Discussion: **DUE:** Virginia Woolf selections

February 3: Women, Work and the Professions in Colonial America

5: Discussion **DUE:** Cowan, Chapters I-III

10 : Economic and Cultural Sources of "The Cult of Domesticity"

12: Women's "Calling": Evangelization

17: Women's "Calling": Voluntarism

19: Discussion   **DUE:**   Sklar, Catherine Beecher

24: The Feminization Process: The American Woman
Schoolteacher

26: Discussion **DUE** : Dudden, Serving Women

March   3 : "Scribbling Women":The Profession of Authorship

5: Antebellum Medicine: The Decline of the Female Midwife

10: FILMS:"Master Smart Woman" (a film about 19th century
author Sarah Orne Jewett) and "Daughters of Time" (a film
about the history and current practice of midwivery)

12: Women Doctors in 19th Century Boston and Upstate
New York

17: **DUE:** Morantz and Drachman articles

19: MID-TERM EXAM

SPRING BREAK - MARCH 22-MARCH 29

MARCH   31:   The Rise of the Trained Nurse, 1850-1910

APRIL   2: **DUE** : The Physician's Hand

            7: The Controversy Over Higher Education For Women/The
               Experience of the First Generation

            9: **DUE:** Women at Cornell

           14: Science and Women's Work: Home Economics at
               Cornell, 1900-1930
               DUE: Rossiter, pp. 1-99

           16: Botany But Not Physics: The Exclusion of Woman
               Scientists
               DUE: Rossiter, pp. 160-217; 267-316

           21: Social Work and Progressive Reform: Jane Addams and
               Alice Hamilton
               DUE: Sklar article

           23: Women in The Depression and World War II
               DUE: Hine article

           28: FILM: "Rosie The Riveter"

May   5: **DUE:** Cowan, Chapters III, V, VI, VII

            7: 1950-1980: From "The Feminine Mystique" to "Superwomen":
               The Case of Women in Law

THE FINAL EXAM COVERS MATERIAL FROM THE MIDTERM TO THE END OF THE
TERM. YOU WILL HAVE ONE ESSAY QUESTION BASED ON THE
BRUMBERG-TOMES ARTICLE THAT YOU WILL BE ABLE TO PREPARE
BEFOREHAND.

PAPER ASSIGNMENT:

Each student is expected to complete an additional paper. You may select an assignment from one of the three areas listed below. Each paper has a different due date which reflects the amount of work and level of difficulty that the assignment requires.

All papers must be typed and double-spaced. Students are expected to pay attention to the rules of grammar, punctuation, and citation. You are graded on how you write because writing is an indication of how you think.

OPTION #1 DUE: APRIL 16
 A Critical Analysis of a Secondary Historical Work:

This assignment involves doing a book review of no more than 1500 words (six double- spaced pages) of Ruth Schwartz Cowan's More Work For Mother. Your review should include (1) a synthesis of the thesis as well as the content of the book (2) some analysis of the method and sources used by the author (3) a discussion of how the subject and the interpretation relate to the history and future of women in the professions.

OPTION #2 DUE: APRIL 23
A Critical Analysis of the Autobiography of a Progressive Reformer

Two of the most important women of the Progressive Era, Jane Addams and Alice Hamilton, have autobiographies that are available in paperback. Select either Twenty Years At Hull House (Addams) or Exploring The Dangerous Trades (Hamilton). Using evidence from the book, discuss (in an essay of no more than 2000 words) the central ideological and social concerns of the author as well as her life and professional accomplishments.

To better prepare yourself for this assignment, read the essay on Addams or Hamilton in Notable American Women, available in Olin and Uris Reference. If you chose Hamilton, be sure to attend the April 21 (4:30 p.m.) lecture by Professor Barbara Sicherman.

184

OPTION #3 **DUE: APRIL 28**
<u>Historical Research in Primary Source Documents:</u>

This option is for students who wish to try their hand at primary source research-- that is, using original documents or published materials from the past: newspapers, magazines, diaries, letters, photographs, etc. This option will require that you spend a good deal of time in Olin Library.

Many opportunities for primary source investigation exist at Cornell. You may want to write about:
 --women faculty or students at Cornell in the late 19th or early 20th century using scrapbooks, yearbooks, literary annuals, diaries or letters available in the Department of Manuscripts and University Archives, Olin Library
--women's work outside the home as discussed in the popular women's periodicals of the 19th and 20th centuries such as <u>Godey's Lady's Book</u> or <u>The Ladies Home Journal</u>
--women who forged careers in areas not covered in this class (architecture; music; art; engineering; business). Students looking for professional women to study can consult <u>Notable American Women</u> in Olin and Uris Libraries; this is an important first step in finding bibliography on this type of women. Do not forget <u>The Reader's Guide to Periodical Literature</u> and <u>The New York Times Index</u> .

You can be as creative as you wish in choosing a subject BUT you must be able to identify a small body of source materials on which to base your paper. STUDENTS DOING OPTION #3 MUST HAVE THE PRIOR APPROVAL OF THE INSTRUCTOR or T.A. Maximum length for paper is 15 pages; students must follow standard footnoting and bibliographic techniques in <u>Chicago Manual of Style</u>. STUDENTS WHO SELECT THIS OPTION AND RECEIVE A GRADE OF "A" MAY BE EXCUSED FROM THE FINAL BY THE PROFESSOR.

EXTRA CREDIT ASSIGNMENT:
During the month of March, Women's Studies will run a series of events as part of the nationwide observance of Women's History Month.There are four March events each at 4:30 p.m.:

> March 5: "When Ladies Go A-Thieving": Women, Kleptomania, and the 19th century Department Store *
> Elaine Abelson (Barnard College)
> March 10:"Patterns of Twentieth Century Feminism"
> Nancy Cott (Yale University)
> March 17: "Women and Science in the Cold War Era"
> Margaret Rossiter (Cornell University)
> March 19: Roundtable Discussion: faculty and graduate students on directions in Women's History
> *April 21: "Alice Hamilton: Founder of Industrial Toxicology"
> Barbara Sicherman (Trinity College)

Students are encouraged to attend this series . Reports on individual lectures will be accepted as extra credit to be considered at the final evaluation. These reports (not to exceed 2 pages) must be submitted within one week of the lecture.

Students who attend any four of the five events and submit a 1000 word paper (5 pages) describing what they have learned about (1) the specific subjects covered by the lectures and (2) general methodology in American women's history may drop their lowest grade.

EVALUATION:

Mid-term Examination = 30%
Paper Assignment   = 30%
Final   = 30%
Class Participation   = 10%

BRUMBERG:
Office hours: Monday, 12:30-2:30, MVR G95
　　　　　　　Tuesday,12:30- 2:30, Uris 332
For appointments on Monday, call Jolan Balog 255-2296
　　"　　　"　　" Tuesday, call Jan Wright 255-6480

CONGER:

University of Rochester

EDC 405/HIS 252/WST 284

WOMEN AND THE PROFESSIONS IN 19TH AND 20TH CENTURY AMERICA

Fall 1986

Professors Lynn Gordon and Ellen More

Office hours:

    Gordon: Lattimore 428, Thurs. 1:30-3:30 and by appt. (X7221)
    More: Rush Rhees 447, Tues. 10:30-21 and by appt. (X   or X2052)

In this course we will examine the historical significance of the rise of professions and the ideology of "professionalism" in the later nineteenth century. We will then consider the relationship of professionalism to American women. In particular we will discuss the following questions: What is a profession? What is "professionalism"? What (if anything) is a semi-profession? What have been the experiences of American women in the professions and how do they fit into more general history and theories about women's work? How have women balanced the claims of family and career? What does "feminization" mean and what does it imply for the professions in America?

Readings at Bookstore: (also available on reserve under EDC 405)

Addams, Jane, Twenty Years at Hull House
Curley, Jayme, et al., The Balancing Act II
Gold, Michael, A Dialogue on Comparable Worth
Hoffman, Nancy, ed., Woman's 'True' Profession: Voices from the History of Teaching
Lewis, Sinclair, Arrowsmith (required for undergraduates)
Lorber, Judith, Women Physicians
Melosh, Barbara, The Physician's Hand
Rossiter, Margaret, Struggles and Strategies: Women Scientists in America to 1940
Woloch, Nancy, Women and the American Experience

Readings on Reserve Only:

Antler, Joyce, "After College, What? ...New Graduates and the Family Claim"
Bledstein, Burton, The Culture of Professionalism
Clarke, Dr. Edward, Sex in Education or A Fair Chance for the Girls
Cook, Blanche Wiesen, "Female Support Networks and Political Activism" in Nancy
    Cott and Elizabeth Pleck, eds., A Heritage of Her Own
Davis, Katharine Bement, "Why They Failed to Marry"
Derber, Charles, "Managing Professionals"
Etzioni, Amitai, The Semi-Professions and their Organization
Freidson, Elliott, Profession of Medicine
Hummer, Patricia, Decade of Elusive Promise
James, Janet, "Isabel Hampton Robb" in Morris Vogel and Charles Rosenberg, eds.,
    The Therapeutic Revolution
Komarovsky, Mirra, Dilemmas of Masculinity

EDC 405/HIS 252/WST 248 (Cont.)

Komarovsky, Mirra, Women in College
Lasch, Christopher, Haven in a Heartless World
Lewis, Sinclair, Ann Vickers
May, William, "Code or Covenant"
Morantz, Regina, et al., eds. In Her Own Words
Morantz-Sanchez, Regina, Sympathy and Science
Ruddick, Sara and Pamela Daniels, eds., Working It Out
Stricker, Frank, "Cookbooks and Lawbooks" in A Heritage of Her Own

Class Handouts:

Joan Brumberg and Nancy Tomes, "Women in the Professions: A Research Agenda"
Laura Consiglio Fantarella, "Faculty: Two Career Families"
Lynn D. Gordon, "Katharine Bement Davis"
Darlene Clark Hine, "Mabel K. Staupers and The Integration of Black Nurses Into the
    Armed Forces"
Gerda Lerner, ed., Black Women in White America, pp. 75-146
Maude Radford, "When Men Come In"

Course Requirements

All students will be required to complete a final examination. Undergraduates
will also have a take-home midterm and write a short critique (5 pages) of gender and
professionalism in the Sinclair Lewis novels listed above. Graduate students will write
a historical paper on a topic of their choice after consultation with one of the
instructors. All students will be required to submit a rough draft of their
paper/critique before the final paper can be accepted. **Exams and papers must be
completed on time. No exceptions will be made.**

Assignments and Class Schedule

Note: Where author's name appears, read entire selection unless specific pages or
articles are indicated.

Sept. 9   **Introduction: Women's Work: Victorian Ideals vs. Victorian Realities**
                Woloch, pp. 88-94, chapters 6, 8
                Brumberg and Tomes (undergrads, optional)

Sept. 16   **The Progressive Era and the "New Woman"**
                Antler
                Clarke, pp. 11-60, 118-161
                Woloch, chapters 10, 12

Sept. 23   **Women and Work in the 20th Century**
                Hummer, IV
                Stricker
                Woloch, chapters 18, 20
                Gold, 1-54

Sept. 30   **Professionalism: Theory and Practice**
                Freidson, 1-84
                Bledstein, pp. 80-92, 129-158
                Hummer II, III

EDC 405/HIS 252/WST 248 (Cont.)

Oct. 7   **Professionalization and Gender: Some Critiques**
        Lasch, pp. 8-21
        Etzioni, Introduction
        Derber
        May
        Rossiter, chapters 4, 10, (11, optional)

    Sinclair Lewis critique assigned for undergraduates
    Rough drafts due November 11th; final copy due December 9th

Oct. 14   NO CLASS—FALL BREAK

Oct. 21   **Social Work**
        Addams, chapters 1-11, 13, 14
        Gordon, "Katherine Bement Davis"

TAKE-HOME MIDTERM ASSIGNED TO UNDERGRADUATES: Due Oct. 28

Oct. 28   **Teaching**
        Hoffman, Introduction, Parts I and III
        Lerner

MIDTERM DUE (undergraduates)

Nov. 4   **Medicine**
        Morantz-Sanchez, chapters VII, IX-XI
        Lorber, chapters I, III, VI, VIII, and Coda

Nov. 11   **Nursing**
        Hine
        James
        Melosh, chapters I, II, IV, V and Concl.

ROUGH DRAFTS OF PAPERS AND CRITIQUES DUE

Nov. 18   Instructor/student conferences on papers

Nov. 25   **Academia**
        Rossiter, chapters 1-3, 5, 7
        Keller, in Working It Out

Dec. 2   **Feminism and Professionalism**
        Hummer, V
        "Katherine Sturgis" in Morantz, In Her Own Words

Dec. 9   **A Delicate Balance: The Personal and the Professional**
        Cook
        Curley, read two case studies and conclusion
        Davis
        Fantarella
        Komarovsky, Dilemmas, chapters 1 and 2
        Komarovsky, Women in College, chapter 8, pp. 313-319

FINAL VERSIONS OF CRITIQUES AND PAPERS DUE

Hofstra University

History 394
Spring, 1985
Alice Kessler-Harris

Women's Work Culture in the U.S.

A major dispute in feminist theory surrounds the issue of
whether there exists a women's "culture," and if so, how it is
defined and identified. In contrast, U.S. labor historians (those
who study women as well as those who study men) have
traditionally assumed that such notions as ethnicity, race, and
class provide the parameters within which we can interpret the
work lives and choices of various groups. This course is designed
to explore, in tandem, the historical and theoretical literature
of women's work with an eye to exploring the notion of women's
culture, as well as to evaluating the the literature as a whole.

You will be asked to read widely, skimming, where necessary, over
a range of literature. I expect you to come to class prepared to
take an active role in the discussion of the day. Each student
will be responsible for focusing the discussion in one class. In
the readings suggested below, all students should read the
required materials. The student who is "on" that day should also
familiarize herself with the supplementary literature. These
supplementary suggestions are by no means comprehensive. You are
encouraged, indeed urged, to investigate the literature as widely as
possible. As you begin to choose paper topics, you will find these
supplementary materials increasingly useful.

You will be asked to write a 10-15 page historiographical paper
on a topic of your choosing, and which may be related to your
presentation.

The following books are available for purchase in the University
bookstore:

    Sarah Eisenstein, Give Us Bread, But Give us Roses
    (Routledge and Kegan Paul)
    Leslie Woodcock Tentler, Wage-Earning Women (Oxford)
    Hasia Diner, Erin's Daughter's in America (Hopkins)
    Carol Gilligan, In a Different Voice (Harvard)
    Louise Kapp Howe, Pink Collar Workers (Avon)
    Alice Amsden, The Economics of Women and Work (Penguin)
    Alice Kessler-Harris, Out to Work (Oxford)
    Harry Braverman, Labor and Monopoly Capital (Monthly Review)

Items starred below are available for borrowing in the History
Department office.

The class schedule and readings outlined below are tentative and subject
to modification at the request of the class as the course proceeds.

190

Course outline

January 16 INTRODUCTORY

You might want to begin reading Out to Work
so that you can ask questions about my
perspectiva and approach

January 23 POSING THE HISTORICAL QUESTIONS

Required: Joan Scott, "Women in History: The
Modern Period," Past and Present
101(November, 1983), 141-157

Joan Kelly,"The Socal Relations of the Sexes"
Signs 1(1976) 809-22

Mari Jo Buhle,"Integrating Themes in Labor
History: Gender and Labor History" *

Kessler-Harris, Out to Work

Supplementary: David Brody, "The Old Labor History and
the New," Labor History 20(1979) 111-126

Julie Matthaei, An Economic History of Women in
the U.S. (1982)

Susan Kennedy, If All We Did Was Sit and Weep
(1980)

January 30 THE SEX-GENDER SYSTEM

Required: Gilligan, In a Different Voice

Iris Young, "Feminism, Gynocentrism and
Feminist Politics," *

Supplementary: Gayle Rubin, "The Traffic in Women: Notes
on the Political Economy of Sex," in Rayna
Reiter ed., Toward an Anthropology of Women

Mackinnon, sexual harrassment

Hartsock

February 6 CLASS, IDEOLOGY AND CONSCIOUSNESS

Required: Eisenstein, Bread and Roses,

Catharine A. MacKinnon, "Feminism, Marxism,
Method and the State: An Agenda for Theory".
Signs, 7 (Spring, 1982), 515-544

Jane Humprhies, " Class Struggle and the
Persistence of the Working-Class Family "
in Amsden

Suplementary: Natalie Sokoloff, The Dialectics of Women's
Work

Nancy Schrom Dye, As Equals and as Sisters

Lillian Rubin, Worlds of Pain

Nancy Seifer,Nobody Speaks for Me

Meredith Tax The Rising of the Women

Charles Sabel, Work and Politics

February 13 LABOR MARKET STRUCTURE AND THE ISSUE OF PROTECTIVE LABOR
LEGISLATION

Required: From Amsden, the articles by
Doeringer; Reich, Gordon and Edwards,
and Ruberry

Veronica Beechey, "Women and Production:
A Critical Analysis of Some Sociological
Theories of Women's Work," in Annette Kuhn and
AnnMarie Wolpe Feminism and Materialism R

Heidi Hartmann, "Capitalism, Patriarchy and
Occupational Segregation" Signs I(1977),
137-169

Clyde and Sally Griffen, "The Employment of
Women," Natives and Newcomers, 1978 ch. 11 R

Protective leg. article in FS

Supplementary: Judith Baer, The Chains of Protection
(1978)

Susan Becker, The Origins of the Equal Rights
Amendment (1981)

Elizabeth Faulkner Baker, Technology and
Women's Work (1964) ch. 21

Elizabeth Faulkner Baker, Protective Labor
Legislation (1925)

192

February 20 THE INDUSTRIAL EXPERIENCE

>Required: Thomas Dublin, _Women_ _at_ _Work_ R (1979)

>>Mary Blewett, "Work, Gender and the Artisan Tradition in New England Shoemaking, 1780-1860" Journal of Social History

>Supplementary: Thomas Dublin, _Farm_ _to_ _Factory_

>>Lise Vogel,

>>Joan Jensen and Sue Davidson, eds., _A_ _Needle_ _A_ _Bobbin,_ _a_ _Strike_ (1984)

>>Christine Stansell, " The Origins of the Sweatshop: Women and Early Industrialization in New York City," in Frisch and Walkowitz, _Working-Class_ _America_ (1983) R

February 27 IS IT THE STRUCTURE OF FAMILY AND THE ROLE OF WOMEN WITHIN IT THAT INFLUENCES HOW WOMEN WORK?

>Required: Tentler,_Wage-Earning_ _Women_

>>From Amsden, articles by Scott and Tilly and Mincer.

>Supplementary: Elizabeth Pleck, "A Mother's Wages: Income Earning among Married Italian and Black Women, 1896-1911," in Cott and Pleck, _A_ _Heritage_ _of_ _Her_ _Own_

>>Tamara Hareven, "Family Time and Industrial Time" _Journal_ _of_ _Urban_ _History,_ I(May, 1975) 365-389

>>Carl Degler, _At_ _Odds_ (1980)

>>Lee Chambers-Schiller, _Liberty's_ _Daughters_ (1984)

>>Judith Smith, "Our Own Kind:Family and Community Networks in Providence," _Radical_ _History_ _Review_ #17 (1978), 99-120

March 13 OR, DOES THE MORE SPECIFIC CULTURE OF ETHNICITY AND RACE PROVIDE A MORE SATISFACTORY EXPLANATION?

>Required: Diner, _Erin's_ _Daughters_ _in_ _America_

>>From Amsden, two articles by B. Bergmann

Elizabeth Pleck, " The Two-Parent Household:
Black Family Structure in late nineteenth
Century Boston, " in Gordon, ed., The American
Family in Social Historical Perspective 152-177
R

Supplementary: Virgina Yans-McLaughlin, Family and
Community

Barbara Klaczynska, "Why Women Work: A
Comparison of various groups,"Labor History
17 (1976) 73-87

M. Cohen, "Italian-American Women in New
York City," in Cantor and Laurie

A. Kessler-Harris, "Organizing the
Unorganizable" Labor History (Winter, 1976)
5-23.

Gerda Lerner, Black Women in White America

March 20 THE NATURE OF CHOICE: DOMESTIC SERVICE AS A FEMALE OCCUPATION

Required: Faye Dudden, Serving Women (1982) R

Evelyn Nakano Glenn, "Dialectics of Wage Work:
Japanese American Women in Domestic Service,
1905-1940" Feminist Studies 6(Fall, 1980)
432-471

Supplementary: David Katzman, Seven Days a Week (1978)

Lucy Salmon, Domestic Service

March 27LIMITS ON CHOICE: THE HOME, THE HOUSEWIFE AND THE HOUSEHOLD

Required: Susan Strasser, Never Done: A History of
American Housework (1982) R

Margaret Benston, " The Political
Economy of Women's Liberation," Monthly Review
21 (1969) 13-27

Heidi Hartmann,"The Family as the locus of
Gender, Class and Political Struggle: The
Example of Housework" Signs 6(Spring, 1981)
366-394

Supplementary: Ruth Cowan, More Work for Mother (1982)

Nona Glazer, "Housework: Review Essay," Signs
1 (1976), 905-922

Nancy Cott, The Bonds of Womanhood, ch1 and 2

Ann Oakley, *Woman's Work: The Housewife Past and Present*

April 3 OUT OF THE FACTORY AND INTO THE OFFICE: THE IMPACT OF CHANGES IN OCCUPATIONAL STRUCTURE ON WOMEN'S PERCEPTIONS

> Required: Howe, *Pink Collar Workers*
>
> > Cynthia Aaron, "To Barter their Souls for Gold: Female Clerks in Federal Government Offices, 1862-1890," *Journal of American History* 67 (March, 1981) 835-853
>
> > Supplementary: Margery Davies, *A Woman's Place is at the Typewriter* (1982)
>
> > Elyse Rotella, *From Home to Office: U.S. Women at Work, 1870-1930* (1981)
>
> > something on management

April 10 THE SELF-MADE WOMAN: EDUCATION AND PROFESSIONALISM

> Required: Mary Roth Walsh, *Doctors Wanted: No Women Need Apply* R
>
> Roberta Weiner article
>
> Supplementary: Rosalind Rosenberg, *Beyond Separate Spheres* esp. ch 2
>
> > Dee Garrison, *Apostles of Culture: The Public Librarian and American Society* (1979)
>
> > Patricia Hammer, *Decade of Elusive Promise: Professional Women in the U.S., 1920-1930* (1978)
>
> > Barbara Brenzel, *Daughters of the State* (1983)

April 17 MOLDING THE JOB MARKET: TRADITIONS OF RESISTANCE AND MILITANCE AMONG WOMEN IN TRADE UNIONS

> Required: Kessler-Harris, "Where are the Organized Women Workers?" *Feminist Studies* 3 (1975) 92-111
>
> Sharon H. Strom, "Challenging 'Woman's Place': Feminism, the left, and Industrial Unionism in the 1930s," *Feminist Studies* 9 (1983) 359-86

195

Ruth Milkman, "Organizing the Sexual Division
of Labor: Historical Perspectives on Women's
work and the American Labor Movement,"
Socialist Review 10(1980) 95-150

Carole Turbin, " Daughters, Wives, Widows:
Family Relations and Women's Labor Organizing in
a Mid-19th Century Working Class Community," *

Supplementary: Susan Levine, Labor's True Woman, (1984)

Meredith Tax, The Rising of the Women (1980)

Ann Schofield article in FS

April 24   THE IMPACT OF ECONOMIC AND SOCIAL CRISES ON OPPORTUNITY AND
PERCEPTION

Required: Ruth Milkman, "Women's Work and the Economic
Crisis:Some Lessons from the Great Depression,"
Review of Radical Political Economics
8 (Spring, 1976) 73-97

Winifred Bolin, Women's Work and Family Values:
1920-1940 (1981) R

In Amsden, OECD, "The 1974-75 recession and the
Employment of Women,"

Supplementary: Lois Scharf, To Work and to Wed: Female
Employment, Feminism and the Great
Depression (1980)

Julia Kirk Blackwelder, Women of the
Depression (1983)

Karen Anderson, Wartime Women (1981)

Maureen Greenwald, Women, War and Work
(1980)

May 1   ON THE SHOP FLOOR: DO WOMEN HAVE DIFFERENT VALUES?

Required: Barbara Melosh, The Physician's Hand: Work
Culture and Conflict in American Nursing (1982)
R

Susan Benson, "'The Customers ain't God': The
Work Culture of Department Store Saleswomen,
1890-1940" in Frisch and Walkowitz, Working
Class America R

Supplementary: David Montgomery, Worker's Control in
America (1980)

196

Syracuse University

HISTORY 401: Gender and the Professions

Sally Gregory Kohlstedt   Spring, 1986

This course is designed to investigate the participation of women in professional careers, with special attention to the historical development of the professions and their patterns of recruitment and opportunities. The course material will depend on new research and rapidly changing theories. Its purpose is to help students identify issues and analyze answers which they derive from their own experience and from texts and experts. In order to do this, our course will involve lectures, class discussion, reading assignments in a range of journals and textbooks, guest lectures and student presentations. More intensive reading occurs at the beginning of the course and more reliance will be placed on oral presentations and discussion as the course proceeds.

Readings

Three texts are on reserve in Bird Library and available in the Orange Bookstore. Other recommended readings will be available on reserve and some material will be distributed in class.

Sharon Lee Rich and Ariel Phillips, eds. Women's Experience and Education (Harvard, 1985)

Barbara Harris, Beyond Her Sphere: Women and the Professions in American History (Greenwood, 1978)

Carol Gilligan, In a Different Voice (Harvard, 1982)

Assignments

There will be a number of writing assignments, designed both to enhance your learning in this course and to increase your ability to communicate; thinking and writing are intimately connected. Thanks to support from the Mellon Foundation, Delia Temes, a writing specialist, will participate in our writing activities. All students will need an inexpensive plastic three ring binder with looseleaf paper for a reading log and journal. In this you will summarize and also respond to the readings, and these will be shared with the class on occasion. Your journal may also be used for lecture notes and responses. Students will be asked occasionally to write in class in response to questions (microthemes). There will be mid-term and final examinations, both essay format. As a culminating experience to draw our reading and discussion into focus, each student will conduct a research project and prepare it for presentation to the rest of the class.

HISTORY 401:   GENDER AND THE PROFESSIONS

Spring, 1986

Conference Room, Maxwell Hall, T-TH 10:05-11:30

January 14:   Introduction

January 16-23:   The Debate on Education

Who should be educated and how has been a fundamental topic in American cultural life over the past two centuries. In your reading watch to see how gender was part of this discussion as women sought opportunities for education and were recruited for teaching.

Henry Maudsley, "Sex and Mind in Education" (1874)

David Starr Jordan, "The Higher Education of Women" (1902)

Esther Manning Westervelt, "The Higher Education of Women: A Carnegie Study," (1973) and Ordway Tead, "Women's Higher Education" in Women's Education and Experience (hereafter WE&E)

The Educated Woman: Problems and Prospects, pp. 35-51

Reports:

Charlotte Conable, Women at Cornell: The Myth of Equal Education

Barbara Miller Solomon, In the Company of Educated Women

Helen Lefkowitz Horowitz, Alma Mater: Design and Experience in Women's Colleges from the Nineteenth Century to the 1930s

January 26-30:   Social Roles and Gender

Sociologists and anthropologists, especially, have been quite involved in investigating the patterns of gender in culture and the choices available, realistically, to women at different times and places.

Margaret Mead, Sex and Temperament in Three Societies (selected, .)

Terri Sarrio, et. al, "Sex Role Stereotyping in the Public Schools," WE&E

Georgia Sassen, "Success Anxiety in Women..." WE&E

February 4-6: Origins of Modern Professions: Myths and Realities

Burton Bledstein, <u>The Culture of Professionalism</u>, chapts 3, 4, 5

February 11-13: Male-Identified Professions

In this section we will deal primarily with medicine, law, and science, noting the emergence of professional aspirations and structures and the ways in which women were involved.

Barbara Harris, <u>Beyond Her Sphere: Women and the Professions in America</u>

Reports:

Virginia Drachman, <u>Hospital with a Heart</u>

Barbara Sicherman, <u>Alice Hamilton, A Life in Letters</u>

Mary Roth Walsh, <u>Doctors Wanted, No Women Need Apply: Sexual Barriers in the Medical Profession, 1837-1975</u>

Cynthia Fuchs Epstein, <u>Women and the Law</u>

Margaret Rossiter, <u>Women Scientists in America: Struggles and Strategies to 1940</u>

Rosabeth Moss Kanter, <u>Men and Women of the Corporation</u>

February 18-25: "Women's Professions"

Barbara Harris, <u>Beyond Her Sphere: Women and the Professions in America</u>

Reports:

Polly Kaufman, <u>Women and Teaching on the Frontier</u>

Nancy Hoffman, <u>"Women's True Profession"</u> (teaching)

Barbara Meloch, <u>The Physician's Hand: Work Culture and Conflict in American Nursing</u>

Cindy Aron, "To Barter Their Souls for Gold," <u>Journal of American History</u> (March, 1981) (clerical workers and office managers)

Florence Kapp Howe, <u>Pink Collar Workers</u>

Faye Dudden, <u>Serving Women: Household Service in Nineteenth Century America</u>

February 27-March 4: Independent Lives

Women have pursued the education and used the skills found in the professions in sometimes independent ways, not the least of which has been by writing.

Tillie Olsen, "Silences in Liberature"

Alex Kate Schulman's review of Olsen in WE&E

Virginia Woolf, <u>A Room of Ones Own</u>

March 18-April 8: Gender and the Workplace

In this section we will have visitors from a number of social science and professional schools. There will be some analysis of data on employment and opportunity patterns as well as attention to the somewhat more subtle effects of language and style. We will begin with attention to language, consider some work situations, and then deal with some propositions for change.

Section 1: March 18-20, 25

Self-expression and telling women's lives has been important for women in many ways, both reflecting and shaping their private and their public experiences. Moreover women have written for many reasons and using many forms, thus making writing one of women's professions. Their efforts have faced various obstacles and is, in turn shaped by these experiences. Consider some of these influences by reading the following essays and reflecting on the ways in which the issues might apply to other kinds of creative work experience.

Virginia Woolf, <u>A Room of One's Own</u>

Tillie Oleson, "Silences in Literature"

Alex Kate Schulman's review of Oleson in WE&E

Section 2: Life and Work Experience

This section will consider some experiences of women, based on research (on women in communication) and experience (field work on anthropology) where both the subject matter and personal experience inform the guest speakers' professional overview. Working relationships, whether the profession is male or female oriented, are affected by gender and there are a number of specific circumstances that are now being addessed.

March 27: Nancy Weatherby Sharp, Newhouse School of Communication

April 1: Susan Wadley, Department of Anthropology

April 3: Readings and Discussion:

Ann Withorn, "Three Views of Liberation, " WE&E

Catharine MacKinnon, Sexual Harassment of Working Women, chapters 2 and 3

Patricia Meyer Spacks, "A Most Arduous Profession," WE&E

Section 3: Some Fundamentals

April 8:   There are many subtle ways in which gender affects women's work lives. Recent research in the humanities, with regard to language theory and language usage, for example, points out how our language is at its root affected by gender issues.

Julia P. Stanley, "Gender-Marking in American English: Usage and Reference, "

Elinor Lenz and Barbara Meyerhoff, "Feminine as a Second Language," from The Feminization of America

April 10: Individual meetings with Delia Temes

April 15: Discussion

Evelyn Fox Keller, "Gender and Science" and "A World of Difference"

Carol Gilligan, In a Different Voice, along with review by Squier and Ruddick in WE&E

April 17-29: Some Conclusions and New Beginnings

April 17 and 22: Student presentations based on research projects

April 24: Issues for the 1980s: comparable worth; marriage, affirmative action, family and child care

April 29: Careers for the 1990s and beyond

Evaluation

1. The mid-term exam with essay and short answer questions on

March 6 will count for 25% of your grade in the class.

2. There will be a required project (30% of your grade), which will be developed in some area of professional interest to you. A preliminary statement and bibliography are due February 4, a revised proposal is due March 18. Professors Temes and Kohlstedt will be available to assist you while you draft your project, with the first draft due on April 8 and a second on April 17; the oral presentation will be given during the last two weeks of class. The written version is due no later than April 29.

3. There will be a final (possibly take-home) examination (25% of your grade).

4. Class discussion and your other written work will be worth 20% of your grade. There will be, for example, 250 word microthemes at the end of each unit. You will also report on at least one additional book in class (see report sections above).

Sally Gregory Kohlstedt
201 Maxwell   x2349/2210
TTh 11:30-12:15

Delia Temes
113 Euclid, Room 305   x2109

Harvard University

HAMC E-175   (History of American Civilization)

American Women and Professional Identity, from 1790 to the Present

Dr. Barbara Miller Solomon , University Extension Course,

The burgeoning scholarship in the history of women has largely focused on the anonymous workers in industry and in households. Historians are just beginning to address the equally important subject of women's development as professionals. The entrance of middle-class women into the professions is a striking phenomenon of modern society. This course examines the processes by which women gained access to different professions at different times. The divergence in the professional patterns for men and women will be emphasized, as well as the effects of professional careers on women's lives.

Reading will include appropriate scholarly studies, and biographies, and autobiographies of career women. This is a discussion course. Requirements include oral presentations in class and choice of an interpretative essay or research paper of moderate size (15-20 pages).

For undergraduate credit students must meet the requirements described in the syllabus. For graduate students some additional reading will be expected along with a research paper approved by the instructor.

Some articles will be placed on reserve in the Extension library; others will be shared by the instructor.

Bibliography in Solomon, In the Company of Educated Women has most of the citations of books and articles used in this seminar.

Office hours by appointment.

Women and Professional Identity   Spring term 1986
Dr. Barbara Miller Solomon

January 29   Introduction

Defining professionalism, past and present
Nineteenth-century professions; male access;
"woman's sphere" in a changing society

Recent bibliographical essay: Joan Brumberg and Nancy Tomes, "Women in
the Professions: A Research Agenda for American Historians," Reviews
in American History 10,2 (June, 1982), pp. 275-296 (on reserve in
Extension library)

February 5   Women's Access to Formal Education and the Beginning of a Revolution in
Women's Lives

Barbara M. Solomon, In the Company of Educated Women, chapters 1, 2, 3

Reports:

Anne Firor Scott, "The Ever-Widening Circle: The Diffusion of Feminist
Values from the Troy Female Seminary, 1822-72," History of Education
Quarterly 19 (Spring 1979), pp. 3-25

Mary Kelly, Private Woman Public Stage: Literary Domesticity in
Nineteenth-Century America, chapters 5 and 6

February 12 Teaching: Vocation or Profession, Means and Ends

Solomon, In the Company of Educated Women, chapters 4 and 5

Reports:

Richard Bernard and Maris Vinovskis, "The Female Schoolteacher in
Antebellum Massachusetts," Journal of Social History 10 (1977), pp.
332-345

Either   Susan B. Carter, "Women's Educational History: A Labor Market
Perspective," Academy Notes 13, 2 (Winter 1983)
Or   Susan B. Carter and Mark Prus, "The Labor Market and the
American High School Girl, 1890-1928," Journal of Economic
History 42, 1 (March 1982)

February 19   Women in Medicine: Moralism versus Science
              Apprenticeships and Medical Schools

              Mary Roth Walsh, Doctors Wanted: No Women Need Apply (entire)

              Reports:

              Regina Morantz, "Feminism, Professionalism, and Germs: The Thought of
                 Mary Putman Jacobi and Elizabeth Blackwell," American Quarterly 34
                 (Winter 1983), pp. 459-478

              Charlotte Perkins Gilman, The Crux, in Ann Lane, ed., The Charlotte
                 Perkins Gilman Reader

              Virginia Drachman, "Female Solidarity and Professional Success: The
                 Dilemma of Women Doctors in Late 19th-Century America," Journal of
                 Social History 15 (Summer 1982) (handout)

February 26   Women in Higher Education and the Impact

              Solomon, In the Company of Educated Women, chapters 6 & 7

              Reports:

              Carol Lasser and Marlene Merrill, eds., Soulmates: The Oberlin
                 Correspondence of Lucy Stone and Antoinette Brown, 1846-1850

              M. Carey Thomas in Barbara Cross, ed., The Educated Woman in America

March 5   From Voluntarism to Professionalism

              Solomon, In the Company of Educated Women, chapter 8

              Jane Addams, Twenty Years of Hull House, especially chapters 4-10

              Joyce Antler, "After College, What?: New Graduates and the Family
                 Claim", American Quarterly 32 (Fall 1980)

              Reports:

              Paula Giddings, When and Where I Enter, chapter 6

              Gerda Lerner, ed., Black Women in White America, pp. 479-497

              Roy Lubove, The Professional Altruist, chapters 5-6

              Recommended: Mary Church Terrell, A Colored Woman in a White World (not
                 available for purchase)

March 12   Pioneering Women Academics

Rosalind Rosenberg, Beyond Separate Spheres, pp. 1-113

Margaret Rossiter, "'Woman's Work' in Science, 1880-1910," Isis 71 (1980), pp. 381-98

Reports:

Laurel Furumoto, "Mary Whiton Calkins (1863-1930)," Journal of the History of the Behavioral Sciences 15 (1979), pp. 346-356

Also recommended:
Article on Calkins in Notable American Women
Bruce Kuklick, The Rise of American Philosophy, Appendix 4, "Women Philosophers in America," pp. 590-594

March 19   The First Modern College Women and their Expectations in the 1920s and 1930s

Solomon, In the Company of Educated Women, chapters 9 and 10

Report:

Elaine Showalter, ed., These Modern Women: Autobiographical Essays

March 26   No class

Over Spring break, read one or more of the following handouts:

Cindy Aron, "To Barter Their Souls for Gold: Female Clerks in Federal Government Offices, 1862-1890," Journal of American History 67, 4 (March 1981), pp. 833-53

Dee Garrison, "The Tender Technicians: The Feminization of Public Librarianship, 1876-1905" in Clio's Consciousness Raised, Mary Hartman and Lois Banner, eds., pp. 158-178

Janet James, "Isabel Hampton and the Professionalization of Nursing in the 1890s," in The Therapeutic Revolution, Charles Rosenberg and Morris Vogel, eds., pp. 201-244

April 2   Alternatives in the Semi-Professions (discussion of above handouts)
Debate on Marriage and Career from the 1920s

Solomon, In the Company of Educated Women, chapter 11

Joyce Antler, "Feminism as Life Process: The Life and Career of Lucy Sprague Mitchell"

Recommended: Frank Stricker, "Cookbooks and Lawbooks"

April 9   Comparison of Emily Fogg Mead and her daughter Margaret Mead as examples
           combining marriage and career in two generations

           Finish Rosenberg, Beyond Separate Spheres

           Margaret Mead, Blackberry Winter

           Report:

           Susan Ware, Holding Their Own, chapter 6

April 16   Higher Education from World War II; Impact of the Women's Movement in
           1970s and 1980s

           Solomon, In the Company of Educated Women, chapter 12

           Reports:

           Alice Walker, In Search of Our Mothers' Gardens (selections)

           Gloria Steinem, Outrageous Acts and Everyday Rebellions (selections)

April 23   Options in Law and Business

           Rosabeth Kanter, Men and Women of the Corporation, chapters 1-4, 6-8
      or: Cynthia Fuchs Epstein, Women in Law, Introduction, chapters 1-3

           Reports:

           D. Kelly Weisberg, "Barred from the Bar: Women and Legal Education in
           the United States, 1870-1890," Journal of Legal Education 38 (1977),
           pp. 485-507

           Judge Florence Allen, To Do Justly

           Recommended:
           Selections on women in the law and business from Notable American
           Women
           Women Lawyers Perspectives on Success, Emily Couric, ed., 1985

           For other bibliography, see instructor

April 30   Dialogue on Women's Life Choices and Careers

           Reports on some papers in progress for this course

           Solomon, In the Company of Educated Women, "After Thoughts"

AMERICAN WOMEN AND PROFESSIONAL IDENTITY

Guide for Term Papers

1. Choosing a Topic and Developing a Bibliography

In general, papers should deal with women's professional development by looking at either one figure or a group of women, or a significant issue, in a particular historical period. Choose a field or profession of particular interest to you, and a specific topic for which materials are readily available. A substantial paper may be based on published sources such as biographies, memoirs and edited volumes of letters, or transcripts of oral histories, in conjunction with general secondary works on the field, many of which can be found on the course syllabus. Do not do original research unless it is manageable. For example, use materials in the Schlesinger archives only to explore <u>specific</u> questions relating to your topic.

2. Questions to Consider

For an individual woman or group of women, some or all of the following may be relevant:

--Place her in the context of her profession; compare her development to that of other women in her field during the same period, and to that of men.
--What contributed to her development as a professional?
--Did her family help or hinder her work? Did she collaborate with her husband or another family member?
--What was her view of her own achievement? Did she consider herself marginal or central in her field?
--Did she consider herself a feminist?
--What sort of obstacles did she face? Were they general, or specific to women? What strategies did she use to overcome them?
--At what level was her profession at the time she entered it (e.g. established, just beginning, etc.)? Did she pioneer by establishing the field itself or defining a new area in an old profession? Did it then become known as a "woman's profession"?

3. Suggested Topics

Ample secondary materials are available on the following women (but this is by no means an exhaustive list):

> Cecilia Payne Gaposchkin (astronomer)
> Dorothy Thompson (journalist)
> Margaret Mead, Ruth Benedict (anthropologists)
> Martha Eliot, M.D., Alice Hamilton (public health)
> Mary Calderone (sex education)
> Edith Wharton, Willa Cather (novelists)

Oral interviews with a professional woman as the focus for an essay on the factors the individual regarded as important in her "professional" development.

Images of professional women in fiction and/or film.

Write an essay for a foreigner to explain American women's diverse attitudes toward professional careers.

Voluntarism as a productive force in giving direction to a woman's life along with family.

Interviews with an individual who found unpaid work meaningful and productive.

Reading List: *Selected Bibliography on the History of Women and Work in the United States*

Note: This is a (very !) limited <u>selection</u> of the many new and old publications on this topic; I welcome your comments and suggestions for future revisions of the list. The listed books should lead you to primary sources and to more detailed secondary works.

General Overviews

Kessler-Harris, Alice. **Out to Work: A History of Wage-Earning Women in the United States** (Oxford, 1982)

Matthaei, Julie A. **An Economic History of Women in America: Women's Work, the Sexual Division of Labor, and the Development of Capitalism** (Schocken, 1982)

Weiner, Lynn Y. **From Working Girl to Working Mother: The Female Labor Force in the United States, 1820-1980** (North Carolina, 1985)

Theory & Methodology

Blaxall, Martha and Reagan, Barbara. **Women and the Workplace: The Implications of Occupational Segregation** (Chicago, 1976)

Conk, Margo A. "Accuracy, Efficiency, and Bias: The Interpretation of Women's Work in the U.S. Census of Occupations, 1890-1940," **Historical Methods** 14 (Spring 1981):65-72.

Hartmann, Heidi. "Capitalism, Patriarchy, and Job Segregation by Sex," in Elizabeth Abel and Abel, Emily, eds., **The Signs Reader: Women, Gender and Scholarship** (Chicago: 1983):193-226

Kessler-Harris, Alice. "Stratifying by Sex: Understanding the History of Working Women, " in **Labor Market Segmentation,** eds. Edwards et al, (1975), pp. 217-55.

_____, ""Women's Wage Work as Myth and History," **Labor History** (Spring 1978): 287-307.

Oppenheimer, Valerie Kincaid. **The Female Labor Force in the United States: Demographic and Economic Factors Governing its Growth and Changing Composition** (Berkeley, 1970)

Pleck, Elizabeth. "Two Worlds in One: Work and Family," **Journal of Social History** (Winter 1976), 178-95.

By Chronology

Colonial

Spruill, Julia C. **Women's Life and Work in the Southern Colonies** (North Carolina, 1938)

Nash, Gary B. "The Failure of Female Factory Labor in Colonial Boston," **Labor History** (Spring 1979): 165-88.

Antebellum

Cott, Nancy F. **The Bonds of Womanhood: 'Woman's Sphere' in New England, 1780-1835** (Yale, 1977)

Dublin,Thomas,ed. **Farm to Factory:Women's Letters,1830-1860** (Columbia 1981)

_____ . **Women at Work: The Transformation of Work and Community in Lowell, Massachusetts, 1826-1860** (Columbia 1979)

Lerner, Gerda. "The Lady and the Mill Girl: Changes in the Status of Women in the Age of Jackson," **Midcontinent American Studies** (Spring 1979): 5-14

Stansell, Christine. **City of Women: Sex and Class in New York, 1789-1860** (Knopf, 1986)

Later 19th/early 20th centuries
(also see general overviews, occupations, and other topics)

Cantor, Milton and Bruce Laurie, eds., **Class, Sex and the Woman Worker** (Greenwood, 1977)

World War I

Greenwald, Maureen Weiner. **Women, War and Work: The Impact of World War I on Women Workers in the U.S.** (Greenwood, 1980)

1920-1940

Scharf, Lois. **To Work and to Wed: Female Employment, Feminism, and the Great Depression** (Greenwood, 1980)

Wandersee, Winifred. **Women's Work and Family Values 1920-1940** (Harvard, 1981)

Ware, Susan. **Holding Their Own: American Women in the 1930s** (Twayne, 1982)

World War 11

Anderson, Karen Tucker. **Wartime Women: Sex Roles, Family Relations, and the Status of Women During World War II** (Greenwood, 1981).

Campbell, D'Ann. **Women at War with America: Private Lives in a Patriotic Era** (Harvard, 1984)

Hartmann, Susan M. **The Home Front and Beyond: American Women in the 1940s** (Twayne, 1982)

Rupp, Leila. **Mobilizing Women for War** (Princeton, 1978)

Recent America

Chafe, William. **The American Woman: Her Changing Social, Economic, and Political Role, 1920-1970** (Oxford, 1972)

Kaledin, Eugenia. **Mothers and More: American Women in the 1950s** (Twayne, 1984)

Remick, Helen, ed. **Comparable Worth and Wage Discrimination: Technical Possibilities and Political Realities** (Temple: 1984)

By Occupation

Agriculture

Jenson, Joan M. **Loosening the Bonds: Mid-Atlantic Farm Women, 1750-1850** (Yale, 1986)

Domestic Work

Dudden, Faye E. **Serving Women:Household Service in Nineteenth Century America** (Weslyan, 1983)

Katzman, David. **Seven Days A Week:Domestic Service in Industrializing America** (Oxford: 1978)

Education

Bernard, Richard and Maris Vinovskis, "The Female Teacher in Antebellum Massachusetts," **Journal of Social History** 10 (1977)

Hoffman, Nancy ed., **Woman's 'True" Profession: Voices from the History of Teaching** (Feminist Press, 1981)

Kaufman, Polly W. **Women Teachers on the Frontier** (Yale, 1984)

Sklar, Kathryn Kish. **Catharine Beecher: A Study in American Domesticity** (Yale, 1973)

Factory Work

Cooper, Particia. **Once a Cigar Maker: Men, Women and Work Culture in American Cigar Factories, 1900-1919** (Illinois, 1986)

Hirsch, Susan E. "Rethinking the Sexual Division of Labor: Pullman Repair Shops,1900-1969", **Radical History Review** 35 (1986): 26-48.

Health Care

Drachman, Virginia G. **Hospital with a Heart: Women Doctors and the Paradox of Separatism at the New England Hospital, 1862-1969** (Cornell, 1984)

Melosh, Barbara. **'The Physicians's Hand: Work Culture and Conflict in American Nursing** (Temple, 1982)

Morantz-Sanchez, Regina Markell. **Sympathy and Science: Women Physicians in American Medicine** (Oxford, 1985)

Walsh, Mary Roth. **Doctors Wanted: No Women Need Apply: Sexual Barriers in the Medical Profession,1835-1975** (Yale, 1977)

Housework

Boydston, Jeanne. "To Earn Her Daily Bread: Housework and Antebellum Working-Class Subsistence, **Radical History Review** 35, 1986:7-25.

Cowan, Ruth. **More Work for Mother: The Ironies of Household Technology from the Open Hearth to the Microwave** (Basic, 1983)

Ogden, Annegret. **The Great American Housewife: From Helpmate to Wage Earner, 1776-1986** (Greenwood, 1986)

Strasser, Susan. **Never Done: A History of American Housework** (Pantheon,1982)

Office Work

Davies, Margery. **Woman's Place is at the Typewriter: Office Work and Office Workers, 1870-1930** (Temple, 1982)

Rotella, Elyce J. **From Home to Office: U.S. Women at Work, 1870-1930** (UMI, 1981)

Prostitution

Rosen, Ruth. **Lost Sisterhood: Prostitution in America, 1900-1918,** (Pantheon, 1982)

Hobson. Barbara M. **Uneasy Virtue: The Politics of Prostitution and the American Reform Tradition** (Basic, forthcoming, 1987)

Sales Work

Benson, Susan Porter. **Counter Cultures: Saleswomen, Managers, and Customers in American Department Stores, 1890-1940** (Illinois, 1986)

Other Professions

Brumberg, Joan and Nancy Tomes, "Women in the Professions: A Research Agenda for American Historians," **Reviews in American History** (June 1982): 275-96.

Glazer, Penina Migdal, and Miriam Slater. **Unequal Colleagues: The Entrance of Women into the Professions, 1890-1940** (Rutgers, 1986)

Garrison, Dee. "The Tender Technicians: The Feminization of Public Librarianship, 1876-1905", **Journal of Social History**, 10 (March 1977):132-59.

Harris, Barbara. **Beyond Her Sphere: Women and the Professions in American History** (Greenwood, 1978)

Rossiter, Margaret W. **Women Scientists in America: Struggles and Strategies to 1940** (Hopkins, 1982)

Labor Movement

Dye, Nancy Schrom. **As Equals and As Sisters: Feminism, the Labor Movement, and the Women's Trade Union League of New York** (Missouri, 1980)

Foner, Philip. **Women and the American Labor Movement** (Free Press, 1979)

Hall, Jacquelyn Dowd. "Disorderly Women: Labor Militancy in the Appalachian South," **Journal of American History** (Sept. 1986): 354-382.

Jenson, Joan M. & Sue Davidson, eds. **A Needle, A Bobbin, A Strike: Women Needleworkers in America** (Temple, 1984)

Kessler-Harris, "Where Are the Organized Women Workers?" in Kerber and Mathews, eds., **Women's America: Refocusing the Past** (Oxford, 1982)

Levine, Susan. **Labor's True Woman: Carpet Weavers, Industrialization, and Labor Reform in the Gilded Age** (Temple, 1984)

Milkman, Ruth, ed. **Women, Work and Protest: A Century of U.S. Women's Labor History** (Routledge & Kegan Paul, 1985)

Legislation & Reform
Baer, Judith A. **The Chains of Protection: The Judicial Response to Women's Labor Legislation** (Greenwood, 1978)

Boris, Eileen," Regulating Industrial Homework: The Triumph of 'Sacred Motherhood', **Journal of American History** (March 1985):745-63.

Sealander, Judith. **As Minority Becomes Majority: Federal Reaction to the Phenomenon of Women in the Work Force, 1920-1983** (Greenwood, 1983)

Sklar, Kathryn Kish, "Hull House in the 1890s: A Community of Women Reformers," **Signs** 4 (1985):658-77.

Married Women/Mothers
Fraundorf, Martha Norby. The Labor Force Participation of Turn-of-the-Century Married Women," **Journal of Economic History** 34 (June 1979):401-18.

Goldin, Claudia. **Life-Cycle Labor Force Participation of Married Women: Historical Evidence and Implications** (National Bureau of Economic Research, 1983)

Margolis, Maxine. **Mothers and Such: Views of American Women and Why They Changed** (California: 1984)

Single Women
Chambers-Schiller, Lee. **Liberty A Better Husband; Single Women in America: the Generations of 1780-1840** (Yale, 1984)

Goldin, Claudia. "The Work and Wages of Single Women, 1870 to1920," **Journal of Economic History** XL (March 1980): 81-88.

Black Women
Hine, Darlene Clark. **Black Women in the Nursing Profession: A Documentary History** (Garland, 1985)

Jones, Jacqueline. **Labor of Love, Labor of Sorrow: Black Women, Work, and the Family from Slavery to the Present** (Basic, 1985)

Lerner, Gerda, ed. **Black Women in White America: A Documentary History** (Vintage, 1973)

Sterling, Dorothy, ed. **We Are Your Sisters: Black Women in the Nineteenth Century** (Norton, 1984)

White Working Class Women

Kennedy, Susan E. **If All We Did Was To Weep At Home: A History of White Working Class Women in America** (Indiana, 1979)

Tentler, Leslie Woodcock. **Wage-Earning Women: Industrial Work and Family Life in the United States, 1900-1930** (Oxford, 1979)

Culture

Peiss, Kathy. **Cheap Amusements: Working Women and Leisure in Turn-of-the-Century New York** (Temple, 1986)

Reitano, Joanne. "Working Girls Unite," **American Quarterly** 36 (Spring 1984): 112-134.

Document Collections

Baxendall, Gordon & Reverby, eds., **America's Working Women: A Documentary History 1600 to the Present** (Vintage, 1976)

Brownlee & Brownlee, eds., **Women in the American Economy: A Documentary History 1675 to 1929** (Yale, 1976)

Stanford University

HISTORY 265/365

THE HISTORY OF SEXUALITY IN AMERICA

Instructor: Prof. Estelle Freedman   Autumn, 1986
Office: Bldg. 200, room 7   5 units
Phone: 723-4951 or 723-2651 (messages)

CLASS STRUCTURE AND REQUIREMENTS

In this upper level undergraduate/graduate colloquium, we will explore recent historical literature on the social history of sexuality in America. The class will meet once a week for two and a half to three hours. During that time I will usually provide introductory comments on the historical period we are discussing and raise questions about the subject under consideration. Members of the class will be expected to have read all of the required readings thoroughly and to come prepared to raise their own questions about them. We will leave time at the end of each session to discuss the oral and written reports in progress. It is critical to the success of the course that students schedule sufficient time to complete and contemplate the readings each week and to plan the final research project during the quarter.

During two class sessions, students will report on additional readings on selected topics. (Approximately half the class at the first such session and the other half at the second.) I will provide an extensive bibliography to help you select these readings. The oral reports should be from five to ten minutes long, to be followed by questions from the class. A written report on the reading, no longer than five pages, is due the day after the oral presentation, in order to allow you to incorporate issues raised in class.

For undergraduates, the final project for the class is a paper of 10 to 12 pages that draws on original research on a single, clearly defined primary source. The purpose of the project is to integrate your own research findings with the themes raised by the secondary readings you have done for the class. We will discuss topics and sources in class, and I would like to meet individually with students about their proposed topics. (Some examples and guidelines are listed at the end of this syllabus.) A statement of topic and sources must be handed in during the seventh class session; students will discuss their projects at the last class and hand in papers during finals week. Graduate students will write more extensive, historiographical papers, providing a critical review of secondary literature. Written statements of their topics are also due at the seventh class session.

Although I do not require that class members hand in a formal journal, I would like to urge you to keep a written account of your thoughts about the readings and the class discussions every week. Doing so will help you incorporate the themes of the class into your oral report and final project. It will also contribute to the class discussions by identifying problematic themes and providing continuity between class sessions. The work load for this course is heavy, but keeping up with it each week should make the written assignments much easier.

BOOKS

The following books contain required readings. All but the last two have been ordered at the Stanford University Bookstore and through the reserve desks at both Meyer and Green libraries.

Carroll Smith-Rosenberg, Disorderly Conduct: Visions of Gender in Victorian America
Thomas Altherr, ed., Procreation or Pleasure: Sexual Attitudes in American History (the original essays reprinted in this book can also be found in journals in the library stacks if you do not wish to purchase this book)
James Mohr, Abortion in America: The Origins and Evolution of National Policy, 1800-1900
Ruth Rosen, The Lost Sisterhood: Prostitution in America, 1900-1918
Charlotte Perkins Gilman, Herland
John D'Emilio, Sexual Politics, Sexual Communities: The Making of A Homosexual Minority in America, 1940-1970
Ann Snitow, et. al., eds., Powers of Desire: The Politics of Sexuality
Linda Gordon, Woman's Body, Woman's Right: A Social History of Birth Control in America (unfortunately out of print, but on reserve; there might be used copies at local bookstores)
The History 265/365 Course Reader (contains all required readings not listed above), available at Copy Mat, on the corner of University and High Sts.

CLASS TOPICS AND REQUIRED READING

1. INTRODUCTION: SEXUALITY, HISTORY AND THEORY

What do we mean by the history of sexuality? What is sexuality, and how do social scientists and historians approach its study? What questions do you bring to this course? What do you want to learn from it?

John Gagnon and William Simon, Sexual Conduct, chapter 1, "The Social Origins of Sexual Development," pp. 1-26 (Course Reader)
Ellen Ross and Rayna Rapp, "Sex and Society: A Research Note from Social History and Anthropology," in Snitow, Powers of Desire, pp. 51-73
Michel Foucault, The History of Sexuality, Volume 1, An Introduction, Part One, "We 'Other Victorians'," pp. 3-13 (Course Reader)
Robert A. Padgug, "Sexual Matters: On Conceptualizing Sexuality in History," introduction to Radical History Review issue on Sexuality in History, (Course Reader)

2. COLONIAL AMERICA: DEMOGRAPHY, GENDER AND RACE

Social historical research has put to rest the myth of the puritanical Puritans. What new themes emerge from studies of the family, women and slavery? How did demographic factors (especially race and gender) influence sexual life in New England and the Chesapeake, and how did sexual regulation change from the seventeenth to the eighteenth centuries?

Edmund S. Morgan, "The Puritans and Sex," in Altherr, Procreation or Pleasure," pp. 5-16 (originally New England Quarterly, December, 1942)
Robert Oaks, "'Things Fearful to Name': Sodomy and Buggery in Seventeenth-Century New England" (Course Reader)
Robert V. Wells, "Illegitimacy and bridal pregnancy in colonial America,"

(Course reader)

Barbara S. Lindemann, "'To Ravish and Carnally Know': Rape in Eighteenth-Century Massachusetts" (Course Reader)

Winthrop D. Jordan, "Fruits of Passion: The Dynamics of Interracial Sex," (Course Reader)

3. SEXUAL IDEOLOGY AND SEXUAL REFORM: THE "VICTORIANS"

Historians have debated the relationship between ideas about sexuality and actual sexual behavior. To these categories I have added that of sexual politics, particularly the emergence of competing interest groups seeking to regulate sexuality. The literature on Victorianism concentrates on the white, middle classes. For this group, how and why did sexuality change during the nineteenth century? How do historians' interpretations of the Victorians differ?

Estelle B. Freedman, "Sexuality in Nineteenth-Century America: Behavior, Ideology and Politics," (Course Reader)

Nancy Cott, "Passionlessness: An Interpretation of Victorian Sexual Ideology, 1790-1850" in Altherr, Procreaction or Pleasure, pp. 17-29 (originally in Signs Winter, 1978)

Carl Degler, "What Ought to Be and What Was: Women's Sexuality in the Nineteenth Century," (Course Reader)

Peter Gay, The Bourgeois Experience, Victoria to Freud: Education of the Senses, pp 71-108 (Course Reader)

G.J. Barker-Benfield, "The Spermatic Economy: A Nineteenth-Century View of Sexuality" in Altherr, Procreation or Pleasure (originally in Feminist Studies, Summer 1972)

Carroll Smith-Rosenberg, "The Female World of Love and Ritual: Relations Between Women in Ninteeenth-Century America;" "Davy Crockett as Trickster: Pornography, Liminality, and Symbolic Inversion in Victorian America;" and "Beauty, the Beast and the Militant Woman: A Case Study in Sex Roles and Social Stress in Jacksonian America," all in Disorderly Conduct

4. FERTILITY CONTROL AND FAMILY PLANNING

Why and how did Americans reduce marital fertility by half between 1800 and 1900? What is the relationship between fertility control and sexual change?

Linda Gordon, Woman's Body, Woman's Right: A Social History of Birth Control in America, chaps. 2-5 (on reserve)

James Mohr, Abortion in America, chaps. 1-3, 7-9 (the rest is optional)

Carroll Smith Rosenberg, "The Abortion Movement and the AMA, 1850-1880," in Disorderly Conduct

5. STUDENT REPORTS, I:

Half the class will report on additional readings (typically a book or a set of articles) at this session. The topics for the nineteenth century include: utopian societies; slavery and its aftermath; reform/radical biographies (e.g. Sylvester Graham, Frances Wright); gay and lesbian history. See the Bibliography for further suggestions of topics and readings.

6. PROSTITUTION AND ANTI-PROSTITUTION

How do we explain the growth of sexual commerce—economic origins, the double standard, the symbolic role of the prostitute? When and why does anti-prostitution emerge, and with what political strategies?

Kathy Peiss, "'Charity Girls' and City Pleasures: Historical Notes on Working-Class Sexuality, 1880-1920," in Snitow, ed. Powers of Desire, pp. 74-87
Ruth Rosen, The Lost Sisterhood
Lucie Cheng Hirata, "Chinese Immigrant Women in Nineteenth-Century California" (Course Reader)

7. SEX REFORM AND SEX RADICALISM

In addition to anti-prostitution, a number of social movements—both conservative and radical—attempted to change sexual ideas and practices in the early twentieth century. These included social hygiene, birth control, sex education, and sexology. What did they have in common, what political ideas divided them, and how did they relate to larger political movements, including progressivism and feminism? What vision of future sexuality did these movements provide?

Linda Gordon, Woman's Body, Woman's Right, chap 9, "Birth Control and Social Revolution" (on reserve)
Bryan Strong, "Ideas of the Early Sex Education Movement in America, 1890-1920," in Altherr, Procreation or Pleasure, pp. 127-144 (originally in History of Education Quarterly, Summer 1972)
Jacquelyn Dowd Hall, "'The Mind That Burns in Each Body': Women, Rape, and Racial Violence," in Snitow, ed., Powers of Desire, pp. 328-349
Charlotte Perkins Gilman, Herland

FINAL PROJECT PROPOSALS ARE DUE AT THIS CLASS.

8. DEVIANCE, BOUNDARIES AND RESISTANCE

In what ways, and why, did Americans reshape sexual boundaries in the mid-twentieth century? What is the relationship of the so-called "sexual revolution" to the regulation of deviance? What difference did gender make in this transition? What is the relationship of the labelling of deviance and movements of affirmation and resistance?

Eric Garber, "'T'Ain't Nobody's Biznesss': Homosexuality in Harlem in the 1920s," (Course Reader)
Regina M. Morantz, "The Scientist as Sex Crusader: Alfred C. Kinsey and American Culture," in Altherr, ed., Procreation or Pleasure, pp. 145-166 (originally American Quarterly, Winter 1977)
John D'Emilio, Sexual Politics, Sexual Communities

9. STUDENT REPORTS, II

Suggested topics include: venereal disease; divorce; biography/ autobiography (e.g., Emma Goldman, Margaret Sanger); sexology; feminism and sexual politics (e.g. porn debates); abortion and anti-abortion.

10. FINAL PROJECTS

At this class, students will report on their final projects and we will discuss course evaluation. The paper should be handed in to the history department office no later than 5 p.m., December 16th. Some examples of undergraduate projects that use primary sources to explore further the themes we have covered in class:

1. Drawing on our discussion of sexual ideology, look at a sample of published sexual advice literature, e.g. marriage guides from two eras or a sex advice column in a newspaper or magazine, comparing advice on a particular subject over time.

2. Look at some of the early survey research on sexual behavior, such as the Mosher study discussed by Degler and the Katherine B. Davis book. What new questions do you bring to this data, given our class discussions?

3. A microfilm of the Mabel Loomis Todd diary, cited by Peter Gay, is available at Stanford. Does your reading of the diary differ from his? Compare parts of her diary with another nineteenth century diary.

4. Using the published slave narratives, construct a portrait of slave courtship and sexual practice. Use Gutman's book to frame your research.

5. Published court records for colonial Maryland are rich with references to bastardy, adultery and fornication. Read these cases to try to compare the sexual system of the early Chesapeake to that of New England.

6. Select a sample of fiction from popular cultural sources, such as romance magazines, and compare the representation of sexuality with the ideas of sex reformers at the time.

There are many other possibilities for using primary sources. Keep in mind as you design your research project that the sources must be readily available at Stanford and that you should confine the scope of your research to one well defined primary source. In other words, this is an exercise in primary research, not the definitive paper on the subject.

The paper will be evaluated in terms of 1) the integration of secondary readings and class discussions; 2) the use of primary sources; 3) the coherence of the argument or interpretation; 4) the clarity of presentation.

Graduate student projects will depend in part on the discipline from which the student comes. For historians, an historiographical essay (e.g., on the fertility decline question, on prostitution, on class and sexuality) would be useful for preparing for oral examinations.

EVALUATION

The final grade will be based on contribution to class discussions, student reports, and the final project. I would very much appreciate your responses on the standard course evaluation forms and any further comments you would like to give, either in person or in writing, about the course.

Oberlin College

SEX, GENDER AND IDENTITY IN AMERICAN HISTORY
History/ Women's Studies 317

Spring 1987

Joseph Interrante   Carol Lasser
Rice 309   Rice 313
X8524   X8192

This course examines changes in the social construction of
sexuality, masculinity, and femininity in the American context
from the colonial period through the present, concentrating in
particular on the nineteenth and early twentieth centuries. It
provides an introduction both to topics of particular importance
to the history of sexuality and to the various methods used by
historians studying the subject. Of special importance
throughout is the relationship of sexuality and sexual identity
to their changing social context.

Format
        The course meets weekly on Thursdays from 1 pm to 3 pm for
two hours. By 5 pm sharp on Wednesdays, each student is required
to submit a "study question" raising an issue related to the
assigned reading for the week. Study questions will be collected
in an envelope for the course on Mr. Interrante's office door,
Rice 309. Study questions form the basis for classroom
discussion and will be considered as a factor in assessing class
participation.

Books to purchase from the Co-op Bookstore:
        Lillian Faderman, Surpassing the Love of Men
        Walt Whitman, Leaves of Grass
        Ruth Rosen, ed., The Mamie Papers
        Kate Chopin, The Awakening
        E. M. Forster, Maurice
        John D'Emilio, Sexual Politics, Sexual Communities
Optional purchases available from the Co-op Bookstore:
        Ann Snitow, Christine Stansell and Sharon Thompson,
            eds., Powers of Desire
        Nancy Cott and Elizabeth Pleck, eds., A Heritage of Her
            Own
In addition, students will be asked to purchase the following
    from the instructors:
        Carol Lasser and Marlene Merrill, eds., Soul Mates: The
            Oberlin Correspondence Between Lucy Stone and
            Antoinette Brown Blackwell, 1846-1850

221

Schedule of Classes

February 5: Introduction

February 12: Approaches to the historical study of sex and
    gender
        Ellen Ross and Rayna Rapp, "Sex and Society," in Snitow
            et.al., Powers of Desire, pp. 51-73.
        Jeffrey Weeks, Sex, Politics and Society, Chapter 1,
            pp. 1-18.
        Robert Padgug, "Sexual Matters: On Conceptualizing
            Sexuality in History," Radical History Review
            20(Spring/Summer 1979):3-23.
        Joseph Interrante and Carol Lasser, "Victims of the
            Very Songs They Sing: A Critique of Recent Work on
            Patriarchal Culture and the Social Construction of
            Gender," Radical History Review 20 (Spring/Summer
            1979): 25-40.

February 19: Social Structure, Behavior and Identity: The Case of
    Agrarian Patriarchy
        Edmund Morgan, "The Puritans and Sex," in Jean Friedman
            and William Shade, Our American Sisters (second
            edition), pp. 11-23.
        Nancy Cott, "Eighteenth-Century Family and Social Life
            in Massachusetts Divorce Records," in Cott and
            Pleck, A Heritage of Her Own, pp. 107-135
        Jonathan Katz, "The Age of Sodomitical Sin,"
            Gay/Lesbian Almanac, pp. 23-65.
        Winthrop Jordan, Chapter 4, _"The Fruits of Passion:
            The Dynamics of Interracial Sex," in White Man's
            Burden, pp. 69-86
                OR
        Winthrop Jordan, Chapter 4, "The Fruits of Passion: The
            Dynamics of Interracial Sex" in White Over Black,
            pp. 136-179.
        Daniel Scott Smith and Michael Hindus, "Premarital
            Pregnancy in America, 1640-1971: An Overview and
            Interpretation," Journal of Interdisciplinary
            History 5(Spring 1975):

February 26: Hard Facts and Ambiguous Meanings: Interpreting the
    "Demographic Transition"
        Daniel Scott Smith, "Family Limitation, Sexual COntrol
            and Domestic Feminism in America" in Cott and
            Pleck, A Heritage of Her Own, pp. 222-245.
        Linda Gordon, Woman's Body, Woman's Right, Chapters 3-
            5, pp. 47-115.
        Nancy Cott, "Passionlessness," in Cott and Pleck, A

222

Heritage of Her Own, pp. 162-181.
Ellen Rothman, "Sex and Self-Control: Middle-Class
Courship in America, 1770-1870," Journal of Social
History 15:3 (1982): 409-425.

Recommended:
Steven Nissenbaum, "Re-imagining Sex: Repression and
Liberation in Mid-Nineteenth-Century America,"
unpublished paper on reserve.

March 5: Gender, Behavior and Identity: Placing "Sorority" in
Context
Carroll Smith-Rosenberg, "The Female World of Love and
Ritual," in Cott and Pleck, A Heritage of Her Own,
pp. 311-342.
Carol Lasser and Marlene Merrill, Soul Mates The
Oberlin Correspondence of Lucy Stone and
Antoinette Brown, 1846-1850, entire.
Lillian Faderman, Surpassing the Love of Men, pp. 145-
230.

Recommended:
Carol Lasser, "'Let Us Be Sisters Forever': Lucy Stone,
Antoinette Brown Blackwell, and the Sororal Model
of Nineteenth-Century Female Friendship,"
typescript of forthcoming article, on reserve.
Nancy Sahli, "Smashing: Women's Relationships Before
the Fall," Chrysalis 9 (1979): 17-27.
Martha Vicinus, "Distance and Desire: English Boarding
School Friendships," Signs 9:4 (1984): 600-622.
Martha Vicinus, "'One Life to Stand Beside Me':
Emotional Conflicts in First Generation College
Women in England, Feminist Studies 8:3 (1982):603-
628.

March 12: Bonds and Boundaries: The Case of Walt Whitman
Walt Whitman, Leaves of Grass: "The Sleepers" (1855 and
1892 editions), "Song of Myself," " Out of the
Cradle...," and all poems in "Children of Adam"
and "Calamus" sections.
Charles Rosenberg, "Sexuality, Class and Role in
Nineteenth-Century America," in Elizabeth Pleck
and Joseph Pleck, The American Man, pp. 129-254.
Michael Lynch, "'Here is Adhesiveness': From Friendship
to Homosexuality," Victorian Studies, 29:1 (1985):
67-96.

Recommended:
Ernst Schachtel, "On Memory and Early Childhood
Amnesia," in Schachtel, Metamorphosis: On the

> Development of Affect, Perception, Attention and Memory.

March 19: Class, Race, Sex and Power
> Lenore Davidoff, "Class and Gender in Victorian England: Diaries of Arthur J. Munby and Hannah Cullwick," Feminist Studies, 5 (1979): 87-141.
> John Gillis, "Servants, Sexual Relations and Risks of Illegitimacy in London, 1800-1900," Feminist Studies 5(1979): 142-172.
> Ida B. Wells, Southern Horrors: Lynch Law in All Its Phases (photocopy of pamphlet of 24 pages can be purchased from instructor).
> Jacquelyn Dowd Hall, "'The Mind That Burns in Each Body': Women, Rape, and Racial Violence," in Snitow et al., Powers of Desire, pp.328-349.

*****SPRING BREAK******

April 2: Prostitution, Sex, and Class
> Kathy Peiss, "'Charity Girls' and City Pleasures: Historical Notes on Working-Class Sexuality, 1880-1920," in Snitow et al., Powers of Desire, pp. 74-87.
> Judith Walkowitz, "Male Vice and Female Virtue: Feminism and the Politics of Prostitution in Nineteenth-Century Britain," in Snitow et al., Powers of Desire, pp. 419-438.
> Ruth Rosen, ed., The Mamie Papers, selections.

> Recommended:
> Christine Stansell, "Women on the Town: Sexual Exchange and Prostitution," Chapter 9 in City of Women: Sex and Class in New York, 1789-1860171-192.

April 9: Middle-Class Desire and its Discontents in Victorian America
> Kate Chopin, The Awakening, entire.
> Ellen Dubois and Linda Gordon, "Seeking Ecstasy on the Battlefield: Danger and Pleasure in Nineteenth-Century Feminist Sexual Thought," Feminist Studies 9 (Spring 1983): 7-26.
> Carroll Smith Rosenberg, "The Hysterical Woman: Sex Roles and Role COnflict in Nineteenth-Century America," in Disorderly Conduct, pp. 197-217.

April 16: Homosexual Identities in Transition
> E. M. Forster, Maurice, entire.
> George Chauncy, Jr., "Christian Brotherhood or Sexual Perversion? Homosexual Identities and the

Construction of Sexual Boundaries in the World War
One Era," Journal of Social History 19 (Winter
1985): 189-212.
Jeffrey Weeks, Sex, Politics and Society, Chapter 6,
Michael pp. 96-121.
Bronski, "Making of Gay Sensibility," Culture Class,
pp. 22-39.

Recommended:
Jeffrey Weeks, "Inverts, Perverts and Mary-Annes: Male
Prostitution and the Regulation of Homosexuality
in England in the Nineteenth and Early Twentieth
Centuries," Journal of Homosexuality 6
(Fall/Winter 1980-81): 113-134.

April 23: The Twentieth Century Sexual Revolution: New Pleasures,
New Dangers
Paul Robinson, "Havelock Ellis," in The Modernization
of Sex, pp. 1-41.
Ellen Kay Trimberger, "Feminism, Men and Modern Love:
Greenwich Village, 1900-1925 in Snitow et al.,
Powers of Desire, pp. 131-152.
Carroll Smith-Rosenberg, "The New Woman as Androgyne:
Social Disorder and Gender Crisis, 1870-1936," in
Disorderly Conduct, pp. 245-296.
Lillian Faderman, Surpassing the Love of Men, pp. 233-
253 and 297-331.
Christopher Lasch, Chapter 2: "Woman as Alien," and
Chapter 4: "Mabel Dodge Luhan: Sex as Politics,"
in The New Radicalism in America, pp. 38-68 and
104-140.

April 30: Politicizing Sex: Gay/Lesbian Identity and Minority
Politics
John D'Emilio, Sexual Politics, Sexual Communities,
entire.
Lillian Faderman, Surpassing the Love of Men, pp. 357-
416.

May 7: Retrospect and Prospect   Gayle Rubin
Amber Hollibaugh, Deirdre English, "Talking Sex," in
Carol Vance, ed., Pleasure and Danger.
Deirdre English, "The Fear that Feminism Will Free Men
First," in Snitow et al., Powers of Desire, pp.
477-484.

Course Requirements

Students are required to attend class and to submit weekly study questions. In addition, students will write three seven to ten page papers. These papers will be due on the following dates:

> March 5
> April 9
> May 7

Topics will be distributed in advance.

Students are encouraged to discuss their papers with either instructor and/or submit drafts in order to develop their thinking and writing skills.

Papers will be evaluated for both style and content.

Grading

Class participation and study questions will account for approximately one-quarter of the final grade. Each paper will account for one-quarter of the final grade. Improvement over the course of the semester will be considered in the final evaluation.

Cornell University

History 227/Women's Studies 227

Modern American Gender Roles in Historical Perspective

Spring, 1986

Professor M.B. Norton
Ms. Ruth Alexander

This course examines the basic assumptions of twentieth-century American society about the proper behavior of men and women. It emphasizes the gender-role patterns that have developed in the United States since approximately 1870, looking equally at masculinity and femininity. The goal of the course is to help its participants become more aware of the subtle and not-so-subtle ways in which their gender shapes their everyday lives, and to gain an understanding of the historical roots of contemporary gender behavior patterns.

Course requirements: Each student is expected to:

1) attend class regularly and participate actively in discussions. This is not a lecture course. Everyone is an instructor.

2) keep a "gender-role" journal throughout the semester, which must be turned in at the end of the term (it will be read but not assigned a grade) and which will be returned to its author. These journals will be discussed in class each week.

3) prepare a brief report on gender concepts as reflected in a current issue of a magazine not normally read by the student (one intended to be read by the opposite sex), to be presented in class the second week of the course; and a similar report on gender concepts in the popular media (movies, music, or TV), to be presented in class during the ninth week of the course.

4) present an oral report to the class on original research, handing in a 3-5 page written account of that research on the same day.

5) prepare a 10-15 page term paper, due at the last meeting of the class, comparing the lives of a woman and a man (historical or contemporary) in terms of the impact of gender on them.

Grades will be based on: participation in discussion (40%), oral reports (20%), short paper and report (20%), term paper (20%).

227

HISTORY 227/WOMEN'S STUDIES 227 -- Guidelines for
Presentations and Papers

I. Presentations and written reports
   a. Presentations and written reports should deal with contemporary
      problems or issues of gender, but they must place that issue within
      historical context. For example, if a student chooses to examine
      gender roles as put forth by the anti-abortion movement he/she must
      discuss how the anti-abortion movement has developed over time and why
      it has chosen to ally itself with particular conceptions of gender.
   b. Students may choose to work on presentations and written reports in
      pairs. One student may want to focus on the historical aspect of the
      topic, the other on the contemporary. But each student must present
      separate oral and written reports and will be graded separately.
   c. The written report must be footnoted and a bibliography must be
      attached. Furthermore, students should try to write reports that do
      not merely recapitulate the oral presentation. An audience is
      different from a reader. The oral presentation should emphasize
      illustrative features, the written report should be more analytical.
   d. Part of the grade for the oral presentation is based on how much
      interest and discussion the presentation generates and how well the
      speaker responds to questions.

2. Term Papers
   a. All students are required to submit term papers which take as their
      subject the analysis of gender roles and gender perceptions held by one
      man and one woman. The man and woman may be either historical or
      contemporary figures. The need not have known one another or have been
      related, but must be of the same historical period, same race, and same
      class background. The purpose of the paper is to isolate gender as a
      social factor, and to analyze how it affects men and women differently
      who are otherwise of similar background. All subjects must be American
      although they need not be native-born.
   b. The term paper must be based on primary sources.
      1) If you choose to analyze historical figures (ex. Ida Tarbell and
         Upton Sinclair, both early twentieth-century social critics), you
         must locate diaries, journals, essays, etc., written by those
         individuals, which will allow you to assess how gender roles shaped
         their lives and perceptions. You may supplement the primary
         documents with secondary source readings that provide background
         information on the time period or social conditions in which your
         pair lived.
      2) If you choose to analyze contemporary figures (exs. your parents, or
         Diane Feinstein and Edward Koch), you must either interview both
         people or locate essays, autobiographies, transcripts or interviews
         or press conferences, etc. Again, you may use secondary sources to
         help explain the way in which gender has shaped the lives of the
         people you're dealing with, but use of such sources must be kept to
         a minimum. If you plan to conduct interviews you should ask both
         people the same question, but those questions should not be directly
         about gender. For example, don't ask, How did gender affect your
         career choice? Do ask, How and why did you choose your career? It
         is then up to you, the researcher, to interpret the meaning of
         gender in your subjects' lives.
   c. All term paper topics must be approved by Professor Norton or Ms.
      Alexander.

Textbooks:

John D'Emillio, <u>Sexual Politics, Sexual Communities</u>
Barbara Ehrenreich, <u>The Hearts of Men</u>
Sara Evans, <u>Personal Politics</u>
Lillian Faderman, <u>Surpassing the Love of Men</u>
John M. Faragher, <u>Women and Men on the Overland Trail</u>
Charlotte Perkins Gilman, <u>Herland</u>
Elizabeth and Joseph Pleck, eds., <u>The American Man</u>
Sheila Rothman, <u>Woman's Proper Place</u>
Peter Stearns, <u>Be a Man!</u>
Dorothy Sterling, <u>We Are Your Sisters</u>

Assignments for week of:

Jan. 27   Introduction to course

Feb. 3   Reports on contemporary magazines

Feb. 10   Sheila Rothman, <u>Woman's Proper Place</u>

Feb. 17   Peter Stearns, <u>Be A Man!</u> (omit last chapter)
               Joseph and Elizabeth Pleck, eds., <u>American Man</u>, introduction

Feb. 24   Sara Evans, <u>Personal Politics</u>

Mar. 3   Barbara Ehrenreich, <u>The Hearts of Men</u>

Mar. 10   John D'Emilio, <u>Sexual Politics, Sexual Communities</u>

Mar. 17   Lillian Faderman, <u>Surpassing the Love of Men</u>, parts 2 and 3

Mar. 31   Reports on contemporary media

Apr. 7   Joseph and Elizabeth Pleck, <u>The American Man</u>, parts 2 and 3

Apr. 14   Charlotte Perkins Gilman, <u>Herland</u>

Apr. 21   Dorothy Sterling, ed. <u>We Are Your Sisters</u>, parts 1 and 4

Apr. 28   John M. Faragher, <u>Women And Men on The Overland Trail</u>

May 6   General concluding discussion

University of Massachusetts, Amherst

WOST 392S/HIST397S
Professor Kathy Peiss
Herter Hall 633
phone: 545-2785/1330

Fall 1986
Office Hours: MWF,
2:30-3:30 and by
appointment

THE SOCIAL CONSTRUCTION OF SEXUALITY

"Sex, which ought to be an incident of life, is the
obsession of the well fed world." (Rebecca West, 1912)

"It's pitch, sex is. Once you touch it, it clings to
you." (Margery Allingham, 1938)

Dissected, categorized, evaluated, organized and deployed --
sexuality in modern society, and particularly the construction of
our obsession with it, is the primary concern of this course. While
the debate over the nature of sexuality has raged in recent
years, one of the most important modes of analysis to emerge is
that of **social construction**: the position that sexuality is
best understood as a phenomenon determined by history, culture
and politics, rather than a universal, natural force. This
insight, gaining salience with the rise of feminism and the
lesbian and gay liberation movements, is the organizing principle
of the course. Through the semester, we will explore the
different meanings American women and men have attached to sexuality, and
the changing political, economic, social and ideological contexts
in which those constructions have taken place. Our goals will be:

(1) to examine the history of Americans' thinking about
the nature and meaning of sexuality, exploring the
"discourse" developed by the medical, psychiatric and
sex research professions, popular responses to it, and
the changing boundaries between "normality" and
"deviance;"

(2) to examine the relationship between sexuality, the
social relations of gender, race and class, and
cultural norms defining those relations (e.g. social
definitions of femininity and "women's place");

(3) to evaluate the various historical theories
explaining this history; and

(4) to evaluate the feminist contributions to the
ongoing debate over sexuality.

REQUIRED TEXTS: Available at Textbook Annex, Food for Thought
Bookstore, and on Library Reserve

Ann Snitow, et al., eds., POWERS OF DESIRE: THE POLITICS OF SEXUALITY

John D'Emilio, SEXUAL POLITICS, SEXUAL COMMUNITIES
Sigmund Freud, THREE ESSAYS ON THE THEORY OF SEXUALITY
Carroll Smith-Rosenberg, DISORDERLY CONDUCT
Ruth Rosen, THE LOST SISTERHOOD
Linda Gordon: WOMAN'S BODY, WOMAN'S RIGHT

OPTIONAL TEXT: Carol Vance, PLEASURE AND DANGER (Approximately
175 pages, 1/3 of this book, are assigned. You might want to
share copies or use the reserve copy.)

OTHER READINGS: A number of articles are available on reserve
that are simply unavailable in textbooks. These comprise an
essential and required part of the coursework. Please be sure to
plan ahead in weeks where reserve readings are required. They are
marked in the syllabus with **.

COURSE REQUIREMENTS

1. **Regular attendance, completion of reading assignments on
time, and participation.** Your thoughtful engagement with
the readings and willingness to contribute to class discussions
are essential ingredients in this course. (10% of final grade)

2. **Historical document analysis.** You will choose a primary
historical document on sexuality, and write an introduction to
it, analyzing the text and placing it in context. A detailed
assignment sheet will follow. 5-7 page paper (typed,
double-spaced) due October 20. (25%)

3. **Analysis/reaction paper to speaker on sexuality.** From
Oct. 25-30, a Five Colleges Women's Studies conference on
sexuality will be held at Mt. Holyoke, presenting speakers who
have done major work in this field (including some we will be
reading). Attend at least one of the lectures, and
write a brief (2-3) page paper detailing your response to it.
Due November 7. (15%)

4. **Critique of reading/facilitation of one class
discussion.** This involves:

   a) Close reading of week's assignment, **plus** several
   additional readings (at least 2 articles), chosen in
   consultation with me.

   b) Prepare an outline of major questions/issues raised
   in these readings, to be distributed in class on the
   preceding Wednesday; then act as facilitator of that
   Friday's discussion.

   c) Write 5-page paper that analyzes the reading, raises
   criticisms and suggestions, and reports on class
   discussion. This paper is due **one week** after the class
   (unless that date falls in a week when another written
   assignment is due--then take **two weeks** to complete the
   paper). (25%)

5. **Take-home final:** Essay questions will be distributed on
the last day of classes and due in exam week. (25%)

**Note that late work will result in a lowering of the grade.
No incompletes will be given, except in cases of medical or other
emergencies.

COURSE OUTLINE

<u>week of</u>

9/3   **Historicizing Sexuality: The Concept of Social Construction**
        Snitow, Stansell & Thompson, "Introduction," and
        Ross & Rapp, "Sex & Society" in POWERS OF DESIRE, 9-47,51-73

        <u>Recommended</u>:
        Michel Foucault, HISTORY OF SEXUALITY, VOL. 1

9/8   **The Emergence of Victorian Sexual Discourse**
        Smith-Rosenberg, "Hearing Women's Words"; "Bourgeois Discourse
        in the Age of Jackson"; "Davy Crockett as Trickster"; "Beauty,
        the Beast & the Militant Woman" in DISORDERLY CONDUCT, 11-52,79-128
        Nancy Cott, "Passionlessness," SIGNS 4(1978): 219-239**

        <u>Recommended</u>:
        Charles E. Rosenberg, "Sexuality, Class and Role," in
            Rosenberg, ed. NO OTHER GODS: ON SCIENCE & SOCIAL THOUGHT
        Steven Marcus, THE OTHER VICTORIANS
        Ellen Rothman, HANDS AND HEARTS: A HISTORY OF COURTSHIP IN
            AMERICA
                            Sept. 12: meet at Sophia Smith Collection

9/15   **Women's Relationships and Sexuality**
        Smith-Rosenberg, "Female World of Love and Ritual" in DISORDERLY
            CONDUCT, pp. 53-76
        Adrienne Rich, "Compulsory Heterosexuality and Lesbian Existence,"
            in POWERS OF DESIRE, 177-205
        Jonathan Katz, "Passing Women" in GAY AMERICAN HISTORY, 317-350**
        Carl Degler, "What Ought to Be and What Was: Women's
            Sexuality in the 19th Century," AMERICAN HISTORICAL REVIEW
            79 (Dec. 1974): 167-190.**

        <u>Recommended</u>:
        Leila J. Rupp, "Imagine My Surprise: Women's Relationships
            in Historical Perspective," FRONTIERS 5 (1981): 61-70.
        Lillian Faderman, SURPASSING THE LOVE OF MEN
        Nancy Sahli, "'Smashing': Women's Relationships Before the
            Fall," CHRYSALIS 8 (Summer 1979): 17-27

                            Sept. 19-20: "Histories of Sexuality" Conf.

9/22   **Medicalization & the Elaboration of Sexual Categories**

232

Smith-Rosenberg, "Bourgeois Discourse & the Progressive Era";
"From Puberty to Menopause"; "The Hysterical Woman" in
DISORDERLY CONDUCT, 167-216
Vern L. Bullough and Martha Voght, "Homosexuality and Its
Confusion with the 'Secret Sin' in Pre-Freudian America,"
in Bullough, SEX, SOCIETY & HISTORY, 112-124

Recommended:
Barbara Ehrenreich and Deirdre English, FOR HER OWN GOOD;
150 YEARS OF THE EXPERTS' ADVICE TO WOMEN
J. Haller and R. Haller, THE PHYSICIAN & SEXUALITY IN
VICTORIAN AMERICA
George Chauncey, "From Sexual Inversion to Homosexuality:
Medicine and the Changing Conceptualization of Female
Deviance," SALMAGUNDI (1982/83)
Michael Gordon, "From Unfortunate Necessity to Cult of
Mutual Orgasm: Sex in American Marital Education Literature,
1830-1940," in Henslin & Sagarin, THE SOCIOLOGY OF SEX

9/29   **Prostitution: Sexual Boundaries & the Commodification of Sexuality**
Ruth Rosen, THE LOST SISTERHOOD

Recommended:
Judith Walkowtiz, PROSTITUTION AND VICTORIAN SOCIETY
Ruth Rosen & Sue Davidson, eds., THE MAIMIE PAPERS
Mark Connelly, THE RESPONSE TO PROSTITUTION IN THE PROGRESSIVE
ERA
Jane Addams, A NEW CONSCIENCE & AN ANCIENT EVIL
Lucie Chang Hirata, "Free, Indentured and Enslaved: Chinese
Prostitution in 19th Century America," SIGNS 5 (Autumn 1979):3-29

10/6   **Sexual Warfare & Late 19th Century Feminism**
Ellen DuBois and Linda Gordon, "Seeking Ecstasy on the
Battlefield," in PLEASURE & DANGER, pp. 31-49
Judith Walkowitz, "Male Vice and Female Virtue: Feminism and
Politics of Prostitution in 19th c. Britain," in POWERS,
pp. 419-438
Sheila Jeffreys, THE SPINSTER & HER ENEMIES, pp. 1-26, 194-99**
Linda Gordon, WOMAN'S BODY, WOMAN'S RIGHT--begin

Recommended:
Barbara Epstein, "Family, Sexual Morality & Popular Movements
in Turn-of-the-Century America," in POWERS, pp. 117-131
Epstein, THE POLITICS OF DOMESTICITY

10/15   **Contested Terrain: The Struggle for Birth Control & Abortion**
Linda Gordon, WOMAN'S BODY, WOMAN'S RIGHT
holiday Smith-Rosenberg, "The Abortion Movement and the AMA, 1850-1880,"
10/13   in DISORDERLY CONDUCT, 217-244

Recommended:
Rosalind Petchesky, ABORTION AND WOMAN'S CHOICE
David Kennedy, BIRTH CONTROL IN AMERICA
James Mohr, ABORTION IN AMERICA
James Reed, FROM PRIVATE VICE TO PUBLIC VIRTUE: THE BIRTH

CONTROL MOVEMENT & AMERICAN SOCIETY SINCE 1830
Margaret Sanger, AUTOBIOGRAPHY

10/20   **The "New Morality": Sexual Autonomy in the Early 20th C. and Its Limits**
Smith-Rosenberg, "New Woman as Androgyne," in DISORDERLY CONDUCT
Peiss, "Charity Girls & City Pleasures," in POWERS OF DESIRE, 74-88
Trimberger, "Feminism, Men & Modern Love: Greenwich Village,
1902-1925," in POWERS OF DESIRE, 131-53
Christina Simmons, "Companionate Marriage and the Lesbian
Threat," FRONTIERS 4, no.3 (Fall 1979): 54-59**

10/27   **Racism, Sexuality and the Afro-American Experience**
Jacquelyn Dowd Hall, "The Mind That Burns in Each Body: Women,
Rape and Racial Violence," in POWERS OF DESIRE, 328-349
Barbara Omolade, "Hearts of Darkness," in POWERS, 350-367
Rennie Simson, "The Afro-American Female: Historical Context of
the Construction of Sexual Identity," in POWERS, 229-235
Hortense J. Spillers, "Interstices: A Small Drama of Words,"
in PLEASURE & DANGER, pp. 73-100
Allan M. Brandt, "Racism and Research: The Case of the Tuskegee
Syphilis Study," in Leavitt and Numbers, eds. SICKNESS AND
HEALTH, pp. 331-346**

                         **no class 10/31: attend lecture at
                         5-Colleges "Feminism & Sexualities" conf.**

11/3   **The Development of the Psychoanalytic Model: Freud & His Followers**
Freud, THREE ESSAYS ON THE THEORY OF SEXUALITY
Chodorow, "Freud, Ideology and Evidence," in REPRODUCTION OF
MOTHERING, pp. 141-158**
Marynia Farnham & Ferdinand Lundberg, "The Feminist Complex," in
MODERN WOMAN: THE LOST SEX, 140-167**

         Recommended:
Nathan Hale, FREUD AND THE AMERICANS
Jeffrey Masson, THE REPRESSION OF PSYCHOANALYSIS
Juliet Mitchell, PSYCHOANALYSIS AND FEMINISM

11/12   **Sexologists and the Behaviorist Model**
Carole Vance, "Gender Systems, Ideology and Sex Research" in
holiday   POWERS OF DESIRE, 371-385
11/10   Mike Brake, HUMAN SEXUAL RELATIONS, pp. 137-196, excerpts
from Kinsey and Masters and Johnson**

         Recommended:
Paul Robinson, THE MODERNIZATION OF SEX
Thomas Szasz, SEX BY PRESCRIPTION
Janice Raymond, THE TRANSSEXUAL EMPIRE
Regina Morantz, "The Scientist as Sex Crusader: Alfred
Kinsey and American Culture," AMERICAN QUARTERLY 29
(Winter 1977): 563-89

11/17   **The Emergence of Lesbian and Gay Communities and Politics**
John D'Emilio, SEXUAL POLITICS, SEXUAL COMMUNITIES:
THE MAKING OF A HOMOSEXUAL MINORITY

Allan Berube, "Marching to a Different Drummer: Lesbian
and Gay GI's in World War II," in POWERS OF DESIRE
Joan Nestle, "The Fem Question," PLEASURE & DANGER, 232-41
Madeline Davis and Elizabeth Lapovsky Kennedy, "Oral History and
the Study of Sexuality in the Lesbian Community: Buffalo,
N.Y., 1940-1960," FEMINIST STUDIES 12 (Spring 1986):7-26.**

Recommended:
Jeffrey Weeks, COMING OUT: HOMOSEXUAL POLITICS IN BRITAIN
FROM THE 19TH CENTURY TO THE PRESENT
Jonathan Katz, GAY AMERICAN HISTORY
Jonathan Katz, GAY/LESBIAN ALMANAC

11/24 **Romance & Desire in Late 20th C. Popular Culture**
Ann Snitow, "Mass Market Romance," in POWERS OF DESIRE, 245-263
holiday Ann Kaplan, "Is the Gaze Male," in POWERS, 309-327
11/28 Meryl Altman, "Everything They Always Wanted You to Know: The
Ideology of Popular Sex Literature," PLEASURE & DANGER, 115-130
Bette Gordon, "Variety: The Pleasure in Looking," in
PLEASURE & DANGER, 189-203
Sharon Thompson, "Search for Tomorrow: On Feminism and the
Reconstruction of Teen Romance," PLEASURE & DANGER, 350-84
Felicita Garcia, "I Just Came Out Pregnant," in POWERS, 236-244

Recommended:
Barbara Ehrenreich, HEARTS OF MEN
Janice Radway, READING THE ROMANCE
Rosalind Petchesky, ABORTION AND WOMAN'S CHOICE, "Abortion and
Heterosexual Culture: The Teenage Question," pp. 205-240

12/1 **Sex Wars in the 80's: The Pornography Debates, Feminism & the Right**
Ellen Willis, "Feminism, Moralism and Pornography" in POWERS
OF DESIRE, 460-467
Gayle Rubin, "Thinking Sex: Notes for a Radical Theory of the
Politics of Sexuality," in PLEASURE & DANGER, 267-319
Andrea Dworkin, "For Men, Freedom of Speech; for Women, Silence
Please"; Helen Longino, "Pornography, Oppression and Freedom";
Diana E.H. Russell, Pornography and the Women's Liberation
Movement"; Kathleen Barry, "Beyond Pornography"--all in Lyn
Lederer, ed. TAKE BACK THE NIGHT, pp. 40-54; 256-258; 301-12**
Mary Kay Blakely, "Is One Woman's Sexuality Another Woman's
Pornography?" MS. 13 (April 1985): 37-47, 120, 123**

Recommended:
Vance, "Introduction," and "Epilogue" in PLEASURE & DANGER
Andrea Dworkin, PORNOGRAPHY--MEN POSSESSING WOMEN
Catharine MacKinnon, "Not a Moral Issue," YALE LAW &
POLICY REVIEW, 2 (1984): 321-345.
Rosalind Petchesky, ABORTION AND WOMAN'S CHOICE, esp.
chs. 7-10

12/8 **Disease and Morality: From V.D. to AIDS**
Cindy Patton, "Introduction," "Germphobia," and "Erotophobia,"
in SEX AND GERMS, pp. 3-18, 51-66, 103-133 (footnotes pp.
165-6, 168-9, 172-3)**

Recommended:
  Allan Brandt, NO MAGIC BULLET: A SOCIAL HISTORY OF VENEREAL
    DISEASE IN THE U.S.
  Cindy Patton, SEX AND GERMS
  Dennis Altman, AIDS IN THE MIND OF AMERICA

History 444
Spring 1987
Mon. 2:30-4:30

Prof. Margaret W. Rossiter
323 McGraw Hall
Office Hrs: Wed. 3-4 and by
appointment (277-6722)

Historical Issues of Gender and Science

This course is a one-semester survey of women's role in science and engineering from antiquity to the 1970s with special emphasis on the United States in the 20th century. Readings will include biographies of prominent women scientists, educational writings and other primary sources, and recent historical and sociological studies. Hopefully by the end of the semester, we shall have attained a broad view of the problems that have faced women entering science and those that still remain.

There are no prerequisites for the course, although some knowledge of women's history and the history of science would be helpful. The course welcomes the participation of students from scientific and non-scientific backgrounds alike.

Among the topics to be considered this term are:

--attitudes toward the "learned ladies" of the 17th century

--"botany for ladies" and the 19th century popularization of science

--the entrance of women into educational institutions here and abroad

--the accomplishments and troubles of some particularly able women scientists as Mme. du Chatelet, Sonia Kovalevsky, and Marie Curie

--particular fields in which women have been numerous and/or successful, as home economics, crystallography, child psychology and anthropology

--issues surrounding women explorers and fieldwork

--scientific families, including scientific couples, scientist-mothers, daughters and wives

--women scientists and the Nazis (Lise Meitner, Emmy Noether, Ida Noddack and others)

--World War II and the back-to-the-home movement

--Cold War "womanpower" in the U.S. and USSR

--Third World, Japanese and other foreign women scientists

--the "path to liberation", 1964-77

--some "male" styles and cultures in science and engineering

237

Students will be expected to come to class prepared to discuss the week's assigned readings. In addition the requirements for under-graduates are:
--- a 3-5 page book review, selected from a list of biographies to be circulated later. This should be typed and submitted before spring break, i.e. 5:00pm March 20.
--- an oral report to the class on a topic approved in advance.
--- a 12-15 page research paper, probably on the same topic, before the end of the semester.
Graduate students should substitute for the book review a short (5-8 page) historiographical or comparative paper and submit a longer (20-30 page) research paper.

The following books have been ordered at the campus store and placed on reserve in Uris Library:

Margaret Alic. Hypatia's Heritage. A History of Women in Science from Antiquity through the Nineteenth Century (Boston: Beacon Press. 1986) paperback

Margaret W. Rossiter. Women Scientists in America. Struggles and Strategies to 1940 (Baltimore: Johns Hopkins University Press. 1982) paperback

Jean Moliere. Learned Ladies (1672, any edition)

Robert Reid. Marie Curie (New York: E.P. Dutton. 1974) paper, but now out of print

Marie Negri Carver. Home Economics as an Academic Discipline: A Short History (University of Arizona. College of Education. 1979) paper

Mary Catherine Bateson. With a Daughter's Eye. A Memoir of Margaret Mead and Gregory Bateson (New York: William Morrow and Co.. 1984) paperback

Marjorie Farnsworth. A Young Woman's Guide to Academia (New York: Richard Roazen Press. 1974) cloth

Inna Kosheleva. Women in Science [in USSR] (Moscow: Progress Publishers. 1983) paperback

Derek Richter. ed.. Women Scientists: The Road to Liberation [in foreign countries] (London: Macmillan. 1982) cloth

Optional (in case you can't find the Reid biography of Marie Curie above):
Ann Hibner Koblitz. A Convergence of Lives. Sofia Kovalevskaia: Scientist. Writer. Revolutionary (Boston: Birkhauser. 1983) cloth

First assignment: For Monday February 2 is Margaret Alic. Hypatia's Heritage, pp. 1-94 (plus relevant notes and bibliography) and Jean Moliere's Learned Ladies (or in French Les Femmes Savantes)

Additional assignments will be made later.

Harvard University

HISTORY 1605

FEMINISM AND ITS DISCONTENTS:

DEVELOPMENT OF MODERN FEMINIST THOUGHT

PROFESSOR CATHERINE CLINTON   Fall '86
ROBINSON L-24/495-5146   Wed 2-4
Office Hours: Tu & Th. 11:00

This seminar will introduce students to the maincurrents
of modern American feminist thought. Seminar members will be
expected to familiarize themselves with the broad outlines of
social and political change for American women while examining
leading theorists and texts.

Students will be expected to attend every seminar and
participate in discussion of the weekly reading. In addition
seminar members will be given six writing assignments, as follows:

1) UNGRADED ESSAY: Due the second seminar meeting.

Write a three page essay discussing the following issues:
Define American feminism and describe its intellectual origins.
Define anti-feminism and describe its sources. What are the most
significant changes feminism has wrought?

2) GRADED ASSIGNMENT:Each student will be required to
maintain a seminar journal. The journal must include impressions
of the weekly assigned reading and comments on any outside
reading undertaken for the seminar. Thoughts about weekly
discussions and other commentary are encouraged as well.
Notebooks will be handed in (and returned promptly) on a random
basis. Students are required to turn in completed journals.
before Christmas vacation.

3) GRADED ASSIGNMENT: Each student will write a bibliographic
essay on a feminist theorist (3-5 Pages). DUE OCTOBER 22ND.

4) GRADED ASSIGNMENT:Each student will write an essay on the
significance and influence of a feminist text selected from a
list of major works published during the period 1965-1985.
(5-8 pages) DUE NOVEMBER 19TH.

5) GRADED ASSIGNMENT:Each student will do research on the
influence of feminist thought on one of the following academic
disciplines: linguistics, philosophy, anthropology, theology, art

history or computer sciences. (5-8 pages) DUE DECEMBER 17th.

6) GRADED ESSAY: Each student will be given an essay question
on an assigned topic; there will be no outside research or
additional reading for this final paper. (8-10 pages) DUE JANUARY 14th

GRADE DISTRIBUTION:

SEMINAR JOURNAL AND PARTICIPATION IN DISCUSSION: 30%
BIBLIOGRAPHIC ESSAY: 10%
ESSAY ON FEMINIST TEXT: 15%
ESSAY ON FEMINISM AND ACADEMIC DISCIPLINE: 20%
ESSAY ON ASSIGNED TOPIC: 25%

ALL REQUIRED READING IS AVAILABLE FOR PURCHASE AT THE COOP AND/OR
ON RESERVE AT LAMONT AND HILLES.

Mary Jo Buhle	Women and American Socialism
Blanche Cook, ed.	Crystal Eastman: On Women and Revolution
Josephine Donovan	Feminist Theory
Ellen Dubois	Stanton/Anthony
Hester Eisenstein	Contemporary Feminist Thought
Carol Gilligan	In a Different Voice
Sandra Harding	The Science Question in Feminism
Dolores Hayden	The Grand Domestic Revolution
Bell Hooks	Feminist Theory
Dale Spender	Feminist Theorists

SEPTEMBER 24TH	INTRODUCTION
OCTOBER 1ST	PAPER DUE
OCTOBER 8TH	READING: SPENDER
OCTOBER 15TH	READING: DUBOIS, p. 2-85 & 152-193 BUHLE, p. 176-284

OCTOBER 22ND	READING: HAYDEN, p. 67-131 & 183-305
	  COOK, p. 1-98 & 170-231
	  (BIBLIOGRAPHIC ESSAY DUE)

OCTOBER 29TH	READING: DONOVAN
NOVEMBER 5TH	READING: EISENSTEIN
NOVEMBER 12TH	READING: HOOKS
NOVEMBER 19TH	(PAPER ON FEMINIST TEXT DUE)
NOVEMBER 26TH	NO CLASS MEETING

DECEMBER 3RD	FEMINISM AND ACADEMIC DISCIPLINES
	READING: HARDING
	GILLIGAN
DECEMBER 10TH	FEMINISM AND ANTI-FEMINISM
DECEMBER 17TH	NO CLASS MEETING.
	(PAPER ON FEMINISM & DISCIPLINES DUE)
	(SEMINAR JOURNALS DUE)
JANUARY 14TH	FUTURE DIRECTIONS IN FEMINIST THOUGHT
	(FINAL ESSAY DUE)

ALL WORK TURNED IN LATE WILL BE PENALIZED ONE-THIRD OF A GRADE PER DAY, I.E. AN 'A' PAPER TURNED IN ONE DAY LATE IS MARKED AN 'A-', TWO DAYS LATE 'B+', ETC.

ANY EXTENSIONS FOR WRITTEN WORK MUST BE OBTAINED ONE WEEK IN ADVANCE OF THE DUE DATE. EXTENSIONS WILL BE GIVEN FOR A PERIOD OF NO MORE THAN FIVE DAYS. EACH STUDENT WILL AUTOMATICALLY BE GRANTED AN EXTENSION FOR ONE OF THE FIVE GRADED WRITING ASSIGNMENTS. ANY STUDENT WILL AUTOMATICALLY BE GRANTED AN EXTENSION FOR MEDICAL REASONS. ALL OTHER CIRCUMSTANCES WILL BE EXAMINED ON A CASE BY CASE BASIS.

St. Olaf College

History 83

Dr. Joan Gundersen

HISTORY OF TWENTIETH CENTURY FEMINIST THOUGHT

Students should purchase the following:

Lois Banner, Women in Modern America, 2nd ed.
Charlotte Perkins Gilman, Women and Economics
Rosalind Rosenberg, Beyond Separate Spheres
Sylvia Plath, The Bell Jar
Betty Friedan, The Feminine Mystique
Mary Daly, Beyond God the Father
Gayle Graham Yates, What Women Want
Mary C. Lynn, Women's Liberation in the Twentieth Century

Course Objectives: This is a level III course, and as such students should expect to participate in the seminar format. The course intends to give students a chance to study the development of feminist thought throughout the twentieth century and the intellectual social currents reflected in that thought. Students should expect to sharpen their skills in writing and analytical reading. As a course fulfilling the level III for both women's studies and history, it will expect students to employ the perspectives of both disciplines, but to keep in mind that the materials we read are not necessarily themselves history, but rather the documents from which history is written.

Course Assignments: There will be no in-class exams. There will be several writing assignments and oral presentations. Each student will be part of a group which will be responsible for leading discussion on a particular day. Each group will meet with me to plan that session. In addition, each student will prepare a 20 minute oral presentation on a particular person or group active in defining feminism. This report will be the basis of a paper due two class sessions after your report. Each student will also write three book reviews. The particulars for all of the assignments come below:

1. Discussion--- 10% of the grade. Students will work in groups of no more than three persons to prepare to lead discussion on a set of assigned readings. The students are not expected to prepare mini-lectures nor conduct bull sessions. Rather they are to plan ways that the class as whole may explore the meaning, context, and premises of the readings. Groups will lead discussion on these dates: February 18, March 18, March 20, April 22, April 24, May 13.

2. Oral Report--- 15% of the grade. See the accompanying list of topics. Each person will choose a topic from this list and prepare a report which analyzes the person from the perspective of her contribution to feminist ideology and the general topic for the day.

242

3. Written Report --- 20% of the grade. The written version
of the oral report should include complete footnotes,
bibliography, and be 10-15 pages in length. These reports
are not to be solely biography, but rather to use
biographical data and historical knowledge to illuminate the
feminist ideology and writing of the person.

4. Book Reviews:

a. Review of Gilman's _Women and Economics_---15% of the
grade. This should be a 2-3 page analytical review, not
a summary. Due February 18.

b. Comparative review of Plath's _The Bell Jar_ and
Friedan's _The Feminine Mystique_---15% of the grade. This
is a 4-5 page review. Be sure to compare and not just
discuss the books in sequence. Due April 24.

c. Book review of Yates' _What Women Want_---25% of the
grade. This should be an extended analysis, 4-7 pages,
making use of insights gathered all semester. It will be
due at the final exam time and takes the place of a
final.

Report Topics:
        February 20 - The Early Critics
                1. Elizabeth Cady Stanton
                2. Matilda Joslyn Gage

        March 4 - Socialist Critics
                1. Emma Goldman
                2. Jane Addams
                3. Crystal Eastman

        April 1 - Feminism Regroups
                1. Alice Paul
                2. Suzanne LaFollette
                3. Mary Church Terrell

        April 8 - The New Scholarship
                1. Mary Ritter Beard
                2. Karen Horney

        April 22 - Adjusting the Role
                1. Ashley Montague
                2. Ruth Hershberger

        April 29 - Feminism Awakes
                1. Alice Rossi
                2. Elizabeth Janeway
                3. Kate Millet
                4. Karen DeCrow

May 6   - Black Feminism
        1. Pauli Murray
        2. Alice Walker

May 8 - Feminism in Full Swing
        1. Germaine Greer
        2. Shulamith Firestone
        3. Rosemary Ruether
        4. Adrienne Rich

Daily Assignments

Feb.	6	Th	Opening Session
	11	T	Beginnings - Background
	13	Th	New Social Sciences Read Banner, Chapter 1
	18	T	DISCUSSION Read C.P. Gilman, Women and Economics, Lynn Part I
	20	Th	Reports - The Early Critics
	25	T	Progressivism Read Banner, Chapter 2
	27	Th	From Justice to Expediency -the Vote
Mar.	4	T	Reports - Socialist Critics
	6	Th	Equality in an Age of Reaction Read Banner, Chapter 4
	11	T	Gopher Prairie & Babbitt
	13	T	No class
	18	T	DISCUSSION Read Lynn Part II
	20	Th	DISCUSSION Read R. Rosenberg, Beyond Separate Spheres
	22-31		SPRING BREAK
Apr.	1	T	Reports - Feminism Regroups
	3	Th	Return to the People

		Read Banner, Chapter 5
8	T	Reports - New Scholarship
10	Th	Freud & Environment
15	T	DISCUSSION Read Lynn Part III
17	Th	Alienation & Existence Read Banner, pp. 230-243
22	T	DISCUSSION and report - Adjusting the Role Read S. Plath, The Bell Jar
24	Th	DISCUSSION Lynn Part IV; B. Friedan, The Feminine Mystique BOOK REVIEW COMPARING PLATH AND FRIEDAN DUE
29	T	Reports - Feminism Awakes
May 1	Th	New Left Read Lynn part V; Banner pp. 243-272
6	T	Reports - Black Feminists
8	Th	Reports - Feminism in Full Swing
13	T	DISCUSSION Read Mary Daly's Beyond God the Father

Penelope D. Johnson
New York University

THE HISTORY OF FEMINIST THEORY

Sept. 20   Introduction

Definitions and Framework
Sept. 27 Alison Jagger and Paula Struhl, Feminist Frameworks ix-5,
            67-156 (and as much more as you have time for.)
            Juliet Mitchell, chap. 5, Woman's Estate
            **TURN IN A CAREFULLY WORDED DEFINITION OF FEMINISM

The Late Medieval Querelle des Femmes
Oct. 4   Christine de Pizan, City of Ladies
            Joan Kelly, "Early Feminist Theory and the Querelle des Femmes
              1400-1789," Signs 8 (1982), 4-28.
            Susan Schibanoff, "Comment on Kelly's "Early Feminist Theory and
              the Querelle des Femmes, 1400-1789," Signs 9 (1983),320-326.
            Beatrice Gottlieb, "The Problem of Feminism in the Fifteenth
              Century," in Women of the Medieval World, ed. Julius
              Kirshner and Suzanne Wemple, 337-364.

Sixteenth and Seventeenth Century
Oct. 11 Baldesar Castiglione, The Book of the Courtier
            Joan Kelly-Gadol, "Did Women Have a Renaissance?"
              Becoming Visible ed. Renate Bridenthal (1977), 137-64.

Oct. 18 Sor Juana Inez de la Cruz,
            Carolyn Merchant, The Death of Nature: Women, Ecology and
              the Scientific Revolution (1980).

Enlightenment and Revolution
Oct. 25 Mary Wollstonecraft, A Vindication of the Rights of Woman
            Miriam Brody, "Mary Wollstonecraft: Sexuality and Women's
              Rights," Feminist Theorists: Three Centuries of Key Women
              Thinkers, ed. Dale Spender (1983).
            Jane Abray, "Feminism in the French Revolution," AHR 80 (1975).
            Condorcet, "On the Admission of Women to the Rights of
              Citizenship."

Three Modern Male Theorists
Nov. 1   John S. Mill, The Subjection of Women
            "Along the Suffrage Trail," Feminist Papers ed. A. Rossi.
            **FIRST PAPER DUE IN CLASS

Nov. 8   F. Engels, The Origins of the Family, Private Property and the
              State intro., 87-170, 217-237
            Karen Sacks, "Engels Revisited," Woman, Culture and Society,, ed.
              Michelle Rosaldo and Louise Lamphere.

Nov. 15 Sigmund Freud, Dora: An Analysis of a Case of Hysteria
         Juliet Mitchell, chap. 9, "Psychoanalysis and the Family,"
         Woman's Estate, 159-172.
         Charlotte Perkins Gilman, The Yellow Wallpaper

Modern Female Theorists
Nov. 22 Alexandra Kollontai, Selected Writings 13-73, 127-149, 201-311.
         Beatrice Farnsworth, "Bolshevism, the Woman Question and
             Aleksandra Kollontai," Socialist Women, ed. Marilyn Boxer
             and Jean Quataert
         Bernice Rosenthal, "Love on the Tractor: Women in the Russian
             Revolution and After," Becoming Visible, ed. Bridenthal.

Nov. 29 Virginia Woolf, A Room of One's Own
         Naomi Black, "Virginia Woolf: The Life of Nautral Happiness,"
             Feminist Theorists, ed. Dale Spender.
         Renate Bridenthal, "Women Between the Two World Wars," Becoming
             Visible

Dec. 6   Simone de Beauvoir, The Second Sex, 3-67, 74-91, 109-155, 755-814
             are required. Try to read the entire book if possible.
         Mary Evans, "Simone de Beauvoir: Dilemmas of a Feminist Radical,"
             Feminist Theorists, ed. Dale Spender.

Dec. 13 Betty Friedan, The Feminine Mystique
         Margaret Mead, "Sex and Temperament", Feminist Papers, ed.
             A.Rossi.
         **SECOND PAPER DUE IN CLASS

Possible New Directions
Dec. 20 Schulamith Firestone, The Dialectic of Sex
         Carol Gilligan, In a Different Voice

Course Requirements

Careful preparation, attendance, and class participation are the basis for
this course. The reading is heavy, but not undue since the only written
assignments are two brief analytic essays.

Two short, critical papers are also required. (1) The first is to be on a
secondary source. You are to define the author's thesis, examine how
s/he establishes the central argument, and discuss what sorts of evidence
are used to underpin the thesis. (2) The second paper is to be your
presentation of what you believe to be a defensible and livable feminist
theory for today. Each paper is to be between 5-8 pages in length. The
first paper is due on Nov. 1, and the second is due on Dec. 13; both are
due in class. Late papers will be downgraded one grade per day.

Classes will be prepared for and led by students, by a schedule to be
arrived at during the first class meeting.

Oberlin College

ROOTS OF FEMINIST ANALYSIS

History/Women's Studies 319   Carol Lasser
Spring 1986   Rice 313
                                               X8192

    This course explores the historical development of
feminist thought in the United States. Based on close
readings of the classic texts of feminist theory, it traces
the evolution of a cumulative body of thought as well as the
emergence of divergent points of view on "the woman
question." In so doing, it seeks to understand the how
thinkers came to identify and conceptualize key issues in
American feminism including: the nature of difference
between men and woemn; the significance of socially
determined roles; the economic, intellectual and political
status of women; the implications of women's reproductive
capacities; the relationship between women's public and
private lives; and the actions to be taken to overcome
woman's subordinate status.

Format
    The course meets weekly on Tuesdays from 1pm to 3pm for
two hours. By 7:30 pm sharp on Monday evening, each student
is required to submit a "study question" raising an issue
related to the assigned readings for the week; study
questions form the basis for classroom discussion and will
be considered as a factor in assessing class participation.

Books to purchase from the Co-op Bookstore:
        Mary Wollstonecraft, VINDICATION OF THE RIGHTS OF
            WOMAN (Norton Critical Edition)
        Joel Myerson, ed., MARGARET FULLER
        Alice Rossi, ed., ESSAYS ON SEX EQUALITY BY JOHN
            STUART MILL AND HARRIET TAYLOR MILL
        Ellen DuBois, ELIZABETH CADY STANTON/SUSAN B.
            ANTHONY: CORRESPONDENCE, WRITINGS, SPEECHES
        Frederick Engels, ORIGIN OF THE FAMILY, PRIVATE
            PROPERTY AND THE STATE
        Charlotte Perkins Gilman, WOMEN AND ECONOMICS
        Jane Addams, TWENTY YEARS AT HULL HOUSE
        Emma Goldman, ANARCHISM AND OTHER ESSAYS
        Hester Eisenstein, CONTEMPORARY FEMINIST THEORY

    Items to purchase from the instructor:
        Sarah Grimke, LETTERS ON THE EQUALITY OF THE SEXES

        Jane Addams, SELECTED ESSAYS
        Carol Lasser and Marlene Merrill, eds., SOUL

MATES: LETTERS BETWEEN LUCY STONE AND
ANTOINETTE BROWN BLACKWELL, 1846-1850

Schedule of Classes

February 4   Introduction: Defining woman's rights,
feminism, and feminist thought. The relationship of
American feminist thought to the history of the woman's
rights movement.
REQUIRED READING:
    Eleanor Flexner, CENTURY OF STRUGGLE (entire).

February 11   Formulating the Woman Question in Eighteenth-
Century Anglo-America
REQUIRED READING:
    Margaret George, "From 'Goodwife' to 'Mistress:' The
Transformation of the Female in Bourgeois Culture," Science
and Society 37(Summer 1973): 152-177 (on reserve).
    Mary Wollstonecraft, VINDICATION OF THE RIGHTS OF WOMAN
(Norton Critical Edition), pp. 1-193.
FOR FURTHER READING:
    Wollstonecraft, VINDICATION OF THE RIGHTS OF WOMAN
(Norton Critical Edition), pp. 202-234.
    Melissa Butler, "Early Liberal Roots of Feminism: John
Locke and the Attack on Patriarchy," American Political
Science Quarterly 72 (March 1978): 135-150.
    Linda Kerber, WOMEN OF THE EARLY REPUBLIC.

February 18   The Woman Question and American Antislavery
REQUIRED READING:
    "Sarah and Angelina Grimke," NOTABLE AMERICAN WOMEN
II:97-99 (Library Reference Section; Call # CT 3260/ .N57)
    Angelina Grimke, "Appeal to the Christian Women of the
South," in Alice Rossi, ed.,FEMINIST PAPERS, pp. 296-304 (on
reserve).
    "Pastoral Letter," in Rossi, ed., FEMINIST PAPERS, pp.
305-306.
    Sarah Grimke, LETTERS ON THE EQUALITY OF THE SEXES
(entire).
FOR FURTHER READING:
    Gerda Lerner, THE GRIMKE SISTERS FROM SOUTH CAROLINA.
    Blanche Glassman Hersch, THE SLAVERY OF SEX.

February 25   Transcendentalism, American Romanticism, and
the Woman Question: or, What if the "representative man" is
a woman?

REQUIRED READING:
    "Margaret Fuller," NOTABLE AMERICAN WOMEN I:678-682.
    Joel Myerson, ed., MARGARET FULLER, pp. 82-208, 303-310, 367-370, 379-380.
FOR FURTHER READING:
    Myerson, ed., MARGARET FULLER. The following pieces in this collection give some indication of Fuller's commitment to antislavery: "Frederick Douglass," pp. 294-296; "Cassius Clay," pp. 325-328; "Fourth of July," pp. 297-300; and "What Fits a Man to be a Voter?" pp. 362-365. For the range of Fuller's other concerns, see, for example, "The Prevalent Idea that Politeness is too great a Luxury to be given to the Poor," pp. 291-293; "Saint Valentine's Day," pp. pp. 277-281; ""Consecration of Grace Church," pp. 349-351; "Darkness Visible," pp. 338-348. Also notable is the excerpt from SUMMER ON THE LAKES, pp. 62-81.
    Paula Blanchard, MARGARET FULLER: FROM TRANSCENDENTALISM TO REVOLUTION.

March 4   Antebellum women's networks and the solidarity of sisterhood; or, is feminism culture or politics?
REQUIRED READING:
    Carroll Smith-Rosenberg, "The Female World of Love and Ritual," Signs 1 (Autumn 1975): 1-30; or in Carroll Smith-Rosenberg, DISORDERLY CONDUCT, pp. 53-76 (on reserve).
    Carol Lasser and Marlene Merrill, eds., SOUL MATES: LETTERS BETWEEN LUCY STONE AND ANTOINETTE BROWN BLACKWELL, 1846-1850.
    "Lucy Stone," NOTABLE AMERICAN WOMEN III:387-390; and "Antoinette Brown Blackwell, NOTABLE AMERICAN WOMEN I:158-161.
    "Seneca Falls Convention," in Rossi, ed., FEMINIST PAPERS, PP. 413-421.
FOR FURTHER READING:
    Alice Stone Blackwell, LUCY STONE.
    Elizabeth Cazden, ANTOINETTE BROWN BLACKWELL.
    Ellen DuBois, FEMINISM AND SUFFRAGE.

March 11   Classic Liberal Feminism
REQUIRED READING:
    John Stuart Mill and Harriet Taylor Mill, ESSAYS ON SEX EQUALITY (entire).
FOR FURTHER READING:
    Evelyn Pugh, "John Stuart Mill, Harriet Taylor, and Women's Rights in America, 1850-1873," Canadian Journal of

<u>History</u> 13 (October 1978):423-442.
      Zillah Eisenstein, THE RADICAL FUTURE OF LIBERAL
FEMINISM.

March 18   The Great American campaigners: theorists or
activists?
REQUIRED READING:
      Ellen DuBois, ELIZABETH CADY STANTON/ SUSAN B. ANTHONY:
CORRESPONDENCE, WRITINGS, SPEECHES, pp. 9-69; 78-85; 88-124;
139-200; 208-215; 222-254.
FOR FURTHER READING:
      Elisabeth Griffin, ELIZABETH CADY STANTON.
      Alma Lutz, CREATED EQUAL.

April 1   Early Socialist reflections on the woman
question
REQUIRED READING:
      Karl Marx and Frederick Engels, THE COMMUNIST MANIFESTO
(on reserve).
      Frederick Engels, THE ORIGIN OF THE FAMILY, PRIVATE
PROPERTY AND THE STATE, Chapters 1, 2 and 11.
      August Bebel, WOMAN UNDER SOCIALISM/PAST PRESENT AND
FUTURE, Chapter numberings vary; please read chapters
entitled: "Introduction," "Sexual Instinct, Wedlock, Checks
and Obstructions to Marriage," and "Woman's Position as a
Breadwinner, Her Intellectual Faculties Darwinism and the
Condition of Society" (on reserve).
FOR FURTHER READING:
      Karen Sacks, "Engels Revisited," in either Rayna
Reiter, ed., TOWARDS AN ANTHROPOLOGY OF WOMAN or Rosaldo and
Lamphere eds., WOMEN, CULTURE AND SOCIETY.

April 8   American Socialism meets American Feminism
REQUIRED READING:
      "Charlotte Perkins Gilman," NOTABLE AMERICAN WOMEN
II:39-42.
      Charlotte Perkins Gilman, WOMEN AND ECONOMICS (entire).
FOR FURTHER READING:
      Gilman, THE LIVING OF CHARLOTTE PERKINS GILMAN.
      Gilman, THE YELLOW WALLPAPER.
      Edward Bellamy, LOOKING BACKWARD.

APRIL 15   The Progressive Reformer as Feminist activist
and theorist
REQUIRED READING:
      "Jane Addams," NOTABLE AMERICAN WOMEN I:16-22.

Jane Addams, TWENTY YEARS AT HULL HOUSE
Chapters 4-6, 9, 11.
Jane Addams, "Filial Relations," from DEMOCRACY AND
SOCIAL ETHICS (1902) (photocopy collection)
Jane Addams, "Utilization of Women in City Government,"
from NEWER IDEALS OF PEACE (1907) (photocopy collection).
Jane Addams, "A Reveiw of Bread Rations and Woman's
Traditions," and "Personal Reactions In Time of War" from
PEACE AND BREAD IN TIMES OF WAR (1922)

April 22   Feminism and Anarchism: Free Love or Class
Struggle?
REQUIRED READING:
"Emma Goldman," NOTABLE AMERICAN WOMEN II:57-59.
Emma Goldman, ANARCHISM AND OTHER ESSAYS, pp. 41-78 and
167-240.

April 29   The Rebirth of American Feminism: Something
old and something new?
REQUIRED READING:
Alice Rossi, "Equality Between the Sexes: An Immodest
Proposal," in Lifton, ed., THE WOMAN IN AMERICA (1964) (on
reserve).
Zillah Eisenstein, "Developing a Theroy of Capitalist
Patriarchy," in Z. Eisenstein, ed., CAPTIALIST PATRIARCHY
AND THE CASE FOR SOCIALIST FEMINISM, pp. 5-40 (on reserve).
Adrienne Rich, "Compulsory Heterosexuality and Lesbian
Existence," Signs 5 (Summer 1980): 631-660 (on reserve).
Hester Eisenstein, CONTEMPORARY FEMINIST THEORY, pp. 1-
68.

May 6   Motherhood as Womanhood: A new essentialism?
REQUIRED READING:
Sara Ruddick, "Maternal Thinking," Feminist Studies 6
(Summer 1980): 342-367 (on reserve).
Laura Lederer, ed., TAKE BACK THE NIGHT: WOMEN ON
PORNOGRAPHY (selections to be announced) (on reserve).
Deidre English, Amber Hollibaugh and Gayle Rubin,
"Talking Sex: A Conversation on Sexuality and Feminism,"
Socialist Review 58 (July-August 1981): 43-62 (on reserve).
Hester Eisenstein, CONTEMPORARY FEMINIST THOUGHT, pp.
69-145.

Requirements
    Students are required to attend class and to submit
weekly study questions. In addition, students will write
three six to ten page papers.
    All students must submit their first paper due <u>Monday,</u>
<u>March 3</u>. Papers will focus on some aspect of works by Mary
Wollstonecraft, Sarah and Angelina Grimke and Margaret
Fuller. A list of specific paper topics will be distributed
in class on February 18. Students who wish to write on a
topic other than one described in the assignment distibuted
must consult the instructor.
    Students may choose to write any <u>two</u> of the following
three papers on some aspect of works of the authors
generally described below and due on the dates listed;
specific topics will be distributed approximately two weeks
before the papers are due:

> April 1   Lucy Stone, Antoinette Brown Blackwell,
>   John and Harriet Taylor Mill, Elizabeth
>   Cady Stanton, Susan B. Anthony.
> April 28   August Bebel, Frederick Engels,
>   Charlotte Perkins Gilman, Jane Addams
> May 10   Comparison between contemporary feminist
>   thought and at least two nineteenth-
>   century predecessors.

    Students are asked to consider carefully their
interests as well as the timing of their workloads in other
courses in order to select the two papers that will best fit
their schedules and their educational goals. Paper due
dates are firm deadlines; late papers will not receive
comments and will be penalized according to their degree of
lateness.
    Students are encouraged to discuss their papers with
the instructor and/or to submit drafts in order to develop
their thinking and writing skills.
    Papers will be evaluated for both style and content.

Grading
    Class participation and study questions will account
for approximately one-quarter of the final grade. Each
paper will account for one-quarter of the final grade.
Improvement over the course of the semester will be
considered in final evaluation.

University of Pennsylvania

HISTORY / WOMEN"S STUDIES 200.

POWER, GENDER, LANGUAGE AND IDEOLOGY

MAUREEN QUILLIGAN

CARROL SMITH-ROSENBERG

Monday. 9-12, College Hall 204

COURSE DESCRIPTION

In recent years, history and literary criticism have gone through various revolutions; questions of gender and language have become newly central to both. Equally significantly, practitioners of both disciplines now recognize that the techniques of the one are essential to the analysis of the other. Historians, influenced by Hayden White, Michel Foucault, and the new cultural historians, have come to realize that we know the past indirectly, that is, primarily through the stories peoples and groups have told about their experiences, using languages that must remain partial in all the meanings of that word. How can we learn to read those stories? What relationships do those stories have to the social experiences of the tellers? to the languages and ideas those tellers inherited (for we are all the products of our collective pasts)? What can literature teach us about reading those stories and translating the social languages of past cultures?

Literary critics, for their part, have come to realize that their own practice is historically determined, and that through an "ahistorical" method they have only been imposing on past texts a present ideology. How can we learn to read "literature" historically, sensitive to the political function of fiction in past societies? How can we read literary texts as continuous with their social context--and with non-literary texts, with sermons, medical and legal treatises, and political speeches? As

English 998/ Women's Studies 200
Maureen Quilligan/Carroll Smith-Rosenberg

Monday, 9-12, College Hall 204

A graduate seminar in conjunction with the undergraduate
women's studies course in theory. Extra bi-weekly meetings
with graduate students, time to be arranged.

Is there a theory of women's studies? Can there be a theory
able to embrace the various methodological and disciplinary
approaches that have become an integral part of the study of
women's experiences throughout history? What would the language
of this theory look like and what part will contemporary
feminist criticism play in this project? How can Angle-American
critical practice be made to connect to marxist and continental
(French psychoanalytic) theory?

Beginning with a survey of the social function of language as
considered/constructed by socio-linguistics and anthropology,
the course will focus on the interplay between language, gender,
and ideology in the analysis of 19th-century American narratives
about class and gender in selected novels and in some less
"literary" doctuments. After a consideration of the various
theories (Foucault, Bakhtin, Raymond Williams, Barthes) empowering
a reading of the entire cultural "text" (in which literature is
seen as having no special independent status, but as being
an ideologically functioning part of its society), the course
will consider the critical notion of the canon as a construct
that has, until now, disbarred the authority of specifically
female writing and reading. Taking note of Virginia Woolf's
remark that feminism only begins when the middle class woman
begins to write, we will begin to unpack the question of class
in a different register, moving back through time to discover
the problematic construction of the middle class subject in
the representations of gender in selected plays by Shakespeare.
The first term will end with a reading of the first feminist
polemic in western history, <u>The Book of the City of Ladies</u>
by Christine de Pisan, written in 1405, that is, at a moment
when the class organization of the modern state had not yet
had an impact on the gender arrangements against which Christine
writes.

The second term will open with study of contemporary
French feminist theory, move to a consideration of marxist
theory and gender, and end with a segment on the interplay
between class, gender, and race in the Afro-American experience.

both historians and literary critics, how can we read words as simultaneously constructing and reflecting their worlds?

This course, taught by a literary critic and a cultural historian, looks at language as the problematic ground of experience in the disciplines of history, literature, anthropology and socio-linguistics. The specific question about langue the course asks is: what is the function of gender in the construction of discourse and social relations as understood by these various fields? By asking the same question of the different disciplines, the course aims to explore the area shared among them, and ideally to weave from their different methodological strains a set of textual theories on which to base the interdisciplinary work in history, literature and women's studies.

Week 1: Sept. 8.

INTRODUCTION: What are the relations between power, gender and language in the world and in the word?

Week 2: Sept. 15.

AN OUTLINE OF THE PROBLEMATICS.
Socio-linguistics. Dell Hymes.
History. Carroll Smith-Rosenberg.
Literature. Maureen Quilligan.
READING. "Hearing Women's Words" in CSR, Disorderly Conduct.

Week 3: Sept. 22.

SOCIO-LINGUISTICS.
Dell Hymes.

Week 4: Sept. 29.

ANTHROPOLOGY.

Week 5: October 6.

THE PROBLEMATICS OF HISTORY: Class and Gender as Linguistic onstructions of Power in America and England.
Carroll Smith-Rosenberg

READINGS: Barbara Welter, "The Cult of True Womanhood," in Cott and Pleck, ed, A Heritage of Her Own.
CSR, "Female World of Love and Ritual"
"The Cross and the Pedestal"
"The AMA and the Abortion Debate"
"The New Woman as Androgyne"
in Disorderly Conduct,

Mary Poovey. xeroxes of two papers on the construction of gender in 19th century British professional discourse
Judith Walkowitz. "Jack The Ripper's London"

Week 6. Oct. 13.

Yom Kippur. no class. additional readings to be discussed on Week 7.

THE PROBLEMATICS OF HISTORIAL READING: THE MALE CONSTRUCTION OF NATIONALITY -- HEROES AND TRICKSTERS.

John Ward. Andrew Jackson. Symbol of an Age
C.S-R. "Davey Crocket as Trickster" in Disorderly Conduct.

Week 7. Oct. 20.

THE PROBLEMATICS OF HISTORICAL READING. BODY LANGUAGE AND THE CONSTRUCTION OF CLASS
    Carroll Smith-Rosenberg

READINGS: Mrs. Manville. Lucinda, the Mountain Mourner.(microfilm)
            Susanna Rowson, Charlotte Temple
Hannah Foster, The Coquette
            Female Moral Reform Society. Advocate of Moral
                                        Reform(microfilm)
            C.S-R. "Mis-Remembering Richardson" xerox.
unpublished paper.

Week 8. Oct. 27   FALL BREAK -- readings to be discussed week 9

            READINGS. CLASS DEVELOPMENT.
            Mary Ryan. Cradle of the Middle Class, ch 2.
            Sean Willentz. Chants Democratic. selected
chapters.
            Susan Hirsch. selected chapters.

Week 9. Nov. 3

    SOCIAL CON-TEXTS. Class and national identities in The New Nation, America 1790-1850.
    Carroll Smith-Rosenberg.

        REPUBLICAN IDEOLOGY.
            Joyce Appleby, "Republicanism and Ideology"
            Linda Kerber, "Republican Ideology of the
Revolutionary Generation,"
            both in American Quarterly v. 37, Fall,1985.

Week 10. Nov. 10.

    THEORETICAL APPRAOCHES TO READING TEXTUAL CON-TEXTS.

Carroll Smith-Rosenberg.

READINGS. Roland Barthes, "Myth Today," in Mythologies
        M.M. Bakhtin. Dialogic Imagination selected
            chapters.
        Gareth Stedman Jones. "Introduction" in Languages
            of Class

Week 11. Nov. 17.

    FEMINIST LITERARY CRITICISM AND THEORIES OF READING: the
problem of the canon.

        Maureen Quilligan/Sandara Gilbert
        READINGS: Catherine Belsey,Critical Practice
                The New Feminist Criticism, ed. Elaine Showalter
                Lilian S. Robinson, "Treason our Text"
                Annette Kolodny, "A Map for Misreading"
                Sandra Gilbert and Susan Gubar,
                Madwoman in the Attic, Ch. I. Patriarchal Poetics
                Judith Fetterly, The Resisting Reader
                Ruth Kosopfsky Sedwick, Between Men

Week 12. Nov. 24.

    AMERICAN FEMINIST LITERARY CRITICISM AND THEORIES OF
WRITING: opening up the canon.
        Maureen Quilligan
        READINGS: The New Feminist Criticism:
                Jane Tompkins, "Sentimental Power: Uncle Tom's
        Cabin Politics of Literary History."
                Elaine Showalter, "Feminist Criticism in the
Wilderness"
                Nina Baym, Women's Fiction (selections)
                Mary Jacobus, Women Writing (selections)

Week 13. Dec. 1.

    LITERARY CRITICISM AS HISTORICAL PRACTICE: The problem of

periodization.

     Maureen Quilligan/Catherine Belsey

     READINGS: Margaret Ferguson, Maureen Quilligan and Nancy Vickers, "Introduction" to <u>Rewriting the Renaissance</u>

           Catherine Belsey, <u>The Subject of Tragedy</u> (selections)

              Shakespeare, <u>The Taming of the Shrew</u>
                         <u>Othello</u>

Week 14. Dec. 8.

     CHRISTINE DE PIZAN: THE FIRST FEMINIST.
     Maureen Quilligan
     READING: <u>The Book of the City of Ladies</u>

HISTORY 610.

SUPPLEMENTAL READINGS

WEEK 5: OCTOBER 6.

THE PROBLEMATICS OF HISTORY.

additional readings in the history of women and American social
history.

Christine Stansell, City of Women (Rosengarten - page proofs)
Gerda Lerner. Black Women in White America.
plus additional readings in the history of Afro-American women.

WEEK 6: OCT. 13.

J.G.A. Pocock. The Machievellian Moment. Part 3.

WEEK 7; OCT. 20.

Terry Eagleton. The Rape of Clarissa
Terry Castle, Clarissa's Ciphers

WEEK 8: OCT. 27

Victor Turner, Ritual Structures
Gordon Wood, The Creation of the American Republic -- selected chapters
OR
Cathy Davidson, The Origins of American Fiction

WEEK 9: NOV. 3.

Gordon Wood or Davidson -- finished.

261

WEEK 10. NOV. 10.

M.M. Bakhtin. Rablais and His World (selected chapters)

Wayne Booth, "Freedom of Interpretation: Bakhtin and the
Challenge of Feminist Criticism," Critical Inquiry, 9 (1982),
45-72.

WEEK 11. NOV. 17.

Stanley Fish. Is there a Text in this Class?
T.S. Elliot. Traditionals and the Individual Talent
Northrop Frye, Anatomy of Criticism
Walter Jackson Bate, The Burden of the Past and the English Poet
Harold Bloom, A Map of Misreading

WEEK 12. NOV. 24.

Mary Jacobus, Reading Women
Margaret Homans, Women Writers and Poetic Identity
Christine Froula, "When Eve Reads Milton<" Critical Inquiry 10
(1983),321-47.

WEEK 13. DEC 1.

Peter Stallybrass, "Patriarchial Territories " in Rewriting the
Renaissance, ed. Ferguson, Quilligan and Vickers

Joel Fineman," The Turning of the Shrew," in Shakespeare and the
Question of Theory, ed. Parker and Hartmann

Catherine Belsey, essay in Alternative Shakespeare, ed. Finfield.

Joan Kelly, Women, History and Theory, especially "Did Women have
a Renaissance ?"

Ian McClean, The Renaissance Notion of Women

Francis Barker, The Tremulous Private Body

WEEK 14. DEC.7

Jean de Meun. The Romance of the Rose
Boccaccio. On Famous Women

Religion 65-1
Spring, 1987
Carleton College

Ann Braude
Leighton 321, x4229
Office Hours: M 4:30-5:30
Th 2-3:30

WOMEN IN AMERICAN RELIGIOUS HISTORY

Required Texts:
  Patricia Hill, The World Their Household
  Marla Powers, Oglala Women: Myth, Ritual and Reality
  Janet James, Women in American Religion
  Marabel Morgan, The Total Woman
  Nelle Morton, The Journey is Home
  Elizabeth Stuart Phelps, The Gates Ajar

Recommended Texts:
  Rosemary Ruether and Rosemary Keller, Women and Religion in America:
      Volume I, The Nineteenth Century
  Rosemary Ruether and Rosemary Keller, Women and Religion in America:
      Volume III, The Twentieth Century
  Carroll Smith-Rosenberg, Disorderly Conduct: Visions of Gender in
      Victorian America

INTRODUCTION TO WOMEN'S HISTORY

  March 31 T   Introduction

  April 2 Th Smith-Rosenberg, "Hearing Women's Words: A Feminist
                Reconstruction of History"
              Gloria Hull and Barbara Smith,"The Politics of Black
                Women's Studies," in Hull, Scott and Smith, But Some of
                Us Are Brave.

WHO GOES TO CHURCH?

  April 7 T Mary Maples Dunn, "Saints and Sisters: Congregational and
                Quaker Women in the Early Colonial Period"
              Gerald F. Moran, "Sisters In Christ: Women and the Church in
                Seventeenth-Century New England"
              Mary P. Ryan, "A Woman's Awakening: Evangelical Religion and
                the Families of Utica, New York, 1800-1840.
              Mary J. Oakes, "Catholic Sisters in Massachusetts"
              [All in James]

PIETY AND FEMININITY IN AMERICAN CULTURE

April 9 Th Barbara Welter, "The Cult of True Womanhood," (in <u>Dimnity</u>
            <u>Convictions</u>, on reserve).
            Nancy Cott "Passionlessness," (in <u>A</u> <u>Heritage</u> <u>of</u> <u>Her</u> <u>Own</u>, on
            reserve)
            "The Marian Century" in (Atkinson, Buchanan, Miles,
            <u>Immaculate</u> <u>and</u> <u>Powerful</u>, on reserve)
            Rosemary Ruether, "The Cult of True Womanhood," <u>Commonweal</u>,
            XCIX (1973).

April 14 T NO CLASS -- PASSOVER

April 16 Th Elizabeth Stuart Phelps, <u>The</u> <u>Gates</u> <u>Ajar</u>.

WOMEN IN RELIGIOUS LEADERSHIP

April 21 T Jean McMahon Humez, <u>Gifts</u> <u>of</u> <u>Power</u>: <u>The</u> <u>Writings</u> <u>of</u> <u>Rebecca</u>
            <u>Jackson</u>, <u>Black</u> <u>Visionary</u>, <u>Shaker</u> <u>Eldress</u>, Introduction.
            Ann Braude, "Spirits Defend the Rights of Women," (in
            Haddad and Findlay, <u>Women</u>, <u>Religion</u>, <u>and</u> <u>Social</u> <u>Change</u>,
            on reserve)

April 23 Th Smith-Rosenberg, "The Cross and the Pedestal,"
            Ruether, "Women in Utopian Movements," (Ruether, V.I);
            Mary Farrell Bednarowski, "Outside the Mainstream: Women's
            Religion and Women's Leadership in Nineteenth-Century
            America," <u>JAAR</u>, 48 (1980), 207-231.
            *Paper topics due.

April 28 T Patricia Hill, <u>The</u> <u>World</u> <u>Their</u> <u>Household</u>, chs. 1-3

April 30 Th Patricia Hill, <u>The</u> <u>World</u> <u>Their</u> <u>Household</u>, chs. 3-6

WOMEN AND CULTURAL CONFLICT AND CONTINUITY

May 5   T Marla Powers, <u>Oglala</u> <u>Women</u>, chs. 1-6

May 7   Th Marla Powers, <u>Oglala</u> <u>Women</u>, chs. 7-12

May 12 T Norma Fain Pratt, "Transitions in Judaism," (James)
           Ann Braude, "Jewish Women's Encounter With American
           Culture," (Ruether, V.I)
           Ann Braude, "Jewish Women in the Twentieth Century,"
           (Ruether, V.III)

May 14 Th Robert Anthony Orsi, <u>The</u> <u>Madonna</u> <u>of</u> <u>115th</u> <u>Street</u>, excerpts
           (on reserve)

THE FEMINIST CRITIQUE OF THE CHURCHES AND THE RELIGIOUS CRITIQUE OF
    FEMINISM

    May 19   T   Marabel Morgan, The Total Woman

    May 21   TH   Matilda Joslyn Gage, Woman Church and State, excerpts (on
                   reserve)

    May 26   T   Nelle Morton, The Journey is Home

    May 28   Th   Nelle Morton, The Journey is Home

    June 2   T   Conclusion

Course Requirements

This class will be taught on a seminar format, so careful reading of all
assignmnets and readiness to participate in a critical discussion of the
texts are essential.

Each student will pursue a research topic throughout the term, and will
report on the project at several stages.

   One page description of the topic with bibliography, due on April 23.

   Oral presentation of research topic and preliminary findings in class.
      Presentations will be scheduled at appropriate points in the term.

   Fifteen page paper due June 2. Students have the option to submit a
      first draft for comment, before writing the final version of the
      paper. First drafts are due May 19.

Discussion Leading: Each student will make a brief oral presentation on
the assigned readings for one class, and help lead that day's discussion.
A one-page, typed outline of the presentation should be handed in by noon
the day before the presentation.

Cheryl Greenberg
Trinity College

Out of the Mainstream: Subcultures in American History

This seminar focuses on the ways in which men and women of different non-"mainstream" groups dealt with pressures to assimilate into American white Protestant middle class culture.

American history, typically, centers around great events, chronologically presented. When blacks, women, the poor, immigrants, or other groups are studied, these courses follow similar patterns, focusing on great events of importance to the group being examined. These courses further assume a one-way path of cultural transmission or transformation: that is, that American culture affected these minority groups, but they did not affect culture. The melting pot theory of the early 20th century posited a new blend of American, but the emphasis remained on white middle class norms becoming all-pervasive. Only recently have scholars begun to examine the impact of minority groups on mainstream culture itself. Subcultures, groups which retain a certain amount of cultural autonomy, alter existing cultural norms or expectations to fit better with their own attitudes and beliefs; this has only recently become the subject of serious scholarly examination. Only recently has it been accepted that not all non-mainstream groups necessarily sought to join the general society and adopt all its values completely.

This course seeks to broaden our understanding of this phenomenon of cultural interaction and ambivalent assimilation by examining it through the lens of yet another distinction, that of gender. The study of women thus far has offered historians a new vision of past family life, and placed women back into our historical understanding. Studying history through the perspective of women's concerns has in some cases even altered our sense of periodization, or at least called into question the equal relevance of that periodization for everyone living at the time. For example, Jacksonian democracy, the pivotal change of the early nineteenth century, seems less significant a change to women, who did not vote, than other changes occurring in family structure and social ideology, such as the emergence of the cult of true womanhood and women's expanded role within the sphere of domestic life. (Every non-mainstream group offers us a new perspective on traditional history in a similar way of course. Jacksonian democracy did not affect blacks, to take another group, as much as did the invention of the cotton gin and the closing of the slave trade.)

Women's history, however, can also teach us much about mainstream history. The study of women is also the study of limits -- to what lengths will a society allow its members to go, before declaring their behavior somehow inappropriate? Women as a group (also racial and ethnic groups, "deviants," children, or the poor), with sharply defined but often marginal roles, are a perfect test of social limits. When women stray too far from prescribed roles, they are punished, thus making visible the boundaries of acceptable social life.

The study of women can also offer new insights into the understanding of subcultures. Immigrants, blacks, workers, and other groups generally seen as monolithic subcultures consisted of both men and women who ordinarily have different roles from each other. Yet the different gender roles within each group affect the ways in which individuals view mainstream society and adapt to it. For example, if a particular group advocates a role for women at home, then those women will have a different sense of outside culture than will their men who interact more directly in that outside culture. Thus contrasting the views of both men and women toward mainstream culture can be a useful and instructive way to better understand the dynamics of adaptation.

Further, gender itself implies the possibility of a subculture. This female culture can be no more monolithic than any other, and can also be approached through contrast, this time by the race and class differences among women.

Thus the course will consist of three parts: women as definers of social boundaries; the view of mainstream society by women of different subcultures (labor, immigrants, American Indians) and class; and racial differences in women's subcultures (suburban experience by class, women's and family life by race).

This course is designed topically, with most units spanning several time periods. This is not to negate chronology, but to recognize the similarity of issues facing women from different subcultures in different times.

Units and Readings

1. Deviance and the Puritans:
    This unit examines the ways in which women's experience highlighted the limits of the Puritan social order, focusing specifically on the Puritan family, witchcraft, and antinomianism.

Readings:
Puritan women's roles: Laurel Ulrich, Good Wives
Witchcraft: Paul Boyer and Stephen Nissenbaum, Salem Possessed
Antinomianism: The trial record and testimony of Anne Hutchinson
    Lyle Koehler, "The Case of the American Jezebels: Anne
        Hutchinson and Female Agitation during the Years of
        Antinomian Turmoil, 1636-1640,"
Women as Defining Limits: Kai Erikson, Wayward Puritans
    David Stannard, The Puritan Way of Death
    Nancy Cott, "Divorce and The Changing Status of Women"

2. American Indians and responses to assimilation pressures -- the Sioux as case study:
    The Sioux Indians faced extensive pressures to Americanize, and to become Christian in the nineteenth century. They responded by dividing into two factions, the Christian, and the "resisters" who supported a messianic religion called the Ghost Dance in the 1880s (which led to the Wounded Knee Massacre). Do men's and women's different views on the question of the Ghost Dance and on the prospect of assimilation tell us anything new about these strains on Indian communities?

Readings:
Overall view: James Mooney, The Ghost Dance Religion and the
    Sioux Outbreak of 1890
A Male view: Charles Eastman, From the Deep Woods to
    Civilization: Chapters in the Autobiography of an Indian
A Female View: Kay Graber, ed., Sister to the Sioux: The Memoirs
    of Elaine Goodale Eastman, 1885-91 (please note both chose
    the side of the Christians. There are no women's accounts
    from the side of the Ghost Dancers.)

3. Immigrants and assimilation:
    Given the different employment patterns, traditional
expectations, and American social pressures on immigrant men and
women, how did the view of assimilation and of culture differ
between the two sexes?

Readings:
The Jews:
    Male: Abraham Cahan, Yekl, The Imported Bridegroom, and
        Other Tales (you might also want to read The Rise of
        David Levinsky)
    Female: Anzia Yezerskia, Hungry Hearts (you might also want
        to read Bread Givers)
The Poles:
    Letters to and from immigrants in William Thomas and Florian
    Znaniecki, The Polish Peasant in America, pp. 712-791.
The Chinese:
    Maxine Hong Kingston, Woman Warrior, China Man

Some historical analyses of immigrant women, as contrast
(recommended):
Irish:
    Hasia Diner, Erin's Daughters in America
Italians:
    Virginia Yans-McLaughlin, Family and Community: Italian
        Immigrants in Buffalo 1880-1930

4. Labor:
    The gender split in employment is nowhere more pronounced
than in the lower classes. This unit examines the different
patterns of work and expectations about work for men and women at
three points in time: the transition from women to immigrant
labor at the Lowell Mills, the emergence of the Women's Trade
Union League in New York, and the labor market's division by
gender in the Great Depression.

Readings:
Thomas Dublin, Women at Work
"Rules and Regulations, Poignaud and Plant Boarding House, Lowell
    Manufacturing Company," in Rosalyn Baxandall, Linda Gordon,
    Susan Reverby, eds., America's Working Women
Nancy Schrom Dye, As Equals and As Sisters

Dorothy Richardson, <u>The Long Day</u>: <u>The Story of a New York Working Girl</u> (reprinted in William O'Neill, ed., <u>Women at Work</u>)
Leon Stein, ed., <u>Out of the Sweatshop</u> (selections)
Ruth Milkman, "Women's Work and the Economic Crisis"

5. Women's culture in the suburbs:
   The postwar flight to the suburbs solidified and intensified a divergence in roles, expectations, and desires of the men and women who lived there. In this unit we focus specifically on women's lives, using class as a further division.

Readings:
Betty Friedan, <u>The Feminine Mystique</u>
Marilyn French, <u>The Women's Room</u> (early chapters)
Lillian Rubin, <u>Worlds of Pain</u>
Herbert Gans, <u>The Levittowners</u>
Nancy Rubin, <u>The New Suburban Woman</u>

6. Black women as a subset of women's culture:
   Women in slavery, freed black women in the north and the south, and contemporary black women did (and do) not have the same concerns as white women. How are their lives and their concerns different, and how can an understanding of their experience expand our vision of women's culture, women's lives?

Readings:
Jacqueline Jones, <u>Labor of Love, Labor of Sorrow</u>
Dorothy Sterling, ed., <u>We Are Your Sisters</u> (selections)
Hull, Scott, and Smith, <u>All the Women Are White, All the Blacks Are Men, But Some of Us Are Brave</u> (selections)
Zora Neale Hurston, <u>Their Eyes Were Watching God</u>
Carol Stack, <u>All Our Kin</u>

Indiana University

WOMEN AND THE CONSTITUTION

H750   Prof. Joan Hoff-Wilson

This seminar will explore the historical developments surrounding
changes in the legal status of women from the colonial period to the present.
Particular attention will be paid to historical circumstances prompting women
reformers to place various degrees of emphasis on achieving equality through
equity procedures, litigation (concentrating on major Supreme Court
decisions), amendments to the constitution, and public policy legislation.
Thus, the following legal topics will be placed in historical perspective:
equity jurisprudence, dower rights, Married Women's Property Acts, legal
actions brought by members of the First Women's Movement, protective
legislation, treatment of rape victims, decisions involving professional and
working women, suffrage, the Fourteenth Amendment, equal pay, Titles VI, VII
and IX, divorce and family law, legal views on contraception and abortion,
the ERA, comparable worth, pregnancy benefits, sexual harassment on the job,
pornography, and special versus equal rights.

Background Readings:

The concentrated nature of this seminar requires a certain amount
of background reading. This is particularly true for
understanding the ways in which women's legal status has changed
over time; the ways in which women's views of rights and justice
differ from men's; and the ways in which scholars have written
about the general constitutional neglect which women have
experienced until the last twenty years. The following readings
provide the essentials of this historical background (and if
possible, should be read in the order listed). Specific
assignments from other texts, casebooks and journals listed below
will be designated later in the semester.

Richard B. Morris, Studies in the History of American Law
    (Octagon reprint, 1974), pp. iii-xiii; 9-68, 126-200.

George L. Haskins, "Reception of the Common Law in Seventeenth-
    Century Massachusetts: Case Study (of Dower Rights)," in
    George Athan Billias, ed., Selected Essays: Law and
    Authority in Colonial America (Barre, Mass.: Barre
    Publishers, 1965), pp. 17-31.

Mary R. Beard, Woman as Force in History (Macmillan, 1946), pp.
    7-19, 77-169. If you use the 1962 Collier paperback edition
    the pages are 13-30, 87-180.

D. Kelly Weisberg, Women and the Law: A Social Historical
    Perspective Volume II, Part IV (Schenkman Publishing
    Company, Inc., 1982), pp. 95-155.

Linda Kerber, Women of the Republic (University of North Carolina
    Press, 1980), pp. 139-184.

Joan Hoff-Wilson, "'Hidden Riches': Colonial Legal Records and
    Women" in Woman's Being, Woman's Place: Female Identity and
    Vocation in American History edited by Mary Kelley (G.K.
    Hall, 1979), pp. 7-25.

Abbie Sachs and Joan Hoff-Wilson, Sexism and the Law (Free
    Press, 1979), pp. 67-132.

Marylynn Salmon, "Equality or Submersion? Feme Covert Status in
    Early Pennsylvania," in Women of America: A History edited
    by Carol Ruth Berkin and Mary Beth Norton (Houghton
    Mifflin, 1979), pp. 92-113; idem, "'Life, Liberty, and
    Dower': The Legal Status of Women After the American
    Revolution," in Women, War and Revolution edited by Carol
    Ruth Berkin and Clara Lovett (Homes and Meier, 1979); idem,
    "Women and Property in South Carolina: Evidence from
    Marriage Settlements, 1730-1830," William and Mary

271

Quarterly, 3rd Series, 39 (October 1982): 655-85; "The
Legal Status of Women in Early America: A Reappraisal," Law
and History Review (1983): 129-151.

Susanne D. Lebsock, "Radical Reconstruction and the Property
Rights of Southern Women," Journal of Southern History 43
(May 1977): 195-216; The Free Women of Petersburg
(Norton, 1984), pp. xiii-xx, 15-145, 237-49.

Peggy Rabkin, Fathers to Daughters: The Legal Foundations of
Female Emancipation (Greenwood, 1980); or idem, "The
Origins of Law Reform: The Social Significance of the
Nineteenth-Century Codification Movement and Its
Contribution to the Passage of Early Married Women's
Property Acts," Buffalo Law Review 24 (Spring 1975): 683-
760.

Norma Basch, In the Eyes of the Law: Women, Marriage, and
Property in Nineteenth-Century New York (Cornell University
Press, 1982); and idem, "Invisible Women: The Legal
Fiction of Marital Unity in Nineteenth-Century America,"
Feminist Studies 5 (Summer 1979): 346-66.

D. Kelly Weisberg, Women and the Law: A Social Historical
Perspective Volume II, Part V (Schenkman Publishing
Company, Inc., 1982), pp. 227-283.

Marlene Wortman, editor, Women and American Law: From Colonial
Times to New Deal (Holmes and Meier, Fall, 1986).
Collection of legal documents and excerpts from Supreme
Court cases.

Carol Gilligan, In a Different Voice: Psychological Theory and
Women's Development (Harvard University Press, 1982), pp. 1-
23, 64-74, 128-174; and idem, "Women's Different Voice; the
ethic of Care," Radcliffe Quarterly 68, no. 3 (September
1982): 6-7.

Textbooks and Monographs:

Judith A. Baer, The Chains of Protection: The Judicial Response
to Women's Labor Legislation (Westport, Connecticut:
Greenwood Press, 1978); idem, Equality Under the
Constitution: Reclaiming the Fourteenth Amendment (Ithaca:
Cornell University Press, 1983).

Susan Becker, The Origins of the Equal Rights Amendment; American
Feminism Between the Wars (Westport, Connecticut: Greenwood
Press, 1981).

**Margaret A. Berger, <u>Litigation on Behalf of Women</u> (Ford Foundation, 1980).

Mary Frances Berry, <u>The Defeat of the ERA</u> (Indiana University Press, 1987).

Eve Cary and Kathleen Willert Peratis, <u>Woman and the Law</u> (National Textbook Company, 1977).

Leslie Frieman Goldstein, <u>The Constitutional Rights of Women</u> (Longman, 1979).

Joan Hoff-Wilson, <u>Rights of Passage: The Past and Future of the ERA</u> (Indiana University Press, 1986).

Albie Sachs and Joan Hoff-Wilson, <u>Sexism and the Law</u> (Free Press, 1979), pp. 147-167; 210-232. (An updated appendix of recent Supreme Court decisions through 1986 will be provided in class.)

<u>Forthcoming Texts</u>:

Joan Hoff-Wilson, <u>Balancing the Scales: Changing Legal Status of American Women From the Colonial Period to the Present</u> (Indiana University Press, Winter 1987).

Z. I. Giraldo, editor, <u>Women and American Law: New Deal to the Present</u> (Holmes and Meier, forthcoming). Collection of legal documents and excerpts from Supreme Court cases.

<u>Casebooks</u> (latest editions):

Kenneth M. Davidson, Ruth Bader Ginsburg, and Herma Hill Kay, <u>Text, Cases and Materials on Sex-Based Discrimination</u> (West Publishing Co., with 1983 supplement).

Barbara Allen Babcock, Ann E. Freedman, Eleanor Holmes Norton, and Susan C. Ross, <u>Sex Discrimination and the Law: Causes and Remedies</u> (Little, Brown and Company, with supplement).

<u>Journals</u>:

<u>Women Law Reporter</u>, a bimonthly legal service.

<u>Women Lawyers' Journal</u>, published by the National Association of Women Lawyers.

<u>Women's Newsletter</u>, published by National Lawyers' Guild.

<u>Women's Rights Law Reporter</u>, quarterly published by Rutgers Law School.

**Individual copies can be ordered directly from the Ford Foundation for $4.00.

University of Iowa
Graduate Colloquium
History 16:287

Professor Linda K. Kerber

"Why Should Girls Be Learn'd and Wise?"

The Capacities of Women's Minds

> And why should girls be learn'd or wise,
> Books only serve to spoil their eyes.
> The studious eye but faintly twinkles
> And reading paves the way to wrinkles.
>
> --John Trumbull

The history of women's education is usually treated as a
species of social history. But much of the debate over the
appropriate forms of women's education also involved taking a
position on whether women's minds were fit for the rigors of
intellectual discipline. This course is a venture in
intellectual history as well as social history; an exploration
of ideas about the capacities of women's minds as well as a
review of the institutional settings in which these minds were
nurtured.

I regret to report that there is no succinct and reliable
history of women's education in America that covers elementary,
secondary and collegiate levels; those books that claim to be
general surveys give little attention to women. We will need to
construct our own from a wide variety of sources. Thomas Woody,
A History of Women's Education in the United States (1929) has
been placed on reserve. Happily, the recent publication of
Barbara Miller Solomon, In The Company of Educated Women: A
History of Women and Higher Education in America provides a rich
account of the history of higher education; that has been placed
on reserve and is available in the bookstore. It is a basic
text.

I.   Introductory

274

II. The Social Implications of Literacy

Thomas Wentworth Higginson, "Ought Women to Learn the Alphabet?" in _Women and the Alphabet_

Walter J. Ong, "Latin Language Study as a Renaissance Puberty Rite, " in _Rhetoric, Romance, and Technology_

Lawrence Stone, "Education and Literacy in England, 1600 - 1900," in _Past and Present_

Kenneth Lockridge, _Literacy in Colonial New England_

Linda Auwers, "The Social Meaning of Female Literacy: Windsor, Connecticut, 1660-1775," _Historical Methods Newsletter_

II. Anne Hutchinson as Cautionary Case

Emery Battis, _Saints and Sectaries_

David Hall, ed., _The Antinomian Controversy_

Lyle Koehler, "The Case of the American Jezebels, " _Wm. and Mary Quart._ Jan. 1974 or chapter on Hutchinson in _The Search for Power_

Mary Maples Dunn, "Saints and Sisters," _American Quarterly,_ 1978.

III and IV . The Revolutionary Era: The Political implications of Reading and Education

Rousseau, _Emile_, Part IV

Mary Wollstonecraft, _Vindication of the Rights of Woman_ [preferably Penguin edition with introduction by Miriam Kramnick]

Charles Brockden Brown, _Alcuin_

Linda K. Kerber, _Women of the Republic_, chapters 7, 8, 9

Benjamin Rush, "Thoughts on Female Education"

Maria Edgeworth **Letters for Literary Ladies,** (1810) Readex Microcard

V. The Early Republic: The Transformation of Educational Institutions

Anne Firor Scott, "What, Then, is the American: This New Woman?" _Jnl Am Hist,_ Dec. 1978, pp. 679-703

Anne Firor Scott, "The Ever Widening Circle: The Diffusion of Feminist Values," _History of Education Quarterly,_ (1979)

Emma Willard, _An Address to the Public_ (1819)

Kathryn Kish Sklar, _Catharine Beecher_

Maris Vinovskis and Richard Bernard, "The Female School Teacher in Antebellum Massachusetts," _Jnl Soc Hist_ X (1977) 332-345.

Maris Vinovskis and Richard Bernard, "Beyond Catharine Beecher: Female Education in the Antebellum Period," _Signs_ III (1978) 856-869

VI. The Mind at Work

Susan Conrad, _Perish the Thought: Intellectual Women in Romantic America_

Margaret Fuller, _Woman in the Nineteenth Century_

Gale Bell Chevigny, _Margaret Fuller_

Read as much as you can in Robert Hudspeth, ed. _The Letters of Margaret Fuller_

VII and VIII The Capacities of Women's Minds: The Invention of Higher Education for Women

Helen Thompson, _The Mental Traits of Sex_ (1903)

Edward Clarke, _Sex and Education_

Ronald Hogeland, "Coeducation of the Sexes at Oberlin College," _Jnl of Social History_ VI (1972-73) 160-176

Robert Belding, "Iowa's Brave Model for Women's Education," Annals of Iowa 43 (1976) 342-48

E. S. Eppright and E. Ferguson, A Century of Home Economics at Iowa State University, chs. 1 and 2

Annie Nathan Meyer, Barnard Beginnings

Rosalind Rosenberg, Beyond Separate Spheres

Margaret Rossiter, Women Scientists in America

Helen Horowitz, Alma Mater: Design and Experience in Women's Colleges

Regina Morantz-Sanchez, Sympathy and Science: Women Physicians in America

Dolores Hayden, The Grand Domestic Revolution

Margaret Rossiter, "Doctorates for American Women, 1868-1907," History of Higher Education Quarterly, vol. 22 (1982) 159-183.

Myra Strober and David Tyack, "Why Do Women Teach and Men Manage? A Report on Research on Schools," Signs V (1980) 494-503

Myra Strober and Audri Lanford, "The Feminization of Public School Teaching," Signs XI (1986) 212-235

IX. Expansion and Exclusion

Patricia Albjerg Graham, "Expansion and Exclusion: A History of Women in American Higher Education," Signs III (1978) 759-773

H. L. Mencken, In Defense of Women (1928)

Mary Church Terrell, A Colored Woman in a White World (1940)

Patricia Palmieri, "In Adamless Eden," unpublished Ph.D. dissertation, Harvard University [on Wellesley]

Joyce Antler, unpublished dissertation on Lucy Sprague
Mitchell.

Paula Fass, The Damned and the Beautiful: American Youth
in the 1920's (1920)

M. Elizabeth Tidball, "Women's Colleges and Women Achievers
Revisited," Signs V (1980) 504-517.

X. The Implications of Progressive Education

JoAnn Boydston, "John Dewey and the New Feminism,"
Teachers College Record, 76 (1975) 441-444.

Sari Knopp Biklen, "The Progressive Education Movement and
the Question of Women," Teachers College Record, 80 (1978)
316-335

Constance Warren, A New Design for Women's Education (1940
-- Sarah Lawrence]

Helen Horowitz, Alma Mater, part IV.

XI. The Intellectual and the Institution

Margaret Mead, Blackberry Winter

Margaret Mead, An Anthropologist at Work: THe Writings of
Ruth Benedict (19959)

XII. Rethinking Higher Education for Women 1950 - 1975

Lynn White, Educating Our Daughters, (1950)

Mirra Komarovsky, Women in the Modern World: The Education
and Their Dilemmas (1953)

Adlai Stevenson, "Commencement Address at SMith College,"
1955

WEEK EIGHT: THE WOMAN SUFFRAGE MOVEMENT
(Feb. 26)
    Required Reading:

        (1) Elinor Lerner, "Immigrant and Working Class
Involvement in the New York City Woman Suffrage Movement,
1905-1917: A Study in Progressive Era Politics," Unpub. PhD
Diss., UC, Berkeley, 1981.

        (2) Paula Baker, "The Domestication of
Politics: Women and American Political Society, 1780-1920,"
American Historical Review, Vol. 89, #3 (1984).

        (3) Sharon Hartman Strom, "Leadership and
Tactics in the American Woman Suffrage Movement: A New
Perspective from Massachusetts," Journal of Amer. History,
Vol. 62, No. 2, (Sept. 1975).

        (4) Rosalyn Terborg-Penn, "Black women in the
Woman Suffrage Movement," in Sharon Harley & Rosalyn Terborg
Penn, eds., The Afro-American Woman: Struggles and Images
(1978)

        (5) William O'Neill, Everyone Was Brave: A
History of Feminism in America (1969), chapters 3-5.

Also Recommended:

Eleanor Flexner, Century of Struggle: The Woman's Rights
Movement in the United States (1959), chapters 16, 17, 19-24

Aileen Kraditor, The Ideas of the Woman Suffrage Movement,
1890-1920 (1965), chapters 5-9.

Linda Claire Steiner, "The Women's Suffrage Press, 1850-
1900: A Cultural Analysis," Unpub. PhD. Diss., U. of Ill,
Urbana, 1979.

Frances Sizemore Hensley, "Change and Continuity in the
American Women's Movement, 1848-1930: A National and State
Perspective," Unpub. PhD. Diss, Ohio State U., 1981.

Linda G. Ford, "American Militants: An Analysis of the
National Woman's Party, 1913-1919," Unpub. PhD. diss.
Syracuse University, (1984.)

WEEK NINE: AFTER SUFFRAGE
(Mar. 5)
          Required Reading:

          (1) J. Stanley Lemons, The Woman Citizen:
Social Feminism in the 1920's (1973)

          (2) O'Neill, Everyone Was Brave, chapter 8.

          (3)   Nancy F. Cott, "Feminist Politics in the
1920's: The National Woman's Party," Journal of American
History, Vol. 71, #1 (June 1984).

          (4)   Kathryn Kish Sklar, "Why Were Most
Politically-Active Women Opposed to the ERA in the 1920's?"
Joan Hoff Wilson, ed.,   Rights of Passage: The Past and
Future of the ERA (1986).

Also Recommended:

Felice D. Gordon, After Winning: The Legacy of the New
Jersey Suffragists, 1920-1947 (1986)

Willie Mae Coleman, "Keeping the Faith and Disturbing the
Peace: Black Women from Anti-Slavery to Women's Suffrage,"
Unpub. PhD Diss., UC Irvine, (1982)

WEEK TEN: THE 1930'S
(Mar. 12)
          Required Reading:

          (1) Susan Ware: Beyond Suffrage: Women in the
New Deal (1981)

          (2) Jacqueline Dowd Hall, Revolt Against
Chivary: Jessie Daniel Ames and the Women's Campaign
Against Lynching (1979).

Jan 22, 24   THE HISTORICAL TRADITION:
                       DEBORAH, HELEN, CLEOPATRA

               Begin reading John Keegan, The Face of Battle
               Documents: "Song of Deborah" Book of Judges, 5

Jan 29, 31   THE CLASSICAL INHERITANCE
                       IMAGES OF WOMEN IN HISTORY AND MYTH

               Aristophanes, Lysistrata

               Recommended: Antigone [on reserve]

Feb 5, 7   MEDIEVAL AND EARLY MODERN EUROPE;
                       PATRIARCHY AND HIERARCHY

               Christine de Pizan, The City of Ladies
               Documents: "The Trial of Jeanne d'Arc"
                                   ed. W. P. Bennett, 1931

               Recommended: B. Brecht, Mother Courage
               Barton Hacker, "Women and Military Institutions in
               Early Modern Europe: A Reconnaissance, Signs, VI
               (1981) 643-671

               THE AGE OF THE DEMOCRATIC REVOLUTION:

Feb 12   (1)   THE AMERICAN REVOLUTION

               Linda K. Kerber, Women of the Republic, chs. 2, 3
                       4 [on reserve]
               Documents: "The Sentiments of An American Woman"
                                   (1780)
                                   "The Petition of Rachel Wells" (1786)

Feb. 19,21   (2)   THE FRENCH REVOLUTION:
                                   REPUBLICAINES-REVOLUTIONNAIRES

               Darline Levy et al, Women in Revolutionary Paris

Feb 26, 28   NINETEENTH-CENTURY CONFLICTS:

               (1) THE AMERICAN CIVIL WAR

Documents: selections from S. Emma E. Edmonds,
Nurse and Spy in the Union Army; Annie Wittenmyer,
Under the Guns; Dorothy Sterling, ed. We Are Your
Sisters: Black Women in the 19th Century, chs. 14
& 15

(2)   VICTORIAN ARMIES

Document: "Unjustly accused of prostitution," in
Hellerstein, Hume and Offen, eds., Victorian
Women, pp. 423-428

(3)   THE INDIAN MUTINY: THE RANI OF JHANSI
      Guest Lecture: Dr. Sandra Barkan

March 7:   Mid-term examination

March 12, 14   WORLD WAR I:

                (1)   THE WOMEN'S WAR AND THE MEN'S WAR

                Vera Brittain, Testament of Youth

March 19   (2)   WORLD WAR I PROPAGANDA POSTERS
                      Guest Lecture: Professor Alan Spitzer
                      Meet at State Historical Society

March 21   (3)   WOMEN AND PEACE MOVEMENTS

                Document: Kate Richards O'Hare,   "Socialism and
                the World War," in Kate Richards O'Hare: Selected
                Writings and Speeches, ed. Phillip Foner & Sally
                Miller, (1982) 121-181

March 22-30   Spring Vacation

April 2   THE RUSSIAN REVOLUTION
                    SOCIALISM AND FEMINISM

                   Guest Lecture: Ms. Marcelline Hutton

               Documents: Alexy Tolstoy, "The Viper" [short story]; Barbara E. Clements, "Working Class and Peasant Women in the Russian Revolution," Signs, VIII (1982) 215-235

April 4,
9, 11   WORLD WAR II:

               (1)   FREEDOM, DEMOCRACY, AND FASCISM

               Rupp, Mobilizing Women for War
               Documents: Selections from House and Senate Hearings establishing the Women's Auxiliary Army Corps, 1942, 1943

               (2) Two films will be shown on the evening of April 11; please plan your schedules accordingly:

                    Rosie the Riveter
                    Silver Wings and Santiago Blue

April 16   (3)   WOMEN AND THE HOLOCAUST

               Documents: Sybil Milton, "Women and the Holocaust," in Bridenthal, Kaplan, Grossmann, eds., When Biology Became Destiny, (1984) 297-333.

April 18   MODERN WARS OF NATIONAL LIBERATION: ALGERIA

               Document: Interview with Jamilah Buhrayd, in Fernea & Bezirgan, eds., Middle Eastern Women Speak, (1977) 249-262.

April 23   LIBERATION AND PROTEST MOVEMENTS: SOUTH AFRICA

               Guest Lecture: Dr. Sandra Barkan

April 25   CONTEMPORARY DEBATE ON WOMEN AND WAR

            Guest Lecture: Professor Martha Chamallas, College
            of Law

            Documents: Rostker v. Goldberg (1981) 101 S. Ct
            2541 in Herma Hill Kay, et al, Sex Based
            Discrimination pp. 14-26; 1015-1039; William
            Broyles, Jr. "Why Men Love War," Esquire,
            Nov. 1984, pp. 55-63.

May 2   Selected Student Reports:

            [in 1985, the most distinguished students reports
            were on "Joan of Arc in Children's Books," "The
            Image of Women in World War II Popular Film,"
            "U.S. Army Policy toward Gay Men and Lesbians
            During and After World War II."

            Other subjects for term papers included: "Women
            and War in Shakespeare: Coriolanus, Antony and
            Cleopatra, The History Plays," "Women in the
            Paris Commune," "The Career of Clara Barton,"
            "Women in the French Resistance in World War II,"
            "The Career of Golda Meir," "Women in the Israeli
            Army," "Women in the Chinese Revolution."

May 7   TENTATIVE CONCLUSIONS

University of California, Davis

Fall Quarter 1981   Th 1:00-4:00
History 102M

Professor Ruth Rosen
377 Voorhies
Office Hours: T: 4:00-4:45
                Th: 3:30-4:45   and by appointment on Mondays

HISTORY OF WOMEN IN THE AMERICAN RADICAL TRADITION - Undergraduate
                                                       Seminar

Is there a radical tradition in the American past? In answering this question,
historians have frequently asked why there has been no radical tradition,
denied its existence or searched for scattered pieces of evidence of radical
thought and behavior.

This course will examine the nature of this historical debate and explore
some possible answers to the above question. Using the vehicle of the autobiography and biography, we will examine this tradition from a neglected
perspective--from the point of view of women who offered diverse theories
and solutions to America's social and economic ills. As part of the reading,
we will try to determine whether or not the fact of their gender influenced
the kinds of questions they raised, the nature of their perspectives and the
kinds of experiences they encountered in the various movements in which they
became prominent theorists or participants. The course will emphasize selected
topics in the nineteenth and twentieth centuries: abolitionism, suffragism,
anarchism, socialism, industrial unionism, reproductive rights and birth control,
communism, the new left and contemporary feminism.

READINGS: Peggy Dennis, _The Autobiography of an American Communist_

           Mary Hill, _The Making of a Radical Feminist_

           Emma Goldman, _Living My Life_, Vol. I

           Judith Nies, _Seven Women_

           Margaret Sanger, _An Autobiography_

           Sarah Evans, _Personal Politics_

GRADING: Term Paper - 60%

          Seminar Participation - 20%

          Oral Report - 20%

Prof. Ruth Rosen
History 102M

Requirements:

1. All the assigned reading.

2. Responsibility for leading one section.

3. A term paper due December 6 based on the study of one significant radical thinker/writer from the past or present or on an oral interview with such a "radical elder." Instructions forthcoming. Due December 1 in class with no exceptions. Approval for the term paper topic should be obtained before October 13th at the latest.

4. A short oral presentation (20 minutes) describing the results of one's research.

Class Schedule: Readings are for dates listed below.

Oct. 6   Organization meeting - Introduction to Nies, Seven Women

Oct. 13 Abolitionism and the Women's Rights Movement
         Reading: Nies: Sarah Grimke, Harriet Tubman, and Elizabeth Cady
         Stanton

Oct. 20 Anarchism: Goldman, Living My Life

Oct. 27 Socialist and Radical Feminism: Reading: Nies: Charlotte Perkins
         Gilman, Mary Hill, The Making of a Radical Feminist

Nov. 3   Reproductive Right: The Politics of Sexuality
         Reading: Margaret Sanger, Autobiography

Nov. 10 American Communism
         Reading: Peggy Dennis, The Autobiography of an American Communist

Nov. 17 The Origins and Varieties of Contemporary Feminism
         Reading: Sarah Evans, Personal Politics

Nov. 24 Students' reports to the class

Dec. 1   Students' reports to the class

Prof. Ruth Rosen
History 102M

Option 1   Term Paper Possible Topics

For the term paper, if you choose to study some individual writings, the
following will likely result in interesting and fruitful research topics.

Victoria Woodhull - first woman to run for president in 1872, radical,
                     egalitarian, feminist, social revolutionary

Dorothy Day and the Catholic Worker's Movement

Charlotte Perkins Gilman - economist, socialist-feminist

Elizabeth Cady Stanton - suffragist leader

Jane Addams - Hull House founder, social reformer

Jessica Mitford - British woman who became radical political muckraker

Elizabeth Gurley Flynn - leader of the Wobblies

Mary Daly - radical feminist author (Contemporary)

Susan Griffin - radical feminist (Contemporary)

Adrienne Rich - radical feminist poet and essayist

If you pick this option, you will be writing a critical autobiographical paper
of an individual, based on a substantial amount of her writings. Your task is
to integrate the individual's personal history with her political thought,
demonstrating the genesis of her ideas, the significance of her thought and how
she fits into what we have studied about the radical tradition in the U.S.

Option 2. If you pick this option, you will conduct an oral interview with an
elderly person who was an active radical in a prior historical period. Names
and suggestions can be obtained from the instructor. After extensive interviewing,
in which you gain the kind of information which one would know if this individual
had written about her ideas, activities and thought, you will write a documented
biographical study of this individual, based on the data which you have collected
yourself. This option requires some skill in oral history, a tape recorder, and
a willingness to travel to interview the person. The department can loan students
a tape recorder and the instructor will provide training in oral history techniques
for those students who wish to have the first-hand experience of interviewing an
individual in depth. As in option 2, your task will be to integrate the individual's
personal history with her political thought, demonstrating the genesis of her
ideas, the significance of her thought and activities and how she fits into what
we have studied about the radical tradition in the U.S.

Graduate Seminar: History of Women's Education in the U.S.

Maxine S. Seller, State University of New York at Buffalo

I Required texts:

Nancy Woloch, Women and the American Experience
Barbara Solomon, In the Company of Educated Women
Mary Roth Walsh, Doctors Wanted, No Women Need Apply
Maxine Seller, Immigrant Women

II Course requirements

1. Weekly reading assignments. Readings not in above texts are at Lockwood Library Graduate Reserve. (Readings for which last name of author only is provided refer to required texts.)

2. Class presentation of one optional book during the semester. (Suggestions are listed after each week's assignment.) Summarize the book, relate it to the topic and required readings for the week, and raise relevant questions. (20-30 minutes).

3. An essay type, "take-home" final examination.

4. A short (10-15 pages) on a person, institution, or issue in the history of women's education. A one page prospectus is due at week 5. Paper is due week 12.

III Grades 1/3 exam, 1/3 paper, 1/3 class participation

1. Introduction.

2. Defining the Field / Colonial Beginnings

Sol Cohen, "History of Education as a Field of Study" in Don Warren, History, Education, and Public Policy 35-53.
Joan Burstyn, "Women in the History of Education" (xerox)
Woloch, 17-48, 65-80
Julia Spruill, Women's Life and Work in the Southern Colonies, Ch. IX and X.

Options: Edmond Morgan, The Puritan Family; John Demos A Little Commonwealth: Family Life in Plymouth Colony; Thomas Woody, A History of Women's Education, 124-217; Mary Sumner Benson, Women in 18th Century America

3. The Revolutionary Generation

Carol Ruth Berkin and Mary Beth Norton, Women of America 69-91 (The Philadelphia Female Academy)
Linda Kerber and Jane de Hart Mathews, Women's America: Kerber, "Daughters of Columbia: Educating Women for the Republic 1787-1805" 82-92.
Woloch, 80-94

288

Catherine Clinton, "Equally Their Due: The Education of the Planter Daughter in the Early Republic," Journal of the Early Republic 2, spring 1982

Options: Linda Kerber, Women of the Republic: Intellect and Ideology in Revolutionary America; Mary Beth Norton, Liberty's Daughers: The Revolutionary Experience of American Women 1750-1800; Nancy Cott The Bonds of Womanhood

4. Teachers and Students in an Expanding America (1820-1880)

Woloch, 113-148
Berkin and Norton, Women of America, A History, 178-201 (Mary Lyons)
Nancy Hoffman:Woman's True Profession: Voices from the History of Teaching pp. 1-36, 56-74, 90-113, 254-256.
Gerda Lerner, Black Women in America 75-113
Richard M. Bernard and Maris A. Vinovskis, "Beyond Catherine Beecher; Female Education in the AnteBellum Period" Signs 3 (summer 1978)
Solomon, 27-42

Options: Willystine Goodsell, Pioneers of Women's Education in the United States: Emma Willard, Catherine Beecher, Mary Lyons; Kathryn Kish Sklar, Catherine Beecher: A Study in American Domesticity; Polly Welts Kaufman, Women Teachers on the Frontier

5. Beyond the Schoolroom: 19th Century Informal Education

Woloch, 97-112, 151-197
Katz and Rapone, Women's Experiences in America, Barbara Welter, "The Cult of True Womanhood 1820-1860"
Kerber and Mathews, Women's America Carroll Smith-Rosenburg, "The Female World of Love and Ritual: Relations between Women in Nineteenth Century America" 156-171.
Susan Levine, "Labor's True Woman: Domesticity and Equality in the Knights of Labor," Journal of American History, vol 70, no. 2 (Sept. 1983), 323-339.
Karen Blair, The Clubwoman as Feminist : True Womanhood Redefined 1868-1914, Introd-ch. 2,
Nina Baym, Women's Fiction, 22-50

Options: Barbara Berg The Remembered Gate: Origins of American Feminism—the Woman and the City 1800-1860; Gwendolyn Wright, Building the Dream: A Social History of Housing in America; Ellen Dubois, Feminism and Suffrage; Ann Douglas, The Feminization of American Culture; Barbara Leslile Epstein, The Politics of Domesticity: Women, Evangelism, and Temperance in the Nineteenth Century; Susan Conrad, Perish the Thought: Intellectual Women in Romantic America 1830-1860

6 Entering the Professions

Walsh, Doctors Wanted
Seller, 30-32; 94-99
Woloch, 283-287

Options: Margaret Rossiter, Woman Scientists in America; Lois Barker Arnold Four Lives in Science : Women's Education in the Nineteeth Centery; Gulielma Alsop, History of the Woman's Medical College, Philadelphia, Pennsylvania 1850-1950; Jone Mottus, New York Nightingales; The Emergence of the Nursing Profession at Bellvue and New York Hospital 1850-1920; Barbara McLosh, The Physician's Hand; Nurses and the Nursing Profession in the Twentieth Century ; Amitai Etzioni, The Semi-Professions and their Organization:Teachers, Nurses, Social Workers

7 Higher Education: The Great Debate

Solomon, 43-140
Willystine Goodsell, The Education of Women. ch. 2-4
Kerber and Mathews, Women's America: "Creating
    Colleges" M. Carey Thomas, 257-9; Mary McLeod Bethune,
    260-262.
Berkin and Norton Women's America, Rosalind Rosenberg "The
    Academic Prism: The New View of American Women" 319-341

Options:Rosalind Rosenberg, Beyond Separate Spheres: Intellectual Roots of Modern Feminism; Marjorie Dobkin, The Making of a Feminist: Early Journals and Letters of M. Carey Thomas; Sister Mary Mariella Bowler,A History of Catholic Colleges for Women in the United States of America: Mabel Newcomer, A Century of Higher Education for American Women; Dorothy Gies McGuigan A Dangerous Experiment: 100 Years of Women at the University of Michigan

8. Educating Women for Urban Industrial Society

Woloch, 219-249, 293-299
Seller, 81-83, 87-89, 106-112
Seller, Maxine S. "G. Stanley Hall and Edward Thorndike on
    the Education of Women: Theory and Policy in the Progressive
    Era" Educational Studies, vol 11, no. 4 (winter, 1981)
    365-374
Barbara Ehrenreich and Deirdre English, For Her Own Good:
    150 Years of the Experts' Advice to Women, ch. 5-6
Kerber and Mathews, Women's America 242-256,
John Rury, "Vocationalism for Home and Work: Women's
    Education in the U.S. 1880-1930," History of Education
    Quarterly, (1984.)

Options: Dolores Haydon, The Grand Domestic Revolution; Marjorie East, Home Economics: Past, Present, and Future; Margaret Davies, Women's Place Is at the Typewriter: Office Work and Office Workers 1870-1930: Elyce Rotella, From Home to Office: U.S. Women at Work 1870:1930; Frances Blascoeur, Colored Schoolchildren in New York

9 The "New Woman"

Woloch, 253-283, 287-293, 299-303, 363-380
Kerber and Mathews, Women's America: Ray Ginger, "The Women
    at Hull House," 263-274 and Blance Wiesen Cook, "Female
    Support Networks and Political Activism: Lilian Wald,
    Crystal Eastman, Emma Goldman" 274-293
Seller, 259-278,
Nancy Hoffman, Woman's True Profession, 200-217, 254-256,
    273-300
Robert Reid, ed. Battleground: The Autobiography of Margaret
    Haley vii-xxxv
Michael Apple,"Teaching and Women's Work," in Edgar B.
    Gumbert, ed. Expressions of Power in Education: Class,
    Gender, and Race

Options: Ellen Lagemann, A Generation of Women: Education in the
Lives of Progressive Reformers; Robert Reid, ed. Battleground:
The Autobiography of Margaret Haley; Joan K. Smith Ella Flagg
Young: Portrait of a Leader; Jane Addams Twenty Years at Hull House

10 Between Two Wars

Woloch, 381-416, 439-474
Estelle Freedman, "The New Woman: Changing Views of Women in
    the 1920's" Journal of American History 61 (Sept 1974)
    372-393
Kerber and Mathews Women's America:Ruth Schwartz Cowan,
    "The Industrial Revolution in the Home: Household
    Technology and Social Change in the Twentieth Century
    324-335; Margaret Hagood, "Of the Tenant Child..." 338-344.
Patricia Hummer The Decade of Elusive Promise: Professional
    Women in the United States, ch.3-6
Solomon, 141-185

Options:J. Stanley Lemons The Woman Citizen: Social Feminism in
the 1920s; William Chafe, The American Woman: Her Changing
Social, Economic, and Political Roles 1920-1970; Lois Scharf To
Work or To Wed ; Leila Rupp, Mobilizing Women for War: German and
American Propaganda 1939-1945; Elaine Showalter, ed. These Modern
Women: Autobiographical Essays from the Twenties

11. Informal Education in the Twentieth Century

Seller, 174-188, 205-221, 229-239, 310-318
Mary Aickin Rothschild, "To Scout or to Guide? The Girl
    Scout-Boy Scout Controversy 1912-1941 " Frontiers 6,
    fall 1981
Seller, M. "World of Our Mothers: The Women's Page of the
    Jewish Daily Forward: Socialism, Feminism, and
    Americanization" (xerox)
Ehrenreich and English For Her Own Good ch 7
Gerda Lerner, Black Women in White America 477-480, 489-520

James Wood, *Magazines in the United States* (chapter on Ladies Home Journal)
Bernard Weiss, *American Education and the European Immigrant*
R. Mohl, "The Internationl Institutes..."117-134

Options: *Channeling Children: Sex Stereotyping on Prime Time TV*
Bobbie Ann Mason, *The Girl Sleuth: A Feminist Guide*

12 "Togetherness," Civil Rights, and Women's Rights

Woloch 495-536
Solomon 186-212
Berkin and Norton, *Womem of America* "From Aid to Organizer,"
290-313,
Ehrenreich and English, ch. 8
Seller, 70-79, 221-229, 310-327, 235-239.
Gerda Lerner, *Black Women in White Amerioca* 585-602

Options: Betty Friedan, *The Feminine Mystique*; Kate Millett,
Sexual Politics; Nancy Seifer, *Nobody Speaks for Me: Self-
Portraits of American Working Class Women*

13 The Feminist Critique of Education

Nancy Frazier and Myra Sadker, *Sexism in School and Society*,
ch 1, 4-8
Myra Sadker and David Sadker, "Sexism in Teacher Education
Texts" *Harvard Educational Review,* vol 50, no. 1 (1980),
36-46
Andrew Fishel and Janice Pottker, "School Boards and Sex
Bias in American Education" *Contemporary Education,*
winter 1974, 85-89
Julia M. Brown, "Women in Physical Education: The Drible Index
of Liberation" in Joan I. Roberts, ed. *Beyond Intellectual
Sexism*, 365-380.

Options:Cynthia Fuchs Epstein , *Woman's Place, Options and Limits*
; Perun, ed. *The Undergraduate Woman: Issues in Educational
Equity*; Blanche Fitzpatrick *Women's Inferior Education: An Economic
Analysis*, Judith Stacey, et. al *And Jill Came Tumbling After*

14 Reform and Reaction

Cynthia Lloyd and Beth Niemi, *The Economics of Sex
Differentials* pp.
Florence Howe, *Women and the Power to Change*, 15-46, 127-71
Title IX Primer (summary of title IX regulations)
Patricia Graham, "Expansion and Exclusion: A History of
Women in American Higher Education" *Signs* summer 1978, vol
3, no. 4, 759-73
M. Elizabeth Tidball, "Women's Colleges and Achievers
Revisited", *Signs* spring 1980, 517

Naomi Weisstein, "Tired of Arguing about Biological Inferiority" Ms Magazine Nov. 1982

L.H. Fox, E. Fennema, and J. Sherman, Women and Mathematics: Research Perspectives ch. 1

Options: Andrea Dworkin Right Wing Women; Debra Kaufman and Barbara Richardson, Achievement and Women: Challenging the Assumptions; Elizabeth Langland and Walter Gove, A Feminist Perspective in the Academy: The Difference It Makes; Elinor Lenz and Barbara Myerhoff, The Feminization of America: How Women's Values are Changing Our Public and Private Lives

J. About the Editor

Louise L. Stevenson is a member of the history department and the American Studies program at Franklin and Marshall College. Her teaching and research interests embrace nineteenth-century cultural and intellectual history, including women's history. After studying with the late Annette K. Baxter at Barnard College, Stevenson went on to graduate study at New York University, and she received her Ph.D. degree from Boston University.

She has published articles and reviews in the field of women's history. Forthcoming in the series *Educated Women: Higher Education and Professionalism,* edited by Barbara Miller Solomon, are two volumes containing documents from the archives of Miss Porter's School, 1840-1940. The first focuses on student life and contains student letters, diaries, and newspapers, the second on alumnae activities, chiefly a home for working girls that the alumnae maintained from the 1880s through the 1930s.

Stevenson is also the author of *Scholarly Means to Evangelical Ends: The New Haven Scholars and the Transformation of Higher Learning in America, 1830-1890* (Baltimore: Johns Hopkins University Press, 1986), and she is beginning a cultural and intellectual history of the years 1860-1880 for a series edited by Lewis Perry entitled *American Thought and Culture.*